ON CUSTOM IN THE ECONOMY

ON CUSTOM
IN THE
ECONOMY

Ekkehart Schlicht

OXFORD

CLARENDON PRESS

1998

Oxford University Press, Great Clarendon Street, Oxford OX2 6DP
Oxford New York
Athens Auckland Bangkok Bogota Bombay Buenos Aires
Calcutta Cape Town Dar es Salaam Delhi Florence Hong Kong Istanbul
Karachi Kuala Lumpur Madras Madrid Melbourne Mexico City
Nairobi Paris Singapore Taipei Tokyo Toronto Warsaw
and associated companies in
Berlin Ibadan

Oxford is a registered trade mark of Oxford University Press

Published in the United States
by Oxford University Press Inc., New York

© Ekkehart Schlicht 1998

The moral rights of the author have been asserted

First published 1998

British Library Cataloguing in Publication Data
Data available

Library of Congress Cataloging in Publication Data
Data available
ISBN 0–19–829224–4

1 3 5 7 9 10 8 6 4 2

Typeset by J&L Composition
Printed in Great Britain
on acid-free paper by
Biddles Ltd, Guildford and King's Lynn

PREFACE

The aim of this book is to re-establish custom in economics. Current economic theorizing largely neglects the forces of custom that underpin market exchange. Economic sociologists have stressed this repeatedly by referring to the 'embeddedness' of all kinds of economic processes. However, while it is true that market transactions hinge critically on elements of custom, economic processes shape custom in turn. This other causal direction needs more attention than it has hitherto received. The way modern institutional economics has developed points to the same deficiency. Institutional economics initially tried to analyse economic institutions as arising from market processes and competition while avoiding reference to all elements of custom, but it became increasingly clear that the answers so obtained were critically dependent on tacit assumptions about the customary infrastructure. One aim of the book is to provide the necessary link between customary elements and market processes.

A current strand of thought, notably originating with game theory, has tried to understand the emergence of customs by interpreting them as routines that have been adopted because they were competitively successful. This approach takes customs essentially as conventions that solve coordination problems. It is driven by the economic paradigm that interprets behaviour as fully reducible to the interplay of (given) preferences and constraints while neglecting the direct motivational impact of custom. A second aim of the book is thus to harmonize the motivational significance of custom with institutional theorizing in a systematic way. The re-establishment of custom in economics will provide foundations for institutional thinking and will help in reducing some arbitrariness of current thought.

The book addresses issues that are fundamental to economics, sociology, political science, and social psychology. The approach taken transgresses the boundaries between these disciplines. While writing the book, I became increasingly convinced that these boundaries do not organize the division of labour in the social sciences in a useful way, but rather hamper and often frustrate attempts to think about fundamentals. The book concerns these fundamentals.

The enterprise started in 1985–6 at the Institute for Advanced Study, Princeton, with a project on the theory of the firm. I had the good fortune to meet the social psychologist Solomon Asch and the economic historian Eric Jones there. Both of them influenced my thinking in a profound way.

I managed to write a draft in winter 1987/8 during a stay at Brown University, and resumed the attempt in summer 1991 at the University of Minnesota. The result was unsatisfactory. Too many problems remained. The entire approach I had taken seemed wrong. I started from scratch again. This book is the result. The manuscript was conceived and written during the Australian winter of 1995 at the Melbourne Business School, University of Melbourne. Discussions with Eric Jones helped me to devise a new conceptual frame for what I wanted to say. He encouraged me to focus not so much on technical but rather on fundamental and sometimes even methodological issues.

Many other individuals deserve my gratitude. I have to thank my long-time assistant Gisela Kubon-Gilke; she was interested in related issues, and the many discussions we had were important in shaping my ideas. Timur Kuran, David Reisman, and Peter Weise read the entire manuscript and provided penetrating comments and expert advice. Hans Albert, Knut Borchardt, Dieter Grimm, Russell Hardin, Erik Leyers, Florian Mayer-Haßelwander, Peter Mücke, Andreas Nicolin, Stephan Panther, Ray Rees, Rudolf Richter, and Ulrich Witt all read parts of the manuscript; their detailed comments helped me to improve it in many ways. At the Melbourne Business School, Phillip Williams and Leon Mann took an active interest in my work and provided valuable criticism. In a deeper sense, my dear wife is responsible for the book. She urged me to pursue the project and discussed many issues with me. I thank her and our daughters and sons for sustained support.

The following institutions helped by providing research facilities or funding: Institute for Advanced Study, Princeton; Department of Economics, Brown University; Industrial Relations Center, University of Minnesota; Institute for Advanced Study, Berlin; Deutsche Forschungsgemeinschaft, and Thyssen Foundation. The ministers of education in Hessia and Bavaria granted sabbaticals, thereby rendering it possible for me to do scientific work in a serious way. Particular thanks go to the Melbourne Business School and its director, John Rose, for offering an outstanding research environment.

E.S.

Munich
November 1997

CONTENTS

LIST OF FIGURES

INTRODUCTION

Writing about custom makes me feel like a fish reasoning how water rules the life of fish. It is a staggering task.

Custom is ubiquitous in all spheres of life. It shapes habits and convictions, sways emotions and cognitions, and influences motivation and action. Through all these channels, custom pervades social and economic interaction. The many individual effects of custom diffuse and interact throughout the social system. This renders it difficult to isolate single causal chains. Moreover, custom affects motivation, conviction, and behaviour in such a perfectly 'natural' way that the customary undergirdings of social and economic processes appear hardly discernible, and sometimes even invisible. In spite of this imperspicuity, custom exerts, in Alfred Marshall's words, a 'deep and controlling influence over the history of the world'.[1]

Custom eases economic and social interaction in some dimensions while constraining it in others. The advantages of custom for social coordination have been stressed by sociologists in observing that 'effective norms can constitute a powerful form of social capital'.[2] By way of contrast, economists depict the 'yoke of custom' as 'hindering the method of production and the character of producers from developing themselves freely'.[3] These observations point to important aspects of custom. A deeper understanding,

---

[1] Marshall (1890: 465).   [2] Coleman (1990: 311).
[3] Marshall (1890: 73, 465).

however, requires an analysis of how customs form, and how they affect behaviour.

This book proposes a theory of custom which centres on individual cognition, emotion, and action. In this, the theory deviates from prevailing approaches which identify customs with routines that are maintained because of their competitive or instrumental advantage. Such an instrumentalist conception falls short of rendering important non-instrumental aspects of custom comprehensible. It is, of course, sensible to drive on the right-hand side of the road if everybody else does the same. The spread of right-hand driving, so induced, may render right-hand driving customary. This is the easy case. The argument will not explain why people stick to certain rules which are individually costly to observe, like keeping promises, respecting property, or giving gratuities. Such behaviours are maintained by custom. They provide the foundation for all kinds of social and economic institutions. The problem of customary rule obedience requires more than simple instrumental arguments like those accounting for the custom of right-hand driving.

The theory of custom pursued in this book emphasizes the motivational force that arises from the individual's striving for coherence and justification. Custom is portrayed as emerging from the individual's desire to align behaviour, conviction, and emotion tightly with one another. Individuals have a preference for patterned behaviour, for acting according to their convictions, and for forming their convictions in accordance with what they are experiencing. The alignment of behaviour, conviction, and emotion is engendered by processes taking place in the human mind.

These psychological processes—termed 'clarification' processes—are not confined to cognition but structure psychological organization through and through. Pattern recognition, which is largely automatic, can be interpreted in terms of clarification processes. Similarly, routine and habit build on spontaneously perceived regularities which escape our regular deliberation. The emotional dispositions that stabilize routine and habit are engendered by a desire to integrate habit, emotion, and conviction. The phenomenon of custom arises from the intermeshing of behavioural, emotional, and cognitive elements. All this is epitomized in the 'clarity' view which will be developed as the argument unfolds.

1.1 Background

Custom is a fundamental constituent of culture, but the subsequent chapters will not take such a broad perspective. Rather, the theory will be developed by building on everyday experience. It is, however, appropriate to sketch the underlying position regarding some important background issues before entering the main argument.

Viewed in very broad terms, current social theory is dominated by two opposing views concerning the interrelation between culture and economics. One of them, the 'economistic' view, conceives culture as an epiphenomenon generated by more fundamental processes of economic and evolutionary competition; the other, the 'culturalist' or 'post-modernist' approach, posits that social reality is, in any society, a thoroughly social construct—the economic sphere is portrayed as being determined by culture, rather than as determining culture.

The theory of custom proposed here deviates from economistic and culturalist conceptions in denying exclusive superiority either to cultural processes or to functional and competitive considerations alone. Both cultural and economic phenomena are conceived as epiphenomena brought about by the way in which humans think, feel, and act. Customs arise from these psychological regularities in the process of social interaction. Rather than postulating an autonomy of either economic or social processes *vis-à-vis* the individual, as entailed by culturalist or economistic views, the question is raised of how such autonomy may emerge from interaction. This problem is analysed with regard to the formation of custom.

In one sense the approach is individualistic, because it takes the individual as the unit of analysis. In another sense it is not, because it does not deny the reality and (partial) autonomy of groups, customs, and other collective phenomena, and does not assume that the individuals remain unaffected by social processes. Rather, the approach seeks to explain how collective phenomena may attain autonomy up to the point of controlling and even enslaving the very individuals who generated these collective phenomena by their interaction.

Further, the theoretical perspective pursued here deviates from currently prevailing positions regarding questions of ethics. In spite of their antagonism, economistic and culturalist conceptions share the conviction that ethical valuations are basically arbitrary and culture-specific, whereas the present approach suggests a quite different stance. Economistic interpretations reduce social values to individual preferences. These are taken as givens, or as having been brought about by blind evolutionary processes without any moral connotation. In brief, social valuations are taken as arbitrary. The same position flows directly from a culturalist perspective, where everything is conceived as being culturally determined. Both strands of thought depict ethical values as valid only within a given culture. More fundamental ethical judgements (like those concerning human rights) may emerge from universal consensus and cross-cultural agreement, but no further and deeper foundation is available.

In contrast, the position adopted here is universalist. Cultural phenomena, including ethical convictions, are conceived as flowing from fundamental cognitive, emotional, and behavioural dispositions of human beings. These dispositions are shared across cultures and are themselves independent of culture. Ethical convictions, therefore, are not arbitrary tastes, but are systematically linked to the prevailing world-view. The 'social construction of reality' which brought about a given world-view is not an erratic process, but is shaped by experience and the laws that govern our thinking. The non-arbitrariness of ethical judgements is entailed by the non-arbitrariness of human nature and the non-arbitrariness of culture.

The broad topics of cultural and ethical relativism and of culturalism versus economism do not, however, provide the central characters of the subsequent account, and the discussion will not elaborate them any further. The broad issues have been mentioned only in order to sketch the background and set the stage for an argument that portrays the formation of custom commencing from everyday settings. However, the appendices at the end of the book offer some additional material on individualism and on cultural and ethical relativism.

I.2 Overview

The first four chapters elaborate on the nature of custom. Custom is depicted as comprising habitual, cognitive, and emotional aspects. These aspects may be conceived as distinct components, but in practice they are closely interlinked. It is argued that market transactions must rely on customary entitlements and obligations. Such entitlements and obligations form the bedrock of property and exchange. Furthermore, it is explained that customs may change smoothly or abruptly in several dimensions.

The idea of adaptive custom is then advanced in Chapter 5. The view follows Alfred Marshall's exposition of custom. Custom is portrayed as an inertial force adapting tardily to new circumstances. While very helpful in elucidating various changes in custom, the adaptive view falls short of accounting for some important characteristics of custom such as its rigidity and partial autonomy. Hence Chapters 6–10 develop the 'clarity' view of custom. Customary regularities relate to rule perception and learning. The motivational force of custom is conceived as emerging from a preference for regularity and a desire for coherence that tie cognition, emotion, and action together. The force of custom, as well as its rigidity and partial autonomy, derive from this contextual reinforcement.

The second part of the book applies this proposed view of

custom to the theory of property, the theory of the law, and the theory of the firm and the market.

The argument on property follows David Hume's theory of property closely. Property is portrayed as grounded in the same traits of human motivation that shape custom, but the particular forms that property takes emerge from social and economic interaction. The motivational and functional aspects of property are largely running in parallel, mutually reinforcing each other. This parallelism resembles the interplay of theme and counterpoint in a piece of music. Each voice supports the other, but sometimes the interplay occasions dissonance and tension. Similarly, and upon certain occasions, motivational and functional requirements point in different directions. This gives rise to conflict and may occasion severe inefficiencies. The 'counterpoint' argument complements the modern theory of property rights in several ways. It accounts for the persistent inefficiencies that withstand evolutionary pressure and helps to constrain the set of institutional solutions that ompete at a time, thus sharpening ideas about institutional competition.

The approach can be generalized to many aspects of jurisprudence. It offers a fresh view of the antagonism between natural and positive law by delineating the way in which psychological and instrumental demands interact. The law is depicted as a kind of systematized custom that aligns behavioural patterns with perceived regularities and thus influences behaviour in the same way as custom. While older legal theorizing stressed the 'organic' nature of legal evolution, modern evolutionary thinking emphasizes almost exclusively external functional and instrumental aspects. The clarity view emphasizes the 'counterpoint' pattern: both internal 'organic' and external instrumental forces work together in shaping the law.

The firm provides another realm in which the workings of custom can be studied. Firms can be envisaged as islands of specialized customs emerging in the market. Competition weeds out inefficient organizational forms and inefficient customary formations. In this way, custom is confined to those tasks where it is superior to other forms of coordination. In a competitive environment, the sluggishness of custom thus establishes limits to integration and to the size of the firm. Further, the clarity view offers new vistas of the firm by focusing not so much on single and separate organizational features as on the pervasive coherence and internal balance of the entire set of routines, control structures, and firm-specific norms.

Custom serves to organize the division of labour within the firm and in society at large. In this, direct coordination by custom provides an alternative to market coordination, which rests more indirectly on custom. While Adam Smith maintains that it is the size of the market that limits the division of labour, the clarity view entails that the nature of the task delimits the division of labour in another important way. Certain tasks—like writing a block of computer code, or a piece of music—cannot usefully be subdivided any further, irrespective of the size of the market. This suggests a fundamental reformulation of Smith's theorem, and a new view about how the division of labour is organized within firms and across the market.

Thus, the forces of custom surface, in various ways and at various places. They provide the foundation for many economic and social institutions. The concluding chapter stresses the overall pattern of the workings of custom, its pervasiveness, and the way in which it influences social evolution.

1.3 *The Nature of the Argument*

A book such as this may be compared to a building. A building is erected by combining various materials in certain ways, and a book is composed of arguments and observations. In both cases, the product is characterized mainly by the overall structure of its composition, somewhat independently of the materials used. The architectural idea embodied in the building could have been realized by using other materials instead of those actually used— other types of stones and mortar, for instance. Similarly, a book develops a thesis which could be explained by using other building blocks—other arguments, observations, or examples. Just as the design of a building is not reducible to the materials used, and is even somewhat independent of these materials, the main message of this book rests in the overall vision it seeks to communicate.

Part I

THE
AMALGAM OF
CUSTOM

Chapter 1

A WEB OF REINFORCEMENTS

1.1 *Malleable Foundations*

Custom furnishes much of the material from which societies are built. The laws and institutions in any particular society—systems of kinship, forms of property, modes of contracting, and so forth—do not form a self-sufficient complex that is ultimately self-enforcing and could be transplanted around the globe and across time at will. Institutions are not formed in a void. Rather, they rest on behavioural dispositions and legitimizing views inherited from the past—that is, on custom.

Yet custom does not provide a firm foundation for the formation of institutions, because it is malleable itself. It is shaped by the very processes that build on it. If there are reasons to cheat, cheating will spread, customary honesty will be destroyed, and those institutions that build on honesty will be undermined. More generally, customary ways of behaving will be moulded by economic and other incentives. At the same time, these customary ways provide the very footing for those economic and social phenomena. Just as the bed of a river channels the flow of water and is moulded by that flow in turn, custom provides the bed for economic and social processes and is shaped by them.

1.2 *The Concept of Custom*

One approach to custom would be to break it down into a compound of many different phenomena, such as habits, usages, manners, and conventions. Further distinctions could be drawn according to the way in which a custom is maintained. For example, it may be sustained by an imbued habit or by external sanctions and rewards, and it may be deliberately pursued or subconsciously ingrained.[1] An analytic dissection of this kind tends to dissolve custom into a cluster of independent, albeit interrelated, specimens, while evading the general phenomenon.

Such a dissolution by dissection is not intended here. The aim is to ideate custom as a comprehensive, if somewhat abstract, phenomenon that materializes in different ways and may take different forms. The abstract nature of custom may be compared to the abstractness of 'matter' in physics, which lends itself to sundry manifestations but cannot be identified with any set of concrete materials. Unlike 'matter' in physics, however, custom is not a primitive concept that cannot be further reduced. Rather, custom will be conceived as arising from interactions among individuals. Its variegated appearances will be traced to properties of the human mind, and to the ways in which individuals interact. This is not to say that custom reduces to a cluster of individual actions that happen to display certain patterns. An interpretation of this kind would fall short of explaining the 'objective' nature of customary practices the individuals are facing.

The purpose of this chapter is to characterize custom in a preliminary way. While disregarding other influences, custom is initially depicted as arising from tradition and common usage alone. Tradition and common usage shape preferences, behavioural dispositions, and normative convictions simultaneously. Custom is, thus, an amalgam comprising habitual, emotional, and cognitive elements, which cannot easily be separated. There is a strong interplay between habits, emotions, convictions, and

---

[1] See Weber (1922: 29–36); Swedberg (1993: 205).

deliberation. Each supports the other, and influences go back and forth.[1]

1.3 *Conservatism*

If an action is performed over and over again, it becomes habitual. This holds true not only for bodily actions, but for mental processes and preferences as well. Repetition ingrains such actions and processes deeply, up to the point that it is difficult to consider other ways of behaviour, novel ways of thinking, or different ways of evaluating one's surroundings. The reasons for this are various. People may simply have a preference for perseverance, or the human organism may have a tendency to continue with behaviour that has been acquired in the past.

There may also be social motives that strengthen conservatism. Each individual may prefer the others to act predictably, and each individual may gain recognition by satisfying the mutual demand for conservatism.[2]

Conservatism may be useful in several ways. The costs of decision-making can be reduced by sticking to behaviours that were acceptable before, side-stepping fresh decisions. The risks involved in adopting new modes of behaviour can be evaded by maintaining the *status quo*. 'Loss aversion', a commanding concern regarding possible losses and a discounting of possible gains, would induce such behaviour.[3] Further, changes in behaviour engender 'cognitive dissonance': If an individual responds in two different ways to the same situation, one of the responses will be believed to be less appropriate than the other. The individual does not, however,

---

[1] The often-used term 'social values' refers to only some aspects of this amalgam. It is for this reason that I prefer the term 'custom'. 'Culture' comes close to what I have in mind, but puts not enough emphasis on the purely habitual aspects inherent in the term 'custom'. See also S. 2.12 below on entitlements and morality.

[2] This point is further elaborated in Kuran (1995: ch. 6), who further introduces the concept of collective conservatism, as distinct from and somewhat unrelated to 'personal' conservatism discussed above.

[3] Loss aversion will be discussed in S. 8.5.

know which. This prompts uneasiness. By adopting a conservative strategy, such problems can be avoided.

All these various reasons lead to the overall outcome that repetition creates a tendency for further repetition. This applies to action as well as to cognition. There is no need, at the present stage, to distinguish the underlying reasons. It suffices to say that repetition shapes custom, and custom creates a tendency for further repetition.

1.4 Conformity

While conservatism tends to continue what has happened in the past, conformity tends to continue what is observed as an established pattern. People tend to adapt their behaviour to the behaviour of the group they belong to. A custom may emerge in this way rather suddenly. The underlying 'reference group behaviour' may flow from sheer conformity. People may have a desire to behave like the others do, eat what the others eat, read what the others read, and so forth.[1]

Another reason for conformity is related to its usefulness. If a person wants to use a tool but does not know how to handle it, he may aptly imitate a workman who happens to use the appliance. It can be presumed that the expert has developed a good way of handling the tool, and this makes it unnecessary to develop the best technique afresh. Time, effort, and frustration can be saved just by copying observed behaviour. This kind of reasoning applies whenever a person can safely assume that others are better informed. Conformity will be a sensible strategy in this case. Whenever many individuals are involved, the case for conformity will be strong. No individual will believe it likely that he can be better informed than everybody else.[2]

In cases where imitative behaviour works in such a 'rational' manner, the individuals who are best informed will take the lead,

---

[1] This is the starting-point for S.R.G Jones', (1984) analysis of conformity.
[2] This is sometimes called 'social proof'; see Cialdini (1984: ch. 4).

and the rest will conform. This is not an unreasonable strategy. It may even be 'efficient'. Whenever an individual wants to avoid detailed reasoning, or is justified in assuming that others have more experience in handling a particular problem, imitation will be a good strategy.

Once imitation is adopted as a strategy, it may turn into a routine. The individual will imitate without further thought, and a previously rational way of behaviour will then become habitual. In this way, the distinction between functional and emotional reasons for maintaining a custom will be blurred.

A further reason for conformity is related to 'cognitive dissonance'. If an individual behaves differently from others who act under similar conditions, a state of psychological tension arises. While one person maintains that the grass is green, others assert that it is red. Such conflicting statements will induce the individual to search for reasons. He may for instance conclude that the others want to tease him. As individuals have a preference for 'cognitive consistency', they will avoid such tensions.[1]

Social motives may strengthen conformity in much the same way that they strengthen conservatism. Each individual may prefer the others to behave like everyone else, and each individual may avoid disdain by conforming. There may even be reasons for such preferences. If conforming is held to signal certain desirable features of character and is taken to indicate reliable behaviour in the future, conformity will enhance the possibilities for social and economic interaction and may be adopted as a strategy even by those individuals who have no intrinsic preference for it.[2]

1.5 Tacit Knowledge

Great parts of knowledge, thought, and emotion escape any regular deliberation. Many native speakers do not 'know' the rules of

---

[1] For the theory of cognitive dissonance, see Festinger (1957), Colman (1988), Zimbardo and Leippe (1991). Applications to economics are discussed in Akerlof and Dickens (1982) and Schlicht (1984a).
[2] This is an analogy to Bernheim's (1994) theory of conformity.

grammar, for instance, yet they speak correctly and understandably. The formal grammar of any language is distilled from spoken language, but it is so complex that it seems impossible ever to produce a comprehensive grammar. Even if such a comprehensive grammar were produced, moreover, it would not enable the reader to speak the language on the spot. Infants may 'know' the easiest way to gain mastery of a language, but this knowledge seems to involve no explicit formal grammar. Certainly, if adults learn a foreign language in a classroom, they have to absorb a certain number of grammatical rules and to deliberately apply this 'declarative' knowledge in order to form sentences. If full mastery of a foreign language is achieved, however, the formal grammatical rules are often forgotten. The class-taught declarative knowledge has been used as a stepping-stone to generate knowledge of another kind, and becomes dispensable once full mastery is achieved. This other kind of knowledge is known as 'tacit', 'procedural', or 'implicit' knowledge.[1]

It is often impossible to give a verbal account of tacit knowledge. Even if somebody 'can' ride a bicycle, he is usually not aware of 'how' to perform the task, and may be quite unable to put his knowledge into words. It may be easier to demonstrate how to ride a bicycle than to produce an explicit instruction, let alone any analysis of the mechanical forces involved. But even if a certain skill—like driving a car—can be described explicitly in a declarative manner, the mastering of the skill requires automatization. Automatic responses—such as pushing the brake when the traffic light is turning red—are usually quicker than deliberate responses. This may be advantageous.

Effective learning often involves the shaping of automatic responses and, in this sense, the creation of tacit knowledge. This sometimes requires considerable time and effort. It takes a

---

[1] The term 'tacit knowledge' has been introduced and extensively analysed by Michael Polanyi (1962), who speaks also of 'personal knowledge'. Social psychology uses 'procedural knowledge' and 'implicit knowledge'; see Anderson (1980: 223–54); Greenwald and Banaji (1995). Organization theory refers to 'behavioural knowledge'; see Barnard (1938). Although the concepts carry slightly different connotations (not to be discussed here), they refer to the same core phenomenon.

long time to achieve fluency in reading and writing. Musicians have to practise very intensely to achieve the right touch, an open sound, or a natural vibrato. Similar observations apply to many skills. The tacit knowledge created by automatization enhances performance immensely for all kinds of tasks. The benefits flowing from specialization and the division of labour within society are largely rooted here. Specialization enables individuals to engage in particular activities more frequently and to develop more specific skills and appropriate tacit knowledge.[1] It has even been maintained that 'civilisation advances by extending the number of operations which we can perform without thinking about them'.[2]

The tacit aspect of knowledge is of the utmost importance for social organization. Somewhat trivial examples illustrate this in a straightforward manner. Michael Polanyi writes about a new machine for blowing bulbs that had been imported to Hungary but had failed for a whole year to produce a single flawless bulb, while an exact counterpart of this machine was operating successfully in Germany.[3] This illustrates that the instructions given in the manual do not suffice to operate such a machine; practical 'know-how' is also required, and this is typically not susceptible to verbal statement.[4] In a similar vein, the evolutionary theory of the firm has stressed the importance of know-how, routinization, and other kinds of tacit knowledge for economic performance.[5]

Similar observations can be made with regard to administration. The application of administrative rules and procedures may be compared to the mastering of a language. It is nearly impossible to speak just by applying the rules of grammar; mastery requires a tacit grasp of grammar, and the fluent speaker will not be aware of the rules he is actually using; he will not, however, make mistakes. Similarly, a good administrator will work in an intuitive way with administrative rules, relying much more on tacit

---

[1] Adam Smith (1776: 19) observes in this context: 'The difference of natural talents in men is, in reality, much less than we are aware of; and the very different genius which appears to distinguish men of different professions, when grown up to maturity, is not upon many occasions so much the cause, as the effect of the division of labour.'
[2] A. Whitehead, as quoted by Hayek (1945: 528).   [3] M. Polanyi (1962: 52).
[4] Barnard (1938: 291).   [5] Nelson and Winter (1982: 99)

knowledge and 'know-how' than on explicit guidelines which can never be complete. The administrative difficulties encountered after Germany's unification in 1989 illustrate the point. Numerous administrative rules and regulations were extended from the West to the East, but the administrators in the East were not accustomed to these rules and regulations. The ensuing uncertainty about the meaning and implication of various regulations hindered many administrative procedures. Experienced administrators from the West were then invited to provide technical assistance. This created the tacit knowledge necessary for running the administration.

1.6 *Emotional Encoding*

The formation of tacit knowledge is not to be conceived, however, as a somewhat mechanical process that imprints a certain pattern by means of obstinate repetition until full automatization is achieved. Rather, tacit knowledge arises from encoding declarative knowledge in a different mode. An illustration is provided by the way in which grammatical rules are assimilated. The competent speaker has developed a 'linguistic feeling'. This feeling prompts emotional responses to wrong constructions but is not necessarily paired with a proper understanding of the grammatical reasons that cause the uneasiness. Yet the emotional response encodes formal grammar correctly. Conversely, formal grammar may be regarded as a formalization of linguistic feeling. Historically, formal grammar developed in this manner. The formal grammar of classical Latin has been distilled from Caesar's writings, for instance.

Similar encodings and decodings occur in all spheres of life. A person is remembered as unsympathetic, for instance, but the reasons that occasioned the judgement have faded from memory. Certain beliefs are entertained as firm convictions, but the underlying reasons can no longer be recalled. Conversely, certain habits are tacitly and imperceptibly ingrained, like the rules of grammar, or gestures of politeness, and give rise to supporting rationalizations.

The interplay of tacit knowledge and explicit knowledge— encoding and decoding—illustrate the general point that cognitive and emotional phenomena interact strongly. Just as linguistic feeling is disciplined and stabilized by grammatical insight, so grammatical reasoning must build on linguistic feeling. Both elements complement and stabilize each other, and it does not seem helpful to cut them apart.

It is sometimes maintained that tacit aspects of knowledge should be disregarded because they are deemed 'irrational'. Such a view is misleading. Any kind of deliberation depends on tacit assumptions and presuppositions which can in turn be subjected to scrutiny. Knowledge may be conceived as forming a complex so large that it is impossible to consider everything simultaneously. It is only a minor part that can surface to consciousness at any time. This may be, in a sense, 'irrational', but such limited attention is immensely functional, given the limitations of our mind.[1] In a deeper sense, the reliance on tacit knowledge is unavoidable. Even axiomatic mathematical systems must presuppose the truth of formally undecidable assertions. Any insistence on purging all tacit elements under the flag of 'rationality' is, thus, self-defeating.[2]

1.7 *The Tacit and Malleable Nature of Custom*

The forces of custom work often invisibly and tacitly. The inconspicuous routines generated by conservatism and conformity often elude our awareness. Customary attitudes and stereotypes influence thinking and action strongly, yet remain largely imperceptible.

---

[1] This has been stressed by the 'bounded rationality' school; see Simon (1978). The problem is also common in computing. Some programs may run 'in the background' and are brought to the attention of the operator only if some critical events occur.
[2] This alludes to 'Gödel's theorem' (see Hofstadter 1979: 17), but is not to be understood as a defence of irrationality. Rather, something beyond rationality is needed.

They are 'implicit'.[1] The same forces that shape tacit knowledge contribute to the formation and working of custom.

The force of custom emerges, thus, from the way in which attitudes, stereotypes, and habits reinforce each other. A conviction may serve to justify a certain habit, and the habit may reconfirm the conviction. Ideas about the healthiness of food may underpin the customary diet, for instance, and the habitual diet may induce theories asserting its healthiness.

Yet these customs, habits, and convictions are not, as a rule, rigidly 'imprinted' but can be changed in response to new exigencies. However, even if a certain custom is firmly ingrained in all members of a cohort, it must be passed on to new generations. Therefore, it can never persist without being incessantly re-established. Since custom must be conveyed from one generation to the next, changes in the process of transmission may induce changes in custom from one generation to the next. This renders custom malleable in the long run and makes it responsive to outside influences. Custom is not to be equated with passive inertia, although it may give rise to persistence. Stability of custom cannot be assumed *a priori*. Any enduring custom requires an explanation in terms of stabilizing forces and transmission processes, which will be elaborated later.

1.8 *Mutual Reinforcement*

The habitual, emotional, and cognitive aspects of custom cannot usefully be segregated. The interaction of tacit and explicit knowledge renders it impossible neatly to separate the conscious and non-conscious parts of custom. Further, the various elements of a given ingrained practice are mutually reinforcing of each other. Customary ways of action generate convictions and even rituals and theories (or 'rationalizations') stressing their appropriateness.

[1] Recent psychological research has stressed the role of implicit social cognition; see Greenwald and Banaji (1995) for a survey.

Contumaciously actions are avoided and, thus, rarely observed. The desire for coherence integrates thinking, emotion, and action.

The phenomenon is well illustrated by the following anthropological account which describes how the shape of the village relates to the religious and social practices of a Brazilian tribe, the Bororo.

The circular arrangement of the huts around the men's house is so important a factor in social and religious life that the Salesian missionaries . . . were quick to realize that the surest way to convert the Bororo was to make them abandon their village in favor of one with houses set out in parallel rows. Once they had been deprived of their bearings and were without the plan which acted as confirmation of their native lore, the Indians soon lost any feelings of tradition; it was as if their social and religious systems (we shall see at once that one cannot be dissociated from the other) were too complex to exist without the pattern which was embodied in the plan of the village and of which their awareness was constantly being refreshed by their everyday activities.[1]

It is the entire complex of custom that stabilizes each of the elements. The circular arrangement of huts was in turn motivated by social and religious practices. Habit, convictions, tacit knowledge, and practical considerations work together in thus such a reciprocal way. Custom cannot be disassembled without losing its strength. It disintegrates like a cloth decomposed into its fibres; although analytical reasons mandate an inspection of separate fibres and small pieces of texture, contextual reinforcement reigns supreme.

The following chapter will not elaborate further on the nature of custom, but will direct attention to the way in which custom contributes to the coordination of social and economic interaction.

---

[1] Lévi-Strauss 1955: 220–1).

Chapter 2

ENTITLEMENTS AND OBLIGATIONS

2.1 A Treacherous Image

A portrait of society, gathered from surface impressions, may be drawn as follows. There exists a body of legal rules that fixes the framework of social and economic interaction. The law does not determine activity fully, nor does it coordinate everything. It may mandate paying taxes according to a certain schedule, but it does not prescribe what to produce and whom to marry; it only rules out certain types of production and certain marriages.

A prevalent, but deceptive, sequel to these observations runs as follows. Economic processes are governed, within the legal confines, by custom and competition. These are, in the words of John Stuart Mill, 'the two determining agencies' in market economies.[1] Some traditional economies may be entirely governed by custom, but in modern economies the forces of competition will erode all kinds of customary arrangements. It is held that the 'economic sphere' will eventually be coordinated by competition alone. Modernization will supplant customary arrangements by market processes.

Custom, it is maintained, will not be superseded by the market

[1] Mill (1909: 242).

in all dimensions. Many activities cannot, will not, or ought not to be mediated by the market. The 'social sphere' will remain the domain of custom. It comprises diverse areas of social interaction and may be subdivided accordingly. Politics, religion, family patterns, sports, fashion, and others belong to this sphere. While the economic sphere is the domain of economics, the social sphere is the province of the other social and political sciences.

The rough division of fields suggested by this offhand description is deeply entrenched in our society. The academic disciplines dealing with social phenomena are subdivided along these lines: law, economics, and sociology. These disciplines derive their identity from presupposing the division.

This picture is, however, grossly deceptive. Custom, competition, and the law are not of equal standing. It is misleading to depict them, with Mill, as alternative means to solve problems of economic and social coordination. Market processes build on custom and on the law. The law itself is, to a large extent, shaped by custom and works through similar channels. Custom constitutes, so to speak, the primordial soup from which economic and legal relations emerge.

The purpose of this chapter is to depict market processes as thoroughly dependent on elements of custom, and to delineate how the customary support is affected by economic processes in turn. Further, a perspective on social norms is outlined which conceives them as emerging from an intermeshing of individually perceived entitlements and obligations. This contrasts with conceptions that take norms as irreducible social facts.

2.2 *The Nature of Entitlements and Obligations*

The view of social interaction proposed here is as follows. Individuals perceive 'entitlements' and 'obligations' which channel and direct their action. In this way, entitlements and obligations coordinate social interaction. While different societies may entertain quite different sets of entitlements and obligations, they share the feature that social interaction is organized by a system of entitlements and obligations.

Entitlements are rights, as perceived by the individuals. They are not, however, abstract legal rights. Rather, they denote the subjectively perceived rights that go along with a motivational disposition to defend them.[1] Obligations are the counterparts of entitlements. They refer to claims of others that are subjectively accepted, and go along with a motivational disposition to respect these claims.

The distinguishing characteristic of entitlements and obligations is thus their motivational and behavioural component. Entitlements and obligations affect valuations and change behaviour. In this, entitlements and obligations influence social and economic interaction. It will be argued in this chapter that entitlements and obligations are crucial for all kinds of everyday transactions. Exchange and contracting depend on behaviours that are elicited by entitlements and obligations.

Yet entitlements and obligations are not reducible to habit formation. They depend on justifications that conjoin customary experience with current conduct, and flow from convictions about appropriateness, as nourished by custom. An entire complex of diverse reasons and experiences spawns entitlements and obligations.

2.3 Entitlements, Obligations, and Custom

The first and most important source of entitlements and obligations is custom. Repetition over time as well as shared patterns of behaviour within a reference group generate perceptions of entitlement and obligation. Individuals will feel prompted to conform to

---

[1] The usage follows the psychological interpretation by Kahneman *et al.* (1986*b*), which differs from the usage that attaches the term to legal or natural rights; see Calabresi and Melamed (1972: 1090–1). It differs also from the view proposed by sociologists such as Coleman (1990: 306–10), for whom 'obligations and expectations' are created and entertained by 'rational' actors for selfish reasons. The account given here stresses the direct motivational force of entitlements and obligations.

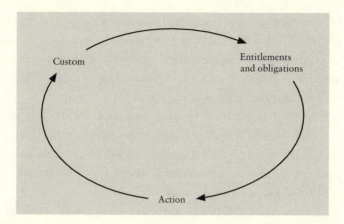

Figure 2.1
Custom, Entitlements, Obligations, Action

customary patterns of behaviour; they will feel entitled to act in customary ways, and will more readily accept demands by others if these demands are affirmed in such a manner.

Repeated action will become ingrained in custom and will in turn add support to the bundle of reasserted entitlements and obligations. In this way, conservatism and conformity will link entitlements and obligations to perceived patterns. Entitlements and obligations will influence action. The working of custom is schematically depicted in Fig 2.1.

2.4 *Entitlements and the Law*

Another important source of entitlements and obligations stems from the law. Laws contribute to the shaping of entitlements and obligations in several ways. First, the law can be imposed by sanctions. The behaviour enforced in this manner will eventually become customary, and perceived entitlements and obligations will adjust to accommodate the new state of affairs.

The law may exert a more direct influence, however. It has been observed that the mere declaration of a law, without imposing any punishment for disobedience, will induce behavioural changes.[1] This 'direct' influence of the law is perhaps most clearly visible when 'contractual presuppositions' command bargaining results. Contractual presuppositions are standard clauses that can be readily replaced by other clauses if the parties wish to do so. Standard clauses are not backed up by sanctions and are, in this sense, weaker than laws. They do not affect the set of permissible contracts, nor the threat points, nor the benefits of the feasible alternatives. Yet it turns out empirically that outcomes are strongly affected by changing contractual presuppositions.

The law by itself will not be sufficient to generate entitlements and obligations, however. Consider the right to free speech. In the former (Communist) German Democratic Republic, the right to free speech was constitutionally guaranteed. Given such a right, it may appear difficult for those in power to suppress free speech. The Communists, however, were largely able to do so by using various sanctions against dissidents. The consequence was that everybody was afraid to dissent. In this way, entitlements were suppressed irrespective of the law. Laws and regulations that play no part in normal life cease to be relevant for generating entitlements and obligations.

Thus, laws can affect entitlements and obligations only within an atmosphere of generalized law obedience. Such generalized law obedience is established by custom. In this sense, the law may be understood as a modifying link in the chain that relates custom to entitlements and obligations. The law is legitimized by custom, and custom plays a part in prescribing the content of the law.

It may be added that many laws may be seen as codifications of usages that came about for quite other reasons. It sometimes follows, rather than guides, custom. This is characteristic of labour legislation or international law, for example.

In another sense, the influence of the law is enigmatic, because people often do not know their own legal position in everyday life.[2]

---

[1] Killias (1985).
[2] See Ellickson (1991: 140) for references to these and other cases.

They largely follow customary patterns when shopping or marry-
ing, but are ignorant of the legal aspects of what they are doing.
Few know about the liability regulations that are brought into
effect by a marriage contract, a lease of a flat, or the purchase of
a power saw. Yet people engage in these transactions and deliberately inform themselves about the legal rights only if something
goes wrong. They follow established patterns. The law affects these
patterns by influencing custom.

While custom is affected by the law, therefore, this effect is not
direct and simple. An appreciation of the law requires a grasp of
the way in which the law moulds entitlements and contributes to
the shaping of custom. Hence any view of custom must offer a
perspective for integrating the influence of law on custom. A later
chapter will suggest such a perspective.[1]

2.5 *Clarity*

It is obvious that all cognition, emotion, and behaviour must be
rooted in the human mind. This holds true for entitlements and
obligations as well as for all other kinds of customary behaviour.
However, it is not feasible to trace all behaviours explicitly to
specific psychological processes. Even if such a reductionist
approach were manageable, it would not yield an appropriate
understanding of very general phenomena such as custom. Yet
the opposite approach of side-stepping all psychological issues
by appropriately demarcating the field of inquiry is not helpful
either. Economic and sociological approaches proceed in this
manner when assuming given 'preferences' or 'social values'.
These approaches must remain powerless with regard to all issues
relating to the formation of preferences and norms. Such questions
are, however, central concerns for any theory of custom.

The theory of custom is thus obliged to build on psychology, but
this does not imply any extreme reductionism. It will suffice to
invoke some broad psychological regularities. Just as economics

[1] Ch. 12.

can deal with price formation in a market while leaving the nature and the precise attributes of the commodities unspecified, the theory of custom can build on fairly general and abstract ideas about human motivation and cognition while remaining tacit about particulars.

The following argument, therefore, will build on a cluster of some general psychological tendencies in learning and motivation relating to psychological 'clarity'. This notion will attain central importance as the argument is developed. A preliminary characterization of clarity in its relation to custom is as follows.

Any custom refers to regularities that must be perceived, learnt, memorized, and passed on. Unclear and complicated rules cannot be handled in this way, and cannot, therefore, be coded by custom. This constrains possible customary patterns. Clarity eases encoding, while unclarity smothers it.

It has been stressed earlier that custom comprises both cognitive and motivational aspects; it is confined neither to the cognitive nor to the emotional sphere alone.[1] Similarly, the notion of 'clarity' is not restricted to mere perceptual or mnemonic simplicity, but comprises multifarious psychological phenomena. It is devised as a portmanteau term referring to psychological consistency between conviction, motivation, and action.

Justifications in terms of custom illustrate some aspects of such consistency. A certain action may be justified by pointing out that it conforms to custom; clarity refers here to the fit of action to custom. Customary behaviour may be justified in terms of its usefulness or appropriateness; clarity refers here to the fit of the practice to the purpose. The everyday desire for justification instances further pertinent clarification processes.

Clarity requirements affect entitlements and obligations in many other ways which will be discussed later. Before doing so, however, it seems appropriate to consider the workings of entitlements and obligations, and how they control social interaction.

[1] See S. 1.6.

2.6 *An Everyday Transaction*

The effect of entitlements and obligations is most easily understood by looking at commonplace transactions. Consider, as an
example, a taxi ride in an unfamiliar town.[1] A person enters a taxi
cab and tells the driver where to go. Upon arrival the taxi driver
points to the taximeter and indicates the fare. The customer pays,
possibly including a tip. The customer leaves, the taxi disappears.
Neither party expects to meet the other again, and no-one thinks
about the episode any further; this is the usual pattern of behaviour. Yet it is not easy to understand the incident in terms of self-
seeking behaviour.

Surely there was an initial contract. The taxi driver promised to
take the person to the place mentioned, and the passenger promised to pay the fare. This initial contract created entitlements:
the passenger obtained an entitlement to the ride, and in exchange
for that the driver obtained an entitlement to the fare. Congruous
obligations were generated simultaneously.

But why do both parties honour the contract? Why do they care
for those entitlements? The passenger, for his part, may consider
leaving the taxi without paying, as he has been brought to the
place where he wanted to go. He may fear, however, that this
would infuriate the taxi driver. As the driver appears to be a
strong and determined person, this appears too high a risk, and
the passenger decides to pay.

However, after having handed over the money, nothing has
changed in the mutual bargaining position: the taximeter reading
is still the same, the physique of the taxi driver appears as threa-
tening as before, and the passenger still has some cash in his
pocket. So why does the taxi driver not insist that the passenger
pay again, and why shouldn't the passenger comply if he did
before?

The taxi driver may think that such a demand would infuriate
the passenger. The passenger could resist, and could consider

---

[1] The following example for anonymous and non-repeated exchange elaborates on
Basu (1984, 5–7) and Schlicht (1993: 179–80).

legal action. So he is content with what he has obtained and drives away.

But if the passenger can threaten the taxi driver by taking legal action, he could do so at the outset and could save the fare. He could falsely pretend that he had already paid, and that the taxi driver was trying to extort him. There is no clear solution to the bargaining problem: if one party has the means to render the other party compliant, this threat could be used right at the beginning, and also repeatedly. It is not at all clear from the mutual options available to the parties why the initial contract is in fact honoured.

2.7 *Compliance and Moralistic Aggression*

The answer suggested in the above episode is that 'moralistic aggression' may serve as an effective enforcement mechanism. The parties may be prepared to defend whatever they perceive as their entitlement, even if they cannot expect any immediate benefit, and even if it involves some cost to them.[1] Under such an assumption, the taxi driver would act aggressively if the passenger tried to walk away without paying, and the passenger would act aggressively if the taxi driver asked him to pay twice. Both expect this. After calculating costs and benefits, both conclude that demanding and paying one fare is the preferred action for both of them. The strategic considerations may even be skipped, as everybody has gone through similar episodes before and has acquired the appropriate strategy as a matter of routine.

Many everyday transactions rely in this way on entitlements that generate a threat of moralistic aggression. This stabilizes the transaction. Such moralistic aggression is irrational in the sense that it would require each of the parties to engage in actions that worsen their position, but it is precisely this psychological dispo-

---

[1] See Klein *et al.* (1978: 305). They built on the work of the biologist R. L. Trivers (1971). See also Kubon-Gilke (1997: s. 4.3.2).

sition to act aggressively in non-normal cases that sustains smooth transactions in the normal case.[1]

Obligations influence action in a parallel way. If a person accepts that somebody is entitled to obtain something from him, this will increase his inclination to actually concede. Obligations spawn compliance.

It is to be noted here that the entitlements and obligations are mental phenomena lacking any 'real' foundation. The taxi driver knows that the passenger has demanded a ride; if the driver had offered a free ride because he was going in that direction anyway, he would not have been entitled to demand a fare. Similarly, the passenger *knows* that he has asked for a ride; if the taxi had not been properly marked, and the passenger were hitch-hiking, he might not feel an obligation to pay the normal fare. Entitlements and obligations reside in the minds of the individuals concerned and in their understanding of a certain situation.

2.8 *Coordination Failures*

Most, if not all, transactions build on perceived entitlements and obligations that influence behaviour and settle the outcome. Without entitlements and their impact on behaviour, many transactions would not be feasible. The taxi driver would, for instance, anticipate that any passenger would leave the taxi without paying and would ask for advance payment. Any passenger would reject such a demand because he would anticipate that the taxi driver would take the money and refuse to make the trip unless paid again, etc. As a result, such transactions would be blocked

---

[1] This type of behaviour may lead to a more desirable outcome in the long run and thus may be considered rational in a wider sense (Frank 1988; 1989: 13). However, Frank (1989: 6) notes a problem with this: 'If there are genuine advantages of being vengeful or trustworthy and being perceived as such, there are even greater advantages in appearing to have, but not actually having, these qualities.' The maxim 'never tell a lie' seems to be individually less efficient than the maxim 'never tell a lie if it can be found out; otherwise tell lies if it is to your own advantage'. Frank terms this the 'problem of mimicry'. But if mimicry is better than truthfulness, truthfulness can be sustained only by forgoing immediate gains.

by strategic considerations. There would be no taxi service available, since it would not be feasible. Taxis would not exist.[1]

In the presence of entitlements, economic and social coordination runs smoothly in the normal case. This is highlighted when things go wrong and incompatible entitlements clash. Consider again the example of the taxi ride. Assume that the taxi driver has erroneously made a detour. He may feel that he is entitled to the full fare as indicated by the taximeter, as he has driven the passenger that distance. The customer may feel obliged to pay somewhat less, since the optimal distance was shorter than that shown on the taximeter, and the detour was caused by the driver's incompetence: the passenger has not asked for it. The passenger may refuse to pay the demanded fare. In an incident of this sort, a female passenger in Munich injured a taxi driver to such an extent that he had to be hospitalized.[2]

Such conflicts are well known. They relate to warranty, delivery, performance, modes of payment, parking, the noise and smell coming from the neighbours' flat, and so forth. On a larger scale, neighbouring groups or nations may perceive entitlements differently—they may for instance interpret history and historical contracts in a different way. This may lead to war even in cases where no party can expect to win. Inaction, or maybe joint military action against some others, would appear a preferable strategy for both parties in such cases, yet the parties choose to engage in a war. On an intermediate scale, industrial disputes that are particularly severe can be observed if 'matters of principle' are at stake.

2.9 Norms

Entitlements and obligations are closely related to social norms. While the importance of social norms is often recognized, it is less

---

[1] The above is just one example of the 'hold up' problem that arises if one party can withhold performance after the other party has performed. Often these problems can be solved by means of hostages (O.E. Williamson 1985: 167–205). In the taxi driver example, the contracting problem might be solved in that manner, but it should be noted that this is not done in practice. It seems more efficient if there is no necessity for pawning. It is also to be doubted if such pawning would not induce other problems elsewhere.   [2] Tochtermann (1992).

common to view those norms as arising from entitlements and obligations on the individual level.

The economic importance of social norms may be illustrated by looking at fairness. Perceptions of fairness influence economic behaviour. In many settings people prefer fair over unfair actions even if these are to their own disadvantage. They are also prone to punish unfairness, even if this involves some costs to them.[1] Fairness judgements arise from judging a given transaction in the light of a 'reference transaction', which serves as a standard for comparison. If the given transaction deviates from the reference transaction, this is considered unfair. Empirical observations have prompted the surprising conclusion that the reference transaction 'provides a basis for fairness judgements because it is normal, not necessarily because it is just'.[2] Fairness standards are, thus, related to normality and custom. As fairness perceptions influence behaviour significantly, the fairness standards, established by custom, shape behaviour.[3]

Fairness standards play an important role in social and economic life. One important function is that they serve to fill the gaps in insufficiently specified contracts. Most transactions and interactions proceed on the assumption that the usual meaning is invoked, and the usual interpretations are applied, whenever something is left open. But even if the singular case obtains that everything is specified in a contract, the interpretation of the terms of the contract is governed by considerations of common usage. In this way, many transactions are carried out smoothly.

It should be clear, however, that standards of fairness are not invariably beneficial. They may ease many transactions, but they may also block beneficial transactions. Customary wage differentials may, for example, be maintained for reasons of fairness, but

---

[1] Kahneman *et al.* (1986*b*: 736). Schmitt and Marvell (1972) summarize their findings, for instance, by asserting that 'a substantial proportion of subjects will forgo rewards to avoid inequitable conditions'. See Güth *et al.* (1982), and Kahneman *et al.* (1986*a*).

[2] Kahneman *et al.* (1986*b*: 730). See also Opp (1982: 144–7) for a theory about the sequence recurrent behaviour–preference formation–norm formation from the point of view of modern social psychology.

[3] Fairness and justice refer here to standards factually entertained by the individuals, not to some absolute philosophical standards.

the wrong wage structure may hinder an improvement in the allocation of resources.

The same may be said with regard to other social norms. They set standards and bias behaviour and thinking in the direction of these standards. The standards themselves refer to normality. It may be argued, as with fairness, that various norm-guided behaviours have some good and some bad consequences, but this is not the concern here. The point is rather that these norms exist and that they strongly influence social and economic interaction. This must be taken into account, and allowance must be made for the fact that these norms are not fixed, but are shaped by social and economic processes.

In all these examples, the term 'norms' can be used interchangeably with 'entitlements and obligations'. Speaking about entitlements seems, however, preferable in most cases. Such a parlance stresses the subjective element and makes it easier to envisage conflict. The coordination failures such as the conflict between the taxi driver and his passenger discussed above can be rephrased in terms of conflicting social norms held by the parties.[1] This appears vexatious since social norms are typically related to shared understandings. 'Conflicting norms' must refer to 'conflicting shared understandings'. Such a parlance requires further refinements to make sense. Therefore, it seems more appropriate to conceive of these cases as arising from conflicting entitlements, and to conceive of social norms as arising from intermeshing perceptions of entitlements and obligations.[2]

The entitlement view permits an analysis of norm formation in terms of psychological processes that shape entitlements and obligations. By treating norms as results of psychological processes that generate entitlements and obligations, issues of norm formation and, more broadly, of custom formation can be addressed. The other position of taking norms as irreducible social facts

[1] See S. 2.8.
[2] The 'dual entitlement' theory of fairness proposed by Kahneman et al. (1986b) derives fairness judgements in a similar—but somewhat more detailed and elaborate—way from entitlements.

would block all understanding of norm formation and the dynamics of custom from the outset.

2.10 Contracting

Economic interaction is intimately related to contracting. The possibility of contracting is tied up with the way in which contracting gives rise to entitlements and obligations. The exchange of one good for another involves mutual agreement on the transaction. Such an agreement—an 'implied contract'—is often implied by acting conclusively. If so, an 'implied' or 'implicit' contract is concluded. In other cases, an explicit contract may govern the transaction.

Market exchange, certainly one of the core themes in economics, is just one form of implicit or explicit contracting. The taxi driver example can be seen in this way.[1] Institutional economics as well as political economics, labour economics, and various branches of microeconomics have stressed that economic activity involves contracting from the outset. Some authors view institutions in general as clusters of contracts between individuals.[2]

Contracting refers to an exchange of promises: one party promises to act under certain conditions in a certain way, and the other party makes a similar promise. Both promises are contingent on one another: if one party does not perform, the other party is not bound to perform either. Further, both promises will restrict behaviour away from what the parties may otherwise prefer to do. A promise to behave strictly selfishly under all circumstances will not fetch a price.[3]

---

[1] See S. 2.6.

[2] The view that institutions are just contracts has been elaborated, e.g. by Jensen and Meckling (1976) and Alchian (1984) with respect to the firm, and may be extended to other institutions. See Ch. 13 below on the theory of the firm.

[3] Contracts are taken thus as dealing with—possibly limited—conflicts, where it is in everybody's interest to default provided the other party observes the contract, and where the other party's obedience is brought about by the other party's promise not to defect. In contrast, pure coordination problems may be solved by simple agreements. Note also that the above discussion is simplified in that third parties are not invoked in the argument. The main conclusion is, however, not affected by that: symbolic action must trigger the behaviour of the parties. This can work only through motivational channels, since no real incentives are changed by uttering the words 'I agree'. The problem that symbolic action must trigger behaviour relates to the problem that 'strategic' speech may destroy communication altogether (Basu 1994: 2).

Contracting is possible because the promises affect behaviour. They are binding. They may be not binding in any absolute sense, but the probability of behaving as promised is increased by the making of the promise. This may come about in several ways.

First, there may be institutions that are responsible for contract enforcement, such as the courts. This 'external enforcement' is certainly of great importance, especially for large-scale explicit contracts.

The second possibility is that contracts are 'self-enforcing' It may be in the mutual interest of the parties to carry them out.[1] The parties may want to do business with one another and promise to meet at a certain place at a certain time. Both would benefit from keeping the promise, and both know this: the 'contract' is 'self-enforcing'. Such 'contracts' ought be termed 'agreements', since they do not restrict future action away from what would be preferable otherwise. They do not pose any particular theoretical problem.

Sometimes this self-enforcement comes about through reputation effects in long-term relationships: in order to continue doing business with the customer, the firm performs as expected— otherwise, the custom may be lost. The danger of spoiling the firm's reputation may provide a sufficient incentive to perform. There are some theoretical problems associated with such reputation mechanisms, but these problems will not be discussed here.

2.11 *Non-enforceable Contracts*

Many contracts rely neither on self-enforcement nor on external enforcement. Such non-enforceable contracts are typical for many everyday transactions, both for business contracts and for contracts between nations. The importance of non-enforceable contracts has been widely recognized in the literature, and it seems

[1] See Telser (1981: 27) and Klein (1985) on self-enforcing contracts.

unnecessary to stress their importance again.[1] The following
remarks are intended to illustrate the nature of these of non-
enforceable contracts.

Every-day interaction is often guided by customary patterns
which trail the law in many cases. For instance, German labour
and commercial law states that common practice is binding in
cases of dispute. In the dozen reported Anglo-American cases in
which ownership of a whale's carcass was contested, judges
regarded themselves as bound to honour whalers' usages which
had been proved in a trial. The usages and property rights evolved
among whalers without any outside interference. When whaling
switched from right (*Balaenidae*) whales to sperm whales, these
practices and customs adapted to the new circumstances. This
happened spontaneously and without any external intervention.[2]
Sometimes custom simply overrides the law. In Shasta County,
California, people settle their disputes by customary rules that
are quite unrelated, and sometimes even contrary, to prevailing
legal arrangements:

When adjoining landowners there decide to split the costs of boundary
fences, they typically reach their solutions in total ignorance of their
substantive legal rights. When resolving cattle-trespass disputes, virtually
all rural residents apply a norm that an animal owner is responsible for
the behaviour of his livestock—even in situations where they know that a
cattleman would not be legally liable for trespass damages.[3]

Business contracts are often rather vague in their contents. They
articulate aims and intentions, rather than tight quality descriptions and formulas linking quantity with price. However, they

---

[1] The literature refers to non-enforceable contracts as 'relational contracts', 'private
ordering', or contracts governed by social norms. Classical papers include Llewellyn
(1931) and Macaulay (1963). O.E. Williamson (1985: 20–2; 163–8) has stressed the
importance of private ordering for business relationships. Ellickson (1991) has inves-
tigated in detail how everyday life in a California county (Shasta County) is governed by
social norms that are unrelated to the pertinent legal norms.
[2] Ellickson (1991: 192;197).   [3] Ellickson (1991: 141).

often contain provisions for arbitration in cases of dispute, presumably to keep the disputes out of court.[1]

Such contracts rely on informal, customary ways of enforcement,
for several reasons. Small-scale contracts cannot count on external
enforcement, because it simply would not be worthwhile to go to
court, and it would be difficult to supply adequate evidence.
Fraudulent taxi drivers exploit this.

Large-scale business contracts require a flexibility that can be
obtained only by keeping the terms vague. Such contracts require
specialized knowledge for interpreting them in an appropriate
manner. The courts with their schematized reasoning, bound by
abstract general rules, and with their ignorance of the many
specifics surrounding a dispute, are poorly equipped to enforce
such contracts sensibly. In consequence, courts are avoided.

International relations are dominated by non-enforceable contracts for obvious reasons. Although international courts do exist,
they have no means of enforcing their rulings other than by
resorting to the help of other nations. There is no supreme agency
for enforcing international contracts, and many contracts are not
self-enforcing. The spontaneous emergence of whaling rights and
the change of these rights in response to changing conditions
illustrates this.

'Non-enforceable' contracts are thus central for our understanding of economic processes. They govern everyday exchanges and
are *a conditio sine qua non* for a proper functioning of any market
system; they are absolutely necessary for the maintenance and
workability of all social structures. Yet they have been often disregarded.[2] Such non-enforceable contracts are concluded because
they affect behaviour, in spite of lacking a supporting enforcement
mechanism. They work, because they create entitlements and
obligations and set the standards that trigger compliance and
moralistic aggression. The contracting parties rely on this

---

[1] Kubon-Gilke (1997: s. 5.3.6).
[2] Modern treatments, such as Lewis (1969), Schotter (1981), or Sugden (1986), have
often been inspired by game theory and rule this out by assumption.

mechanism.[1] In the words of David Hume, 'there must be some act of mind attending these words, I promise; and on this act of mind must the obligation depend.'[2] However, many promises are not kept, and many assertions do not create entitlements. If somebody says: 'I will do my best,' this will not necessarily mean anything more than 'I want to be polite, and I will do the usual.' The entitlements that can be evoked by concluding a contract rely on customary standards of performance.

2.12 *Entitlements and Morality*

The above account of entitlements as the backbone to market transactions covers many of the topics that are usually associated with discussions about social norms and business morality. More specifically, it is held that societies have developed 'implicit agreements of certain kinds of regard for others, agreements which are essential to the survival of the society or at least contribute greatly to the efficiency of its working'.[3]

In the example of the taxi driver, however, it seems a little far-fetched to talk about morality and a mutual regard for others. The ethical connotations may even be unwarranted. They may be quite irrelevant for conducting the transaction. Transactions may even occur under relatively wicked circumstances. Contracting among gangsters or drug traffickers and addicts is remote from current notions of morality but may be covered from an entitlement perspective. It seems confusing rather than enlightening to invoke

---

[1] It may be noted that even very refined notions of self-enforcement, e.g. Bull (1983), implicitly make such an assumption. In Bull, the assumption is that a contract is of relevance because renegotiation is not possible. Any slight deviation from the behaviour specified in the original contract is considered a breach rather than a modification of the original contract and triggers a non-cooperative response.

[2] Hume (1740a: 516).

[3] Arrow (1974: 26). Casson (1991) has used the terms 'morality' and 'trust' in the same sense, as referring to mutually advantageous individual dispositions that enhance economic performance by lowering transaction costs.

moral behaviour in these cases.[1] The entitlement term is morally neutral, and seems also more appropriate in the context of exchange.

Another reason for avoiding reference to morality is as follows. 'Morality' refers not only to conventions and moral values that vary across cultures, but also to ethical core ideas of truth, justice, and human rights that are shared across cultures in spite of different interpretations. Speaking about entitlements and obligations invokes stronger conventional and weaker ethical connotations. If conventional aspects of morality are concerned, the entitlement terminology is preferable, while morality terms are more appropriate when referring to absolute ethical aspects.

---

[1] David Hume (1740a: 532) put this as follows: 'Here are two persons that dispute an estate; of whom one is rich, a fool, and a bachelor; the other poor, a man of sense, and has a numerous family: The first is my enemy, the second my friend. Whether I be actuated in this affair by a view of public interest, by friendship or enmity, I must do the utmost to procure the estate to the latter.' Still, the first may be entitled to obtain the property!

Chapter 3

SMOOTH AND LUMPY CHANGES

3.1 Change

Custom has been depicted as shaping entitlements and obligations and thereby governing economic and social interaction. Yet economic and social developments in turn affect custom. As a consequence, any theory of custom must confront the problem of change in custom.

The issue is, however, an intricate one. Custom comprises various interconnected constituents. The power of custom is not effectuated by any single factor alone, but is engendered by the confluence of many influences. The discussion of change requires envisaging the transformation of the entire complex. This is prohibitively difficult. The present chapter will side-step this complexity by focusing on some simple cases.

The adoption of a new technology provides an example for considering the workings of conservatism and inertia and their interaction with other incentives under simple circumstances. It illustrates how conservatism smoothes the impact of external incentives while conformity induces discontinuity and hysteresis.

The discussion offered in this chapter should be regarded as a preliminary step in the argument. The simple mechanisms described here require modification at later stages. Further, the example of technical change is to be taken as illustrative of a more general pattern. The adoption of new habits and new routines may be conceived in a similar manner, and the formation of convictions that give rise to entitlements and obligations can be understood in an analogy to the adoption of a new technology.

3.2 Conservatism and Inertia

Conservatism tends to maintain what had occurred before. If conditions change, there may be incentives to change behaviour, but conservatism will resist such change and will slow down adaptation. It creates inertia.

Consider a group of workers who perform a certain task. A new practice becomes available that has several advantages. (Think of a new computer software program.) Conservatism among the workers ensures that it will be adopted only slowly. Some workers will change their ways, others will stick to the old practice. All new workers who join the group will start in with the new technique, however. In this way, the new technique will gradually supplant the old one. This is depicted in Fig. 3.1. Without conservatism, the new technique could have been adopted just when it became available. Conservatism does what Marshall attributed to custom: it 'rounds off the edges of change' and plays 'the same part in the moral world that friction does in the mechanical'.[1] It does not block economic or other incentives, but it slows down their effects.

3.3 Conformity and Critical Mass

Conformity works in a different way.[2] Consider again a group of workers facing a new technique. Assume that each worker prefers

---

[1] Marshall (1890: 533; 1961: 140). On diffusion processes, see Rogers (1971).

[2] The following builds on Schelling (1978: 91–110). Interesting developments of critical mass ideas involving discussions of underlying motivational processes can be found in Witt (1986; 1989), Weise (1992), and Kuran (1995).

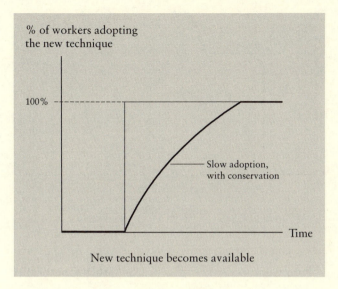

Figure 3.1
Conservatism and the Adoption of a New Technique

to work like the others do and chooses the technique used by the majority of co-workers. More specifically, let us assume for the sake of the argument that all workers will switch to the technique initially used by more than 50 per cent of the co-workers. If less than 50 per cent are using the new technique initially, all workers will use the old technique in the next period; if more than 50 per cent are initially using the new technique, all workers will adopt it in the next period. This pure case is depicted in Fig. 3.2. The abscissa gives the percentage of workers using the new technique initially. This is the 'usage rate'. The solid curve gives the percentage of workers adopting the new technique in the subsequent period: this is the 'adoption rate'. There is a 'critical mass', arbitrarily assumed here to be 50 per cent. Usage rates exceeding this critical mass lead eventually to full adoption, usage rates below the critical mass lead eventually to a rejection of the new technology.

Such critical mass effects also occur in cases where conformity does not take the extreme form depicted in Fig. 3.2. Some workers

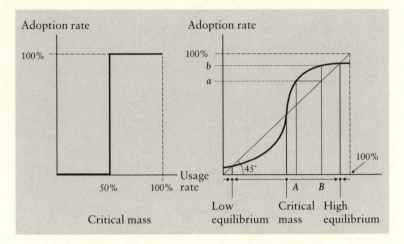

Figure 3.2
Pure Conformity

Figure 3.3
Smoothed Conformity

may have reason to rely on their own judgement, and only those who are insecure may follow the majority. Such a case is depicted in Fig. 3.3. Here, some workers prefer the new technique, even if most do not. Symmetrically, some workers prefer the old technique even if most use the new one. The majority is, however, guided by conformity. To make the story somewhat more realistic, it may even be assumed that the workers differ in their switching behaviour. Some may not be willing to adopt the new technique at first, but will readily join if only a small number of others are doing the same. Still other workers may be prepared to switch only if a large majority has already adopted the new technique. If reference group behaviour is sufficiently strong, a small increase in the usage rate will boost adoption in an intermediate region and a critical mass effect will result.

The adjustment process is as follows. Any given usage rate, such as A in Fig. 3.3, induces a certain adoption rate (a in the figure). This adoption rate will be the usage rate in the next period (B in Fig. 3.3) and will induce another adoption rate (b in the figure). An equilibrium is reached whenever a usage rate induces an adoption rate that equals the usage rate. The equilibria are thus given by the intersections of the solid curve in Fig. 3.3 with the 45° line. There are three such equilibria, labelled 'low equilibrium', 'critical mass', and 'high equilibrium'.

When an equilibrium usage rate is achieved, the usage rate will induce an identical adoption rate which will serve as the usage rate for the next period. The usage rate will thus remain constant over time. Whenever the usage rate induces an adoption rate in excess of the usage rate, the usage rate will increase over time. This is the case between the critical mass and the high equilibrium and also to the left of the low equilibrium point. Whenever a usage rate induces a lower adoption rate, the usage rate will decline over time. This is the case between the low equilibrium point and the critical mass and also to the right of the high equilibrium point. The directions of change in the usage rate are indicated by arrows. The low equilibrium and the high equilibrium are both stable in the sense that usage rates close to these equilibria will induce movements tending towards these equilibria. The critical mass is an unstable equilibrium in the sense that small perturbations will induce movements of the usage rate away from the critical mass. In the long run, usage rates will settle at either the high or the low equilibrium. The critical mass is, so to speak, the watershed separating the regions of attraction of the low and the high equilibria.

3.4 *Dispersed Conformity*

If conformity is dispersed, the critical mass effect disappears. This is illustrated in Fig. 3.4. Here, there is no critical range of adoption rates where many individuals switch their behaviour. Rather, switching points are spread diffusely over the entire range of usage rates. At low usage rates adoption will be above usage, because some individuals are unconditionally preferring the new technique. At high usage rates adoption will be below usage, because some individuals are unconditionally preferring the old technique. As a consequence, usage will increase at low usage rates and

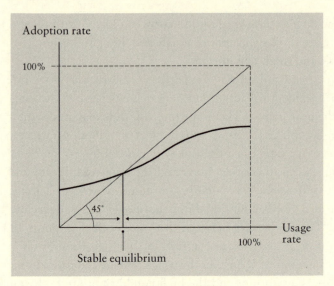

Figure 3.4
Dispersed Conformity

decrease at high usage rates. The process will reach equilibrium where the usage rate equals the rate of adoption.

3.5 *Conservatism, Dispersed Conformity, and Incentives*

Consider next a change in incentives, and how such a change affects the adoption of a new technique. Assume that incentives that are oriented even more towards change render the new technique even more attractive. There is, for example, a new version of the software program embodying further improvements. It can be expected that the better performance of the new version will weaken the impact of conservatism. Adoption will speed up.[1]

In the case of dispersed conformity, increased incentives will lead, for any adoption rate, to higher usage rates, and equilibrium usage rates will increase.[2]

---

[1] The curve in Fig. 3.1, describing adoption over time, will become steeper.
[2] The solid curve in Fig. 3.4. For a discussion of the corresponding multi-dimensional case, see Schlicht (1981).

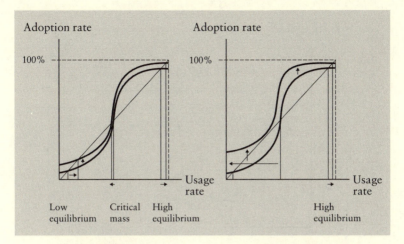

Figure 3.5
**Conformity With
Increasing Incentives**

Figure 3.6
**Further Increases of Incentives
and Cumulative Growth**

In both cases outside incentives are increasing usage rates. This translates to custom: any custom may be viewed as having been brought about by outside influences that are channelled by conservatism and conformity. It is also to be expected that observance of a custom will increase if it becomes more attractive to adopt the custom, and may decrease if it becomes more costly to do so.

3.6 *Conformity and Cumulative Growth*

With strong conformity and critical mass effects, the overall picture changes somewhat. Start again with the old technique. The new technique is introduced, and incentives for adoption are gradually increased. With pure conformity, nothing significant would happen. Since everybody does what the majority is doing, the old technique continues to be used, in spite of slight changes in incentives.[1] This is, however, an extreme case. The standard case would be as depicted in the lower curve of Fig. 3.5.[2] If the new

[1] See Fig. 3.2.   [2] CF. Fig. 3.3.

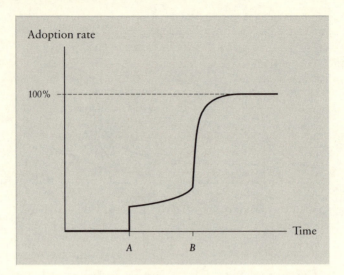

Figure 3.7
Conservatism With Cumulative Growth

technique becomes more attractive, adoption rates will increase at all usage levels, and the curve giving the adoption rate will shift up. This will decrease the critical mass: fewer users will be needed now to excite cumulative adoption. The low equilibrium level will increase, since even at low usage rates there is a stronger incentive for using the new technique. The high equilibrium level will increase for the same reason.

If the incentive for using the new technique is further increased, this process will continue until a position is reached as illustrated in Fig. 3.6. The critical mass has jumped to zero, the lower equilibrium has ceased to exist, and the new technique is adopted quickly and widely. One additional worker tips the balance, and the new practice spreads cumulatively and rapidly. The time-path generated in this way may look like the one in Fig. 3.7. The new technology becomes available at time *A*. Initially it is diffusing slowly, but beyond the threshold point *B* conformity generates a wave of imitation, and the new technique spreads very fast.

Similar patterns will emerge whenever customs, habits, or convictions are governed by conformity. It may, for example, be unsafe to walk home in the dark when the streets are empty, so everybody prefers to take a taxi. If safety improves, the number of those who dare to walk will gradually increase. Once a certain security level is reached, the balance is tipped, and the majority will adopt the habit of walking home in the dark.

The workings of conservatism and of conformity differ. Conservatism induces sluggishness in any kind of response. Conformity stabilizes the *status quo* but may also induce discontinuous changes if the relevant critical masses disappear.

3.7 *Conformity and Sudden Decay*

The process may also work in the other direction. Consider fiscal morality.[1] Assume that everybody is prepared to declare his income correctly only if all the others submit correct tax returns. If an individual knows that many others cheat on taxes, he will be tempted, rationally speaking, to do the same. Information about cheating, statistical and other, is available. In short, fiscal morality is assumed to be strongly governed by conformity. This is— analogously to Fig. 3.6—depicted in Fig. 3.8. 'Tax compliance' on the abscissa gives the percentage of correct tax returns, and 'fiscal morality' on the ordinate, the percentage of correct tax returns made in response to a given degree of compliance.[2] There are two stable equilibria where tax compliance equals fiscal morality, and a critical mass separating these equilibria. Consider a process that starts at the high equilibrium. Tax rates increase. This increases incentives to cheat. It becomes more expensive to be honest. Cheating increases slightly and the high equilibrium moves to the left. The process continues until the critical position is reached. A further tax increase tips the balance, and fiscal morality collapses suddenly. The resulting time-path is depicted in Fig. 3.9.

---

[1] The following draws on Schlicht (1984*a*).

[2] That is, tax compliance corresponds to the usage rate and fiscal morality to the adoption rate, as explained in S. 3.3.

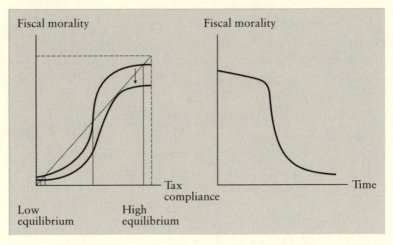

Figure 3.8
**Further Increases in the
Tax Rate**

Figure 3.9
**Conservatism With
Cumulative Decay**

3.8 *Hysteresis*

Conformity channels incentives in a particularly 'lumpy' way. This has been illustrated with the example about fiscal morality. The impact of changing incentives is first impeded and later augmented. There is, so to speak, some limited memory in the system. An established practice will be maintained under conditions in which it would not emerge anew. An analogous phenomenon is well known in physics. If iron is magnetized, it will retain the magnetic polarization even if the external magnetizing field is removed. A magnetic field of reversed polarity is needed to purge the trace of the initial magnetic field.[1]

The critical mass effect will lead to a similar hysteresis phenomenon with respect to custom. Take again the example of fiscal morality. In Fig. 3.10 it has been assumed that the tax rate increases over time. Thus, a graph can be drawn which displays

---

[1] For some formal aspects, see Schlicht (1985*a*: 38–9). In labour market theory, hysteresis has been used recently to denote phenomena of persistence and inertia (e.g. Franz 1990). As this would leave no term for the effect described above, I prefer to use it in the classic sense.

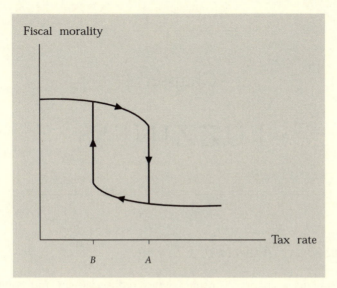

Figure 3.10
The Hysteresis Loop

fiscal morality as a function of the tax rate. This is the upper line
in the figure. Along this graph, fiscal morality is declining with an
increasing tax rate, first slowly and then abruptly.

Consider now a reverse movement. The tax rate is gradually
reduced. Even if tax rates are reduced below point *A*, where the
breakdown of morale occurred previously, no recovery of fiscal
morality occurs. As everyone else continues to cheat, everyone
feels entitled to cheat. Conformity stabilizes cheating, just as it
stabilizes honesty in the reverse process. Only if the tax rate is
reduced much further—below point *B*—will honesty re-emerge.
The advantages from cheating are not great at that point, and the
danger and shame of being caught remain. Fiscal morality will
recover suddenly and quickly.

Such hysteresis may be tarnished by conservatism, which slows
down all processes of adaptation. With conservatism, the hysteresis loop would appear less sudden, the time-scale being stretched
as if in slow motion; but the speed differences characteristic for
hysteresis would remain.

Chapter 4

FUZZINESS

4.1 *Variegating Aspects of Custom*

The previous chapter considered how conservatism and conformity shape custom, but the analysis was confined to an extremely
simple setting. It was assumed that a custom is either observed or
ignored, and other possibilities were disregarded. Such a view is,
however, much too simple. Customs do not fit well into an all-or-
nothing schema. They may change in various dimensions, and
outside influences may affect them accordingly.

This chapter will be devoted to characterizing custom in a
broader setting, where observance of a custom may occur in
varying intensity, and over a varying range of conditions. It will
be argued that this more realistic treatment introduces fuzziness as
an important and pervasive feature of custom.

4.2 *Scope*

A custom establishes a certain regularity. Whenever an event of a
certain type occurs, it requires a certain response. The set of
events to which the custom applies constitutes the 'scope' of the
custom.

As an example, consider tipping. In Germany it is appropriate
to give a tip to the taxi driver. Gratuities are also given to waiters,

guides, chambermaids, and hairdressers. All these occasions are included in the scope of the custom.

This scope is further characterized by the definitions and delineations involved. While a taxi driver may expect a tip, this will not apply to the driver of a shuttle bus, or the pilot of an aeroplane. The waiter may be tipped, but not the chef or the owner of the restaurant, or the personnel in a self-service bistro. Similarly, the guide, or the chambermaid, or the hairdresser, or the nurse would be entitled to receive a tip under certain conditions, and it might be considered offensive to disregard these limits.

Similar considerations apply to all kinds of custom. In Germany, for instance, queues are formed at bank tills or at the airport check-in counters, but not at a bus stop.

It is also evident that the scope of any custom is very different in different countries. In Spain, museum attendants expect a tip, whereas this is not customary in Iceland or New Zealand. England is well-known for queuing, but Germany is not.

4.3 *Level*

Many customs are of an all-or-nothing nature. The practice of queuing may be observed or disregarded. Other customs can, however, be varied in intensity. The tip may be larger or smaller; a bill may be paid upon receipt or with a delay; hospitality may be interpreted more or less extensively; a circumcision may be more or less drastic.

The 'level' of a custom denotes this intensity, if it can be varied. Levels are aspects of a custom that vary greatly across countries. In the United States a waiter will expect 15 per cent of the bill, in Germany only 10 percent.[1]

---

[1] In Germany service is included in the bill, however.

4.4 *Compliance*

Further, a custom may be more or less deeply ingrained and more or less strictly obeyed. Traffic lights are respected in some countries, but not in others. Tipping a guide is not obligatory in Germany.

'Compliance' refers to the degree of obedience. Compliance may be conceived as measuring the relative frequency of obedience in situations where the custom applies. If the code is strictly obeyed, compliance is 100 per cent; if it is observed in only half of the cases, it is 50 per cent.

A given custom—like tipping—cannot, of course, simply be characterized by one single measure of compliance. Across the scope of the custom, compliance will vary. For central cases (tipping a waiter) compliance will be high, while for boundary cases (tipping a hairdresser) it will be low.

Thus, a custom may be characterized by a general rule that links certain actions to certain events. The *scope* of the custom is given by the set of circumstances to which it applies. Its *level* is given by the intensity, if this can be varied. *Compliance* measures the degree to which the custom is observed. In all these dimensions, a custom may be moulded and affected by outside influences.

4.5 *The Fuzziness of Custom*

The three dimensions of custom discussed above—scope, level, and compliance—are also the dimensions in which changes may occur. The changeability of custom is intimately related to its vagueness. Alfred Marshall has described this fuzziness of custom very clearly:

> But in fact the payments and dues, which custom is supposed to stereotype, nearly always contain elements which are incapable of precise definition; while the accounts of them handed down by tradition are embodied in loose and vague impressions, or at best are expressed in words that make no attempt at scientific exactness.

We can watch the influence of this vagueness in the agreements between landlord and tenant even in modern England; for they have always been interpreted by the aid of customs, which have ever been imperceptibly growing and dwindling again, to meet the changing exigencies of successive generations.[1]

The vagueness of contract terms that Marshall notes is related to the level of custom. A similar vagueness applies to seemingly clearcut cases, such as giving a cab driver a 15 per cent tip. Assume that the fare for a taxi ride was £23.80, but the passenger paid £27.00. The tip may have been determined by calculating the normal tip, adding it to the fare, and rounding the result. The result is, however, ambiguous. A tip of 15 per cent would amount to paying £27.37. The passenger settled for £27.00, but he could have decided equally well to pay £27.50 or £28.00 instead, or he could have returned three £1 coins after having obtained the exact change. This would have amounted to paying £26.80. The example illustrates that there is scope for shading the level in one direction or the other even in cases where the rule is fairly definite.

Further, vagueness may also occur in cases of all-or-nothing customs. The Indian custom of burning the widow of a deceased man seems to be very definite indeed. Yet the time-span between the death and cremation may be stretched. Many all-or-nothing customs are actually quite fuzzy if the possibility of delay is taken into account.

Scope is usually fuzzy, too. There are always some borderline cases where ambiguity arises. If the taxi driver can expect a tip, what about the driver of the mini-bus?

Such fuzziness can be found even in apparently clear-cut cases. Consider widow-burning again. What if the man and his widow have lived apart for a long time? What if they had only just been married? In such extreme cases, some fuzziness may occur.

---

[1] Marshall (1890: 638). See also Kuran (1991: 252–5; 1995: 295–7), who stresses the space for discretion generated by fuzziness. This invites 'creative' and even 'self-serving' interpretation, as can be seen for example in the development of some religious interpretations.

4.6 *Ambiguity and Compliance*

A very clear-cut custom can give rise, then, to fuzziness. Ambiguity will arise at the fringes of its scope. Ambiguous instances will induce conflicting perceptions and opinions about appropriate behaviour even in cases where people are motivated exclusively by a concern to follow customary ways, reducing compliance in unclear cases. If there are other motives as well, complexity and ambiguity will be compounded by these other concerns, and the behavioural impact of the custom will be further obscured. As observed behaviour cannot easily indicate whether a custom has been observed in an ambiguous case, or whether other motives have induced the observed behaviour, the forces of conservatism and conformity will be weakened and compliance will be reduced.

Thus, a clear-cut custom may command obedience for core cases, but it will appear less obligatory for borderline circumstances. At the fringes of its scope, and with vaguely defined levels, a custom is vulnerable to outside influences. This opens the way for growth as well as for erosion. The next chapter turns to these issues.

Chapter 5

ADAPTIVE CUSTOM

5.1 *Full Malleability*

With conservatism and inertia working alone, custom would per-
petuate what happened before. Other forces may bend the course
of events by slowly modifying scope, level, or compliance. Fuzziness smoothes the path for such changes. Legal or social enforcement mechanisms cannot work in regions of fuzziness, and
compliance is limited because fuzziness induces conflicting perceptions and opinions. Ambiguity allows for different interpretations,
and there is scope to select the interpretation with an eye to
personal advantage. The custom may be shaded in a self-seeking
manner. Deviations will persist and will appear normal after a
while. In this way, the custom yields to outside forces. Great
fuzziness permits fast change, but for some change to occur, it is
sufficient to have some fuzziness.

Alfred Marshall saw this clearly. He noted that custom may be
evaded by 'gradual and imperceptible changes', and 'short-lived
man has little better means of ascertaining whether custom is
quietly changing, than the fly, born to-day and dead to-morrow,
has of watching the growth of the plant on which it rests'.[1]

Fuzziness thus renders any custom malleable. As a result, outside influences may erode it, starting from the fringes of its scope.

[1] Marshall (1890, 1920: 465, 532).

The converse is also true: the scope of a custom may expand and the level of a custom may increase if there are outside influences that promote growth.

This chapter will consider the formation of custom under the assumption that custom is fully malleable. Custom is assumed to yield to outside forces in all dimensions—scope, level, and compliance. To simplify further, it will be supposed that the only modifying force influencing custom arises from the self-interested behaviour of the individuals concerned. Other possible forces, in particular the cognitive and emotional tendencies relating to clarity, are disregarded for the time being.

The assumption of full malleability captures important features of reality. It is, however, a simplification that overstates the plasticity of custom. With full malleability, it will be argued, custom would just amount to friction. Growth and decay of custom may be fruitfully discussed with the aid of such an assumption, but all customs that are rigid and individually costly to obey elude such an approach. This will mandate a modification of the full malleability assumption at a later stage.

5.2 *The Erosion and Growth of Custom*

Consider first how a custom may erode under the permanent influence of self-interested behaviour. Again, take the example of tipping the cab driver. Assume, as an established norm, that the level of the tip should amount to roughly 15 per cent of the bill. If people were neither self-interested nor altruistic, but were driven only by conservatism and conformity, the prevailing level of tipping would be self-perpetuating. All taxi drivers would feel entitled to obtain a tip of this size, and all passengers would feel obliged to give such a tip.

Consider now how widespread self-seeking behaviour would modify the custom. While the taxi driver may be interested in obtaining a bigger tip, he will not be entitled to obtain it and has no means effectively of claiming it. The customer will be interested in paying somewhat less, but will feel that the taxi driver is entitled to the customary tip. Yet the customary tip is almost never paid exactly, because of rounding. The selfish customers will tend to under-tip, and there will emerge a tendency to shade the custom in cases of doubt. Any given customary level of tipping will, therefore, induce a slightly lower average rate of tipping in the next period. This will lead to 'level erosion': the customary level of tipping will shrink over time.[1]

The argument can be refined in various ways. It may be the case, for instance, that customers wish to give something extra for good service, and to reduce the tip for poor service. In this case, an average service would fetch an average tip. This way of varying the size of the tip with the quality of the service will lead to an average tip being attached to average service, with the average reproducing itself. If self-seeking customers give a smaller tip in cases of doubt, the average will be driven down, and the custom will eventually erode.[2]

If the custom of tipping is fully malleable and gratuities are not intrinsically preferred, but are given only for customary reasons, tipping must be expected to yield to the forces of selfishness and eventually to disappear. Empirically, this is clearly not the case. In Australia, for instance, tipping has spread.

Consider now how the custom of tipping may emerge where it was initially unknown. This may come about because humans have a tendency to reciprocate. Customers may like to reward above-average service by rounding somewhat more generously than usual.[3] As they cannot pay less than the stated price for the service, paying the stated price alone may come to mean paying

---

[1] This is an example of what Kuran (1991: 252–5; 1995: 295–7) termed a 'self-serving interpretation'.

[2] An additional reason working in this direction is related to the phenomenon of 'loss aversion' (see S. 8.5). While people react strongly if the customary standard is not met, they will react less resolutely if it is surpassed. The loss felt by the customer who pays in excess of the customary standard looms larger than the perceived gain obtained by underperforming. This creates an asymmetry favouring erosion.

[3] This tendency to reciprocate is fairly universal and has been the subject of 'equity theory', and 'social exchange theory', see Adams (1963), Blau (1955), Homans (1961). The argument given in the text is refined and formalized by using equity theory in Schlicht (1993: 198–9)

below the average. This will tend to be done only for below-average service. The average level of tipping arrived at in this way will become customary and will be expected for average service. Taxi drivers will expect a corresponding 'normal' tip under normal circumstances, and customers will pay it unless they are dissatisfied. In order to reward good service, those who want to reward it must offer a tip that exceeds the customary level, and the customary level will increase further. The process will stabilize only if people cease to surpass the customary level on average, for some external reason.

In conclusion, the assumption of full adaptability implies that a custom that can be varied in its level—like tipping—will eventually reflect the preferences of the customers. It will have no 'life of its own'.

With full malleability, processes of erosion and growth similar to those discussed above must be expected to occur whenever the level of a custom is changeable. Consider, as another example, periods of grace. Assume that it is customary to pay a bill within a week. This standard has established itself as a kind of average: some customers pay sooner, others pay later. It may, however, be in the interest of the debtors to pay later. On average, they pay just a little too late, but not so much that they have to fear some kind of sanction. This behaviour will drive the average delay up, and the customary period of grace will follow suit. Ultimately, no bill would be paid, and all transactions would have to be carried out in cash.

The problem is of some practical importance. Small businesses in Germany complain about being paid only after great delay while their suppliers insist on prompt payment. They have no easy means of solving the problem because all customers take the long periods of settlement for granted. Even if the law prescribes shorter terms, it will not be feasible to go to court. Yet it is to be noted that the process has to stop somewhere. Under the assumption of full malleability, the establishment of certain customary settlement periods must be attributed to the debtor's preferences.

If the customary period of grace is long, the tendency to prolong it further must be curbed.

Note an important difficulty here. The argument cannot easily resort to notions of fairness and appropriateness as ultimate determinants of modes of payment. Under the assumption of full adaptivity, these notions themselves relate directly to customary, and hence adaptive, standards.

In a similar way, the scope of a custom can be eroded by the attempts of the individuals to pursue their own interests. Consider the occasions where formal dress is required. There are cases of doubt. If the individuals prefer less formal dress and follow their self-interest in the unclear cases, the scope of the custom will contract. Conversely, formal dress may emerge as prescribed by custom on many occasions if people prefer formal to informal dress; this will induce them, in cases of doubt, to select formal dress, and the scope of formal dress will expand. In the long run, the custom will reflect the tastes and will adapt to underlying preferences. It has, again, no life of its own.

5.3 *The Smoothing of Hysteresis*

Phenomena of critical mass and hysteresis appear self-stabilizing and have, in this sense, a life of their own.[1] Yet the apparent lumpiness and rigidity disappears once the issue is considered in depth.

Consider the case of walking home alone at night as long as others are doing the same. A high equilibrium has established itself, as described above.[2] So the custom seems firmly established. The earlier argument about hysteresis suggests that it is stable. If danger increases slightly, no change in behaviour is to be expected, as long as the critical mass is safely maintained. Yet under the assumption of full adaptability, this conclusion would be misleading. It rests on implicitly neglecting details and dimensions that induce fuzziness.

[1] S. 3.3–3.8.   [2] S. 3.6.

Consider the spatial and the temporal aspects of the problem. Regarding space, the safety problem arises in a certain district. In the centre of this district is a bus stop, where people leave the bus and walk home. After dark, there are many other people on the street, and everybody feels safe. Yet not all the streets in the neighbourhood will be equally crowded. There will be more pedestrians at some places, and fewer at other places. Many will pass close to the bus stop and will feel safe there. Those who live farther away, however, will have to walk along some fairly empty streets when approaching their homes. They will feel less safe there. Their decision will thus depend not only on the average number of pedestrians close to the bus stop, but also on safety in the periphery. If the danger increases slightly, some may decide to take taxis more frequently. This will drive the density of pedestrians down, which will reduce overall safety and deminish pedestrian density still further. As a result, the number of people walking home in the dark will react smoothly to external incentives. The lumpiness associated with hysteresis is gone.

The process works also in the reverse. Those living very close to the bus stop will not take a taxi anyhow. They may thus act as a seed crystal for the custom. If the area becomes safer, the number of those who walk home alone in the dark will increase.

A similar argument applies to the temporal aspect of the problem. It does not become dark abruptly. If it becomes a little safer, people may want to walk home at slightly later hours. In the temporal dimension, the custom will react smoothly, too, and the apparent rigidity disappears.

If critical mass phenomena are reconsidered by including further dimensions, fuzziness and ambiguity emerge. All hysteresis, lumpiness, and rigidity vanish, and adaptive custom can be depicted as reacting passively to outside circumstances.

5.4 A Model of Caste

Many recent arguments stressing critical mass effects under headings such as 'network externalities' and 'path dependency' do not take into account the fact that a close look at most customary phenomena reveals some fuzziness, and that fuzziness renders custom adaptive and vulnerable to erosion. It seems, thus, worthwhile to discuss some further examples.

Consider the model of a 'caste' society that has been proposed by Akerlof[1]. This model has been designed to illustrate the possibility of an inefficient self-stabilizing custom. It relies on critical mass in a way that may seem, at first glance, to be immune to erosion, yet this is not the case.

There are several castes of workers. Each caste specializes in a certain type of production. This division of labour is maintained by custom. The caste code prescribes what each worker is permitted to do. If he breaches the code, he is ostracized. Nobody is permitted to have any contact with him; if someone does, he himself is ostracized. It is further assumed that a critical mass effect applies to the ostracized group. If the ostracized group is small, average productivity is low, and it is better not to be ostracized. This prevents each individual from breaching the code. Only if the ostracized group is large will it be possible to capture efficiency gains by disregarding the code, but this is prevented because joint action is excluded.

This code is assumed to be inefficient in the sense that everyone would be better off if everyone were ostracized. It would thus be preferable jointly to abolish the code. Yet it is in the best interest of each member of this society to observe the code, even if he dislikes it. In this way, Akerlof argues, an appalling state of society may be perpetuated in spite of widespread opposition. It seems, thus, that this is a model of an adaptive yet self-stabilizing custom which is entirely inefficient and reproduces itself none the less.

The argument rests, however, on assuming fuzziness away. It assumes that a clear line can be drawn that separates permitted from outlawed activities. This is problematic. If fuzziness is pervasive in reality, then allowance for fuzziness must be made in the model—and fuzziness is pervasive in reality. This is true even with

[1] Akerlof (1976: 34–44).

regard to the caste code. The pariahs may be restricted to working with hides and leather, while everybody else is prohibited from doing so. However, in order to work with leather, one needs other goods, such as needles, yarn, and various tools and chemicals. Obviously, they will be entitled to carry out *some* repairs on their tools. The pariahs will obviously also be entitled to cook for themselves, their relatives, and their guests, although they are not permitted to run a restaurant for other pariahs. Thus, there will be fuzziness regarding the scope of permitted repairs and permitted hospitality. This illustrates just a few aspects of the omnipresence of fuzziness.

Given fuzziness, the caste society sketched above cannot easily be maintained. Fuzziness invites erosion. There cannot be effective sanctions to prevent non-customary behaviour in unclear cases because it is unclear whether or not the custom applies. Thus, the scope of permitted activities may expand or shrink, depending on external incentives. If an improvement can be achieved by shading the custom, the custom will be bent in this direction and will ultimately reflect the underlying interests of all individuals in the community. This is not, of course, what happens.

As a consequence, the adaptive view of custom would necessitate a conception of the caste system as ultimately being supported by individual preferences. Inefficiencies should not occur because people would be interested in finding ways to improve efficiency. Fuzziness would permit them to bend the system in that direction.

It could be argued now that the system may be stabilized through external enforcement, say by a legal or religious organization. However, this neglects two problems. The first is that the enforcement mechanism in the Indian caste system is customary itself and susceptible to erosion.[1] The second is that even formal

---

[1] Kuran (1987: 662–4; 1995: chs. 8 and 12) vividly describes the social mechanisms that contribute to stabilizing the caste system. He advances the argument that people have a tendency to not voice their true opinion in public, but rather to express whatever they think is the socially accepted view. This 'preference falsification' further induces a social process which distorts individual convictions in the direction of whatever is

black-letter law cannot prevent disobedience in unclear cases.[1] The prevailing set of interests and incentives will govern the resolution of ambiguous cases. Actual behaviour will thus respond to incentives in those borderline cases. Since actual behaviour, rather than black-letter law, will shape the perceptions of entitlements, the prevailing set of formal systems of enforcement will ultimately yield to the incessant pressure of self-interested behaviour.

Alfred Marshall has formulated this adaptive view of custom with respect to the Indian caste system quite succinctly:

> I believe that very many economic customs could be traced, if we had only knowledge enough, to the slow equilibration of measurable motives: that even in such a country as India no custom retains its hold long after the relative positions of the motives of demand and supply have so changed that the values which would bring them into stable equilibrium, are far removed from those which the custom sanctions.[2]

Thus, it appears that the adaptive view of custom rules out any true rigidity and firmness of custom in the long run. The view of custom expounded in this book will, however, allow for rigidity and so will go beyond the Marshallian view of custom.

5.5 *The QWERTY Keyboard*

Consider another widely discussed example for critical mass effects, which runs into the same theoretical problems as the caste model. It relates to the QWERTY typewriter keyboard.[3] The

considered 'politically correct'. As a result, preference falsification stabilizes the caste system directly (by the suppression of opposing views, even if widely shared) and indirectly (by deforming the individuals' preferences in the direction of perceived public opinion). The argument seems to me open to the erosion critique, however, unless mechanisms like those outlined in the following chapters prevent public opinion from changing smoothly.

[1] Romer (1984) has argued that a custom may be maintained by a system of sanctions and rewards which render the gains from compliance larger than the gains from defection. This argument, however, neglects the problem of fuzziness which will render sanctions impossible in borderline cases, as it is unclear whether or not the custom has been observed.

[2] Marshall (1885: 169–70). Marshall's theory of custom is splendidly summarized in Reisman (1987: 344–5).

[3] See David (1985), and Liebowitz and Margolis (1990).

layout of this keyboard was developed with the aim of separating keys that are used often in conjunction, in order to prevent jamming. Another reason for the design was simply promotional: salesmen could type the word 'typewriter' incredibly fast, because all required keys are placed on the second row of the keyboard. These aspects suggest that the QWERTY layout is not fully efficient, at least for modern computers. The winners of contests in speed typing routinely use another layout. It appears therefore that an inefficient custom has been stabilized by a kind of critical mass effect.

The mechanism underlying the stabilization of the QWERTY layout has been described as follows. People get accustomed to the QWERTY layout. If they have to buy a new typewriter, they will stick with that keyboard. All firms will buy QWERTY keyboards because all the secretaries they might hire will be accustomed to that layout. All secretaries will be trained on that keyboard because their prospective employers will require it. So the inefficient custom is stabilized.

This argument is not convincing, however. One would expect pairwise changes to occur whenever this is of advantage. There is also considerable flexibility in the layout, as witnessed by the many empirical variants of QWERTY. The German layout starts with QWERTZ, for instance, with the rarely needed Y swapped with the often-used Z. The Swiss–German layout differs from the German, the Swiss–French layout differs from the French, and small typewriters (as well as small computers) have idiosyncratic keyboards to accommodate fewer keys. There is, thus, considerable variation. The choice is not simply between QWERTY and the 'optimal' keyboard in an all-or-nothing sense. Small changes, like swapping two keys, are possible and do take place. Such changes are as easy to learn as differences between small and large keyboard layouts. There is fuzziness again, which opens the way for all kinds of improvements. The argument would lead to the conclusion that QWERTY layouts are 'optimal' in the United States, while QWERTZ layouts are 'optimal' in Germany, simply because these layouts have remained stable.

There is also a spatial dimension to the issue. A large firm would have an incentive to introduce another layout if this were worthwhile, and a better keyboard might spread just as the touch-tone phone has spread, in spite of not being usable everywhere. Optimal keyboard layouts should be expected to emerge.

This is not too far from the truth. Liebowitz and Margolis have argued that the inefficiency of QWERTY is indeed rather small, not exceeding 5 per cent.[1] Yet nobody has argued that the QWERTY is the optimal layout. One possibility is that the layout matters only marginally. Note, however, that there are layouts that are easier to learn. An alphabetic layout is one instance; customers who do not specialize in typing ought logically to prefer such simple layouts. Furthermore, it should not be expected that some keys have multiple functions whereas others have no function at all. Yet the PC keyboard instances a clearly inefficient layout, at least because the 'SysRq' key is without any function with all known software.

Thus, it appears that QWERTY is close to an optimum, in accordance with adaptive custom—but that there are some rigidities and some inefficiencies of the QWERTY layout that pose obstacles to an interpretation of custom based on full malleability.

5.6 *Passive Custom and the Problem of Efficiency*

Adaptive custom is passive. It gives way to changing circumstances, but it will not assume a life of its own. It will not enforce on individuals practices that they dislike. It will give way to all kinds of improvements that can be attained in a gradual fashion.

It is true that custom adapts to changing circumstances in many ways. Rules of traffic change in response to changing conditions, languages change over time, and religious teachings change to accommodate emerging social trends.

The assumption of full adaptability would lead, therefore, to perceiving custom as exerting no significant long-run influence.

[1] Liebowitz and Margolis (1990).

'Cultural Nullity' would be the appropriate assumption to make for any kind of long-run analysis.[1] Such a view would portray custom as adapting to all exigencies. All customary logjams would be conceived as being only of short-run importance. In the long run, custom would change to accommodate all kinds of new exigencies. Inefficiencies could not persist in social evolution, just as ecological niches will not remain unexploited in biological evolution.

Such a view is, however, misleading. Neither biological nor social evolution can be characterized as producing efficient solutions in all cases. The woodpeckers' valuable ecological niche—the consumption of insects in the bark of trees—has remained untapped in Australia, New Zealand, New Guinea, and Madagascar, for instance, although it is, in a sense, easy to exploit.[2] Similarly, very dangerous practices of extreme circumcision have evolved and stabilized in some societies, but not in others. These practices seem highly inefficient. For any function that may be imagined, there are less costly ways to take care of it. Further, circumcisions need not be unnecessarily drastic. (Some practices are indeed extremely cruel.) They also need not be performed at an unnecessarily early age, where they are particularly dangerous.[3] It seems, therefore, a little far-fetched to assume that such practices stabilize because individuals like them, or because they are useful and no better functional substitute is available. Yet these customs persist, and there must have been a time when they emerged.

Custom can, therefore, not be portrayed as fully adaptive. It must exert an influence beyond simply yielding to outside forces in an unstructured and malleable way. Otherwise, the massive inefficiencies mentioned above could not possibly persist over centuries. Other influences must be considered. This is the task of the following chapters.

---

[1] See E. Jones (1995).   [2] Diamond (1991: 191).
[3] See Barley (1986: 49–50) on male circumcision and S. Armstrong (1991: 22–3) on female circumcision. Another example of a persistent inefficient custom was the Chinese practice of binding the feet of girls from infancy on, a practice that was sustained for over a thousand years (Chang 1991: 30–3).

Chapter 6

CLARITY

6.1 *Rigidity*

The adaptive view, expounded in the previous chapter, rules out the possibility of any custom that is individually costly to obey persisting indefinitely. Such custom should be expected to erode, quite irrespective of whether it is socially beneficial or harmful. Yet many customs that are individually costly to observe have endured for a long time. Religious sacrifices provide examples.[1]

Further, the adaptivity argument suggests that custom adapts smoothly to slowly changing conditions. However, custom seems to be rigid in the sense that continuously changing circumstances may go along with discontinuous changes in the associated set of customs.

Rigidity is conceived here as referring to constancy over some range of conditions. It is always local or partial. Only small changes leave a rigid custom unchanged, whereas large changes in certain circumstances may modify the custom or even break it

---

[1] Sometimes it is maintained that human sacrifices may serve useful functions and that this explains their stability over time. Iannaccone (1992), for instance, has argued that sacrifices may serve as screening devices. The general point against this is that many religious sacrifices are economically wasteful and might be replaced by equivalent productive or redistributive sacrifice, which should benefit both the individual and the congregation. But this possibility is usually not acknowledged. (Nobody gains if somebody castigates himself. If he pays an equivalent fine, somebody else would be better off. Still, economically wasteful penances continue to exist.)

down altogether. Rigidity is similar to hysteresis, but it is weaker: it will not necessarily entail a 'memory effect', and the switch point may be the same in both directions.[1]

Rigidity is of central importance for the workings of custom. Any fully adaptive custom, even if very inert, could only slow down the speed of transmission of economic and other incentives. A rigid custom may however channel economic forces in an entirely different direction. As has been argued before, full adaptability would imply that hysteresis would disappear, yet customs like tipping persist in spite of being variable in level and scope. Further, these customs differ in otherwise similar countries such as the United States and Australia. This points to rigidity as well. So some other influences must contribute to rigidity. These influences, it will be argued, derive from the psychological dispositions of the human mind towards simplicity and clarity.

6.2 *The Significance of Rigidity*

The question of whether custom is rigid is of immense importance for social science. Without rigidity, adaptive customs would be eventually moulded by outside forces. Custom would reduce to mere inertia. Its sole effect would be to slow down all movements. It would just work as a device for generating history in slow motion.

Custom, however, is not fully adaptive, and rigidity is important. Rigidity is a prime cause for the partial autonomy of many social phenomena. Several partial rigidities may engender much greater overall rigidity. A set of somewhat rigid customs may, thus, form an interlocking system exhibiting great stability and firmness.

Such a system may appear as an independent, even hostile, set of conditions which 'lock in' the very human actors who create it. In this way, rigidity helps to explain the apparent autonomy of institutions *vis-à-vis* individuals. Social institutions may be con-

---

[1] See S. 3.8. Without a 'memory effect', the two branches of the hysteresis loop in Fig. 3.10 will coincide.

ceived as emerging from the interaction of countless disconnected individuals, detaching themselves from these roots and eventually moulding the individuals in turn. This is obviously one of the central issues in social science.

The following sections will describe some psychological mechanisms that generate rigidity. This psychologically induced rigidity, it will be argued, may bring about critical mass effects even in cases of fuzziness. The argument will be presented in terms of very simple examples.

6.3 *Rounding and Rigidity*

Consider again the tipping example. The fare was £23.80, but the passenger gave £27.00. This was a tip of 13.5 per cent. How will this tip be remembered by the parties?

Everyone will presumably perceive the tip as 'close to 15 per cent', rather than 'somewhat between 13 and 14 per cent': the tip will be rounded and remembered in this way. The other alternative would be to perceive and remember the tip as a 'generous 10 per cent'.

Rounding induces stickiness. Even if the average tip is permanently slightly below 15 per cent, people will perceive it as being roughly 15 per cent, and this will reconfirm the norm. Even if behaviour shades the custom, the custom will remain in place as long as discrepancies are not too pronounced. If they are, rounding will go in another direction, and the custom will adapt to another rigid level suitable for rounding.

In this way, rounding leads to rigidity. The custom will remain constant within a range.

6.4 *A First Glance at Clarity*

This everyday phenomenon of rounding illustrates, in a very modest way, a pervasive regularity of perception, categorization, learning, and recall. Things are conceptualized in terms of adjacent clear cases. These clear cases have been mentioned in the literature under various names, in various connections, and with various shades of meaning. Here is a short, and certainly incomplete, list of names given to various clarity notions: 'prominence', 'salience', 'coherence', 'consistency', 'prototype', 'stereotype', 'ideal type', 'typical case', 'central case', 'balanced case', 'cognitive reference point', 'focal point', 'schema', 'paradigm', 'pattern', 'optimum complexity', 'Gestalt', 'Prägnanz'.[1]

All these terms go along with different shadings and connotations and, in particular, with very special applications. For the present purposes, however, a more general (and less specialized) term is needed which refers not exclusively to one particular set of problems. The portmanteau term 'clarity' will be used in this sense. Because the notion is quite abstract (like 'matter' in physics), it is not easy to explain, and no clear-cut definition can be offered at the present stage of the argument. The notion will be characterized by describing the set of phenomena to which the term is intended to relate, and offering examples. As a starting point, the term 'clarity' is to be understood in its naïve, everyday sense, relating to simplicity, terseness, and good articulation.

6.5 *The War of the Ghosts*

Clarity is obviously important for the formation of custom because clear cases can be perceived and learnt more easily than unclear cases, and also can be memorized and communicated better. Since all these processes are error-ridden, clear customs

[1] Prominence: Albers and Albers (1983); salience: Kelley (1973); coherence: Murphy and Medin (1985); consistency: McGuire (1966), prototype: Rosch (1975); stereotype: Katz and Braly (1933); ideal type: Weber (1949); typical instance: Rosch (1973); central case: Thorndyke (1977); cognitive reference point: Rosch (1975); balanced case: F. Heider (1958); focal point: Schelling (1980); schema: Bartlett (1932), Piaget (1967); paradigm: Kuhn (1970); pattern: Hayek (1964); optimum complexity: Walker (1980) Gestalt: Ehrenfels (1890); Prägnanz: Wertheimer (1922). The specimen best-known in the social sciences is Thomas Schelling's (1980) 'focal point'. Simplicity relates also very closely to clarity. It goes without saying that it would require an extensive historical study to relate all the above-mentioned concepts and to pinpoint where and when they originated, and how they interrelate with each other.

will be less affected by errors of learning and transmission. In this sense, clarity enhances stability. For this reason alone, clear customs will survive better than unclear customs.

Clarity has, however, a much stronger effect on the formation of custom. It not only eases perception, memory, and communication, but actively biases perception and memory towards greater clarity.

This tendency shows up very clearly in various experiments where subjects are required to reproduce a story or a drawing from memory. The classic experiments have been conducted by Frederick Bartlett. Here is the famous story of 'The War of the Ghosts', together with a recall obtained two weeks later.[1]

The War of the Ghosts

One night two young men from Egulac went down to the river to hunt seals, and while they were there, it became foggy and calm. Then they heard war-cries, and they thought: 'Maybe this is a war-party.' They escaped to the shore, and hid behind a log. Now canoes came up, and they heard the noise of paddles, and saw one canoe coming up to them. There were five men in the canoe, and they said:

'What do you think? We wish to take you along. We are going up the river to make war on the people.'

One of the young men said, 'I have no arrows.'

'Arrows are in the canoe', they said.

'I will not go along. I might be killed. My relatives do not know where I have gone. But you', he said, turning to the other, 'may go with them.'

So one of the young men went, but the other returned home.

And the warriors went on up the river to a town on the other side of the Kalama. The people came down to the water, and they began to fight, and many were killed. But presently the

[1] Bartlett (1932: 65,76). For further references, see Anderson (1980: 128–221), and M. W. Eysenck and Keane (1990: 275–94).

young men heard one of the warriors say: 'Quick, let us go home: that Indian has been hit.' Now he thought: 'Oh, they are ghosts.' He did not feel sick, but they said he had been shot.

So the canoes went back to Egulac, and the young man went ashore to his house, and made a fire. And he told everybody and said: 'Behold I accompanied the ghosts, and we went to fight. Many of our fellows were killed. They said I was hit, and I did not feel sick.'

He told it all, and then became quiet. When the sun rose, he fell down. Something black came out of his mouth. His face became contorted. The people jumped up and cried.

He was dead.

After two weeks, the story was recalled as follows.

There were two ghosts. They went on a river. There was a canoe on the river with five men in it. There occurred a war of the ghosts. One of the ghosts asked: 'where are the arrows?' The other said: 'In the canoe'. They started the war and several were wounded, and some killed. One ghost was wounded but did not feel sick. He went back to the village in a canoe. The next morning he was sick and something black came out of his mouth, and they cried: 'He is dead.'

The condensation of the original story exemplifies a broad regularity in perception and recall. Repetition of stories over long time intervals reveals tendencies to structure the story so that it 'makes sense'. Also, as the story grows older it gets shorter, and irrelevant details drop out.[1] Comprehensibility and recall are a function of the amount of inherent plot in the story, independent of the content of the passage. The probability of recalling individual facts from passages read depends on the structural centrality of the facts in question. Subjects tend to recall facts corresponding to higher-level organization story elements, rather than lower levels of details. Story summarizations from memory tend to emphasize general structural characteristics rather than specific content.[2]

[1] This paraphrases the summary of Bartlett's experiments provided by Hilgard and Bower (1966: 250).   [2] Thorndyke (1977: 77).

6.6 *Spontaneous Clarification*

These and related phenomena may be summarized by saying that the human mind strives for clarification. It tries to perceive and comprehend objects in such a way that they make as much sense as possible.[1] This is done in two ways: by *levelling*, and by *sharpening*. Disturbing elements are levelled away, whereas characteristic features are sharpened.[2] This urge for clarification is a pervasive feature of psychological organization. All cognitive psychology starts from here. Even preferences and behaviour are moulded by clarification processes. This is studied in theories about cognitive dissonance and attribution, which will be discussed later. With regard to learning and the transmission of custom, it suffices to focus on cognition.

The mental processes that are involved in the act of clarification account for many 'distortions' in perception and memory. It is here that the tendency is most easily perceived. Many recalls from memory, for instance, involve active reconstructions and inferences rather than passive remembering.[3] This renders it possible to concentrate on essential aspects and to drop inessential information. If the filtering goes wrong, 'distortions' result. This is the unavoidable consequence of all good filtering. Any good filter must work like that. It will at the same time both enhance and distort the picture. This holds true for photography as well as for psychology. Enhancement implies distortion. Thus, the tendency towards clarification that works in the human mind should not be seen as negative. It works, to a much larger extent, in a positive and functional way. Good performance is, however, usually taken for granted. Nobody complains if memory and perception work superbly: it is only if distortions arise that the active part of psychological elements is acknowledged. This puts an undue stress on apparent irrationalities and distortions.

Many optical illusions derive from clarification processes. The

---

[1] This is Wertheimer's 'Prägnanzgesetz'. Various aspects are discussed in Koffka (1935: 110 and *passim*).
[2] Wulf (1922).　　[3] Anderson (1980: 199–208).

Figure 6.1
Watch How Your Mind Tries to Clarify the Picture
Square of Three—Yellow and Black (1964)
by Reginald Neal (1909–1992) Acrylic and lithograph on canvas,
New Jersey State Museum Collection

same factors that permit incredibly good pattern recognition in
many everyday situations also occasion illusions and distortions.
The forces working here are automatic, and they are rather strong.
This is illustrated by the ambiguous pattern depicted in Fig. 6.1.
The lack of clarity induces spontaneous processes in the observer
which aim to structure the picture in a meaningful way. The figure
should be viewed in bright light.[1]

[1] Schiffman (1982: 199).

The earlier assumptions about conservatism and conformity relate also to the urge for clarification. These behaviours engender clarity by aligning behaviour with perceived patterns established in the past, or prevailing in the group.

6.7 *Culture and Clarity*

The spontaneous clarification processes that take place in the human mind are of central importance to the entire argument put forward in this book. It will be contended that clarity contributes to the shaping of custom. Clarification works as an independent force in establishing rigidity and the partial autonomy of custom.

This line of thought requires clarity to be ultimately independent of culture. If clarity judgements themselves were matters of conventional adaptation and cultural influence, clarity could not serve as a foothold for the rigidity of custom.

Clarity must be conceived, therefore, as basically culture-invariant. Clarity judgements must be ultimately 'hard-wired' in the human mind. Such an assumption may strike the reader as somewhat unexpected, and in this crude form it certainly is. The following sections will indicate what is involved here, and in what sense clarity can be conceived as independent of culture.

6.8 *Prominence, Clarity, and Culture*

Consider again the phenomenon of rounding. It rests on the existence of 'prominent numbers', for example (in our culture) 1, 2, 5, 10, 15, 20, 50, 100 and the decimal powers thereof. These numbers are clearer or simpler than the rest. They are the preferred 'benchmarks'. Other numbers, like 7.5, 12.5, and 17.5, are somewhat less clear, but are still more prominent than numbers such as 8.2 or 13.6. In experimental bargaining games it turned out that the bargaining outcomes are typically taken from the set of prominent numbers, quite irrespective of the nature of the game. This would be a highly improbable result unless 'prominence' played a role in actual bargaining processes and affected behaviour.[1]

The phenomenon of prominent numbers may be interpreted in two different ways, which illustrate two different ideas about the origins of the underlying clarity notion. The first is the adaptive interpretation. The prominence feature may be conceived as generated by habituation. More frequent exposure to certain numbers may render them more prominent than others. This would subject the prominence feature itself to smooth adaptation. Prominence would be generated by custom, and stickiness could not be explained. The argument about rigidity and rounding would break down.

However, the adaptive interpretation faces massive problems in accommodating various other observations. It seems highly improbable that one would find the particular distribution of prominence along the range of numbers that is actually observed. Why should powers of 10 be of such practical relevance—why not powers of 7? It also seems strange to think of '11.3' as being less frequently used in practical life than '1,000,000', and it is certainly not more time-consuming to write it down.

This suggests another interpretation, namely, that the number system itself determines prominence. Powers of 10 play an important role in the decimal system as anchors for prominence, because the system itself is decimal. Cases where other number systems are employed illustrate the importance of the number system in determining prominence. Time is measured in a way derived from the Babylonian sexagesimal system, whereby day and night are divided into 12 hours; as a consequence, 2 and 10 are not as prominent as 6 and 'noon'. A related observation is known to all computer programmers who work in the hexadecimal system. There 100hex and 80hex are prominent, but the decimal equivalents 256 and 128 are not. Programmers actually recognize these numbers as prominent in the hexadecimal system even if they are

---

[1] Albers and Albers (1983).

written in decimal form. This illustrates another fairly general feature of psychological organization which will be considered later. The tendency towards clarity seeks to integrate all elements of psychological organization. It aims at overall clarity. This creates overall connections.

The parlance about the number system itself (in contrast simply to frequent exposure) as engendering prominence requires further elaboration. After all, both the number system and the notion of prominence are created by the human mind. Some would say that they are not 'objective', but 'psychological'. Yet they are not 'subjective' in the sense of anybody holding arbitrarily divergent opinions about these notions. It might be said that prominence is objective once the number system is given; the way in which prominence is generated by any number system is 'hard-wired' in the brain. It is, in this sense, objective. Particular prominence attributions are not.

This may be compared to linguistics, where a 'hard-wired' universal grammar is assumed. Without such a grammar, it would be impossible for children to learn a language in a few years with rules that the linguists themselves do not understand fully.[1]

Prominence of numbers refers, then, to a culture-invariant human propensity for perceiving regularities in any given number system. It should be noted further that prominence is not an attribute of a single number taken in isolation. Rather, a number is perceived as prominent because it is embedded in a certain number system. Prominence rests in the relation of the object with its surroundings.

Clarity generalizes the idea of prominence to overall coherence, simplicity, and terseness beyond arithmetic. The following examples are intended to illustrate this culture-invariant nature of clarity. The examples will also illustrate that clarity cannot be attributed to single objects: it is an attribute that relates to objects in their surroundings.

---

[1] See Diamond (1991: Ch. 8) for an excellent account.

Figure 6.2
How Would You Describe This?

6.9 *Clarity and Repetition*

Consider Fig. 6.2, and how it would be described, sketched, and remembered.

There are certainly several ways to describe the figure. It is actually not very clear, and several possibilities for characterizing it come to mind. It may be described as a vanity mirror, for instance. As a matter of fact, the figure is composed out of four identical elements to which the reader has been exposed quite recently many times in quick succession. It is the letter 'n', which has already appeared more than 600 times in this chapter and more than 5,000 times in the text of this book. The picture has been composed out of four mirror images of the letter. The reader has looked at this letter several million times in his life. Yet the n's are not conspicuous. The strength and symmetry of the overall pattern overrules the perception of single elements, in spite of ever-recurring exposure.[1]

Just as prominence in the number system overrides possible effects of frequent exposure, symmetry overrides frequent exposure in visual organization. In order to explain that in adaptive terms, one would have to assume that symmetrical cases occur

[1] The example paraphrases a set of experiments and findings by Gottschaldt (1926).

more often than non-symmetrical cases in visual perception. With regard to point symmetry and horizontal symmetry, such an assumption seems utterly implausible. Symmetry must be taken as ultimately being generated by culture-invariant propensities, and clarity must be related to that.

6.10 *Context Dependency*

This does not imply, however, that certain judgements about clarity will be identical across cultures. Although this seems to be true for many phenomena, it is certainly not true as a general rule. Just as the prominence of a given number rests both in the number and in the number system, clarity refers to an object in relation to its surroundings. Since culture sets such a frame, it will influence all kinds of interpretations.

It is easy, for instance, to change the perception of Fig. 6.2 by adding additional elements that destroy its symmetry, as in Fig. 6.3. This 'framing effect' illustrates again that clarification works on the object as a whole, and not on single elements taken in isolation. The framing effect is, indeed, present almost everywhere. It renders perceptions and cognitions context-dependent. When Jonathan Swift writes 'The handkerchiefs will be put in some friend's pocket not to pay custom', this refers to something different from what David Hume invokes when saying: 'Custom, then, is the great guide of human life.'[1] Each quotation invokes another meaning of the same word, 'custom', without creating any difficulty.

Another everyday example of framing is illustrated in Fig. 6.4. This plays on the identity of the letter 'O' and the digit for zero. It may be read as 'zoom 2004', although both words start with graphically identical symbols. The first three symbols are spontaneously interpreted in conjunction with the fourth symbol such that they make sense. The clearest possible interpretation is

---

[1] Swift (1713: Oct. 10, s.19); Hume (1777a: s.5, pt 1).

Figure 6.3
The Framing Effect

chosen. The perception of the symbol 'O' is thus context-dependent.

This translates to culture as an all-embracing context. Culture surrounds everything in social life; thus, it influences many interpretations. This can be stated briefly by saying that culture works through clarity. The desire for clarification renders human perceptions and thoughts context-dependent. Emotions follow the same pattern.[1] Context dependency renders the influence of culture pervasive.

Context dependency may also be understood with the help of an analogy drawn from data processing. If a set of data is to be stored in a parsimonious manner, it will be coded in such a way that long chains of symbols that occur repeatedly are represented by one single symbol. In this way, the data set is 'compressed' and requires less storage space. This encoding exploits the overall structure of the data set, because the way in which a chain of symbols is encoded depends on the frequency with which this chain of symbols appears in the entire set. The way in which a single element of text is represented will thus depend on the structure of the entire set. The better the compression, the more

---

[1] This will be elaborated in Chs. 9 and 10.

Figure 6.4
Zeros and Os Look Alike

extensive use will be made of the overall data structure, and the more strongly will the representation of each element be affected by the overall context.[1]

6.11 *Culture and Colours*

The influence of culture has its limits, however. Although painting styles differ widely across space and time, all cultures consider the same colours as 'basic', and although musical styles differ enormously, all music builds on certain intervals.

Consider colour first, and how colour perception relates to culture.[2] English, for instance, has eleven basic colour words: black, white, red, green, yellow, blue, brown, purple, pink, orange, and grey. People usually refer to these basic colours when describing and memorizing objects. Non-basic colour words for brownish objects, such as maroon, rufous, sepia, sorrel, russet, mahogany, henna, rust, or olive, are used less often. There is, further, just one hue of red among the entire spectrum of reddish colours that is judged to be the best red. The same holds true for other colours— there is a best blue, a best green, and so forth. These best speci-

---

[1] It may be noted that context dependency is not an exclusively psychological phenomenon, but also arises naturally under diverse circumstances, such as aggregation problems; see Schlicht (1985*a*: 71–9).

[2] The following section is based on Anderson(1980: 385–6). The study on the Danis has been made by Heider (Rosch) (1972). For an extensive study on the influence of culture on visual perception that reaches similar conclusions, see Segall *et al.* (1966). On a more basic level, visual perception obviously relates to clarity; the lens of the eye accommodates to obtain a clear picture with maximum contrast.

mens are known as *focal colours*. English speakers find it easier to remember focal colours than non-focal colours.

There are, however, cultures with languages that have more or fewer basic colour words. The language of the Dani—a tribe in Indonesian New Guinea—provides an extreme example. It has just two basic colour words. *Mili* denotes dark, cold hues and *mola* refers to bright, warm colours. If culture and language affect colour perception, the English distinction between focal and non-focal colours should not have the same bearing on colour remembrance with the Dani as with the English.

It turns out, however, that there is no difference. The English speakers' focal colours turned out to be focal colours for the Dani, too. Dani subjects found it easier to learn nonsense names for focal colours than for non-focal colours, just as the English did. The cultural frame of language seems not to affect colour perception on this fundamental level. The judgement about the clarity of a colour is independent of language and culture.

Some psychologists draw much broader conclusions from such experiments. The following quotation illustrates a widely shared view:

To conclude, the evidence tends not to support the hypothesis that language has any significant effect on the way we think or on the way we perceive the world. It is certainly true that language can influence us . . . but its effect is to communicate ideas, not to determine the kinds of ideas we can think about.

This conclusion that culture has no significant influence on thinking and perception seems perhaps unnecessarily strong, but there is no need to settle the issue here.[1] It suffices for the present purposes to establish the culture invariance of *basic* clarity judgements, and this seems to be a tenable position.

[1] The quotation is from Anderson (1980: 386). I doubt somewhat the validity of this statement with respect to subtleties. One reason for writing this book in English rather than in my mother tongue (German) is that some ideas are easier to express in English than in German. For instance, German has no equivalent for 'custom'. Abstract ideas as well as subtle distinctions can often be better expressed in German, but the German language does not lend itself as easily to hinting at somewhat ill-defined clusters of ideas by instances and allusions. In this sense, language may bias thought by rendering some ideas easier to express and communicate than others.

6.12   *Musical Perception*

The culture invariance of basic clarity judgements may be further
illustrated by pointing to music and music perception. Musical
styles and idioms differ greatly across cultures. Yet the diversity of
music builds on musical universals which are related directly to
clarity. Consider musical intervals. The most prominent interval—
the clearest one—is the octave, which is, technically, a doubling of
frequencies. The octave is particularly easy to recognize. It is, in
this sense, of particular simplicity. If somebody can recognize any
interval, he will be able to recognize the octave.

Not surprisingly, the octave appears in all kinds of music. What
may be surprising, however, is that it is of special significance to
animals as well. If a dog is conditioned on a certain tone, it will
react in a similar manner to the octave of that tone. It will not,
however, react to intermediate tones that are, in terms of frequency, closer to the original sound. Recent studies of musical
perception in animals do indeed suggest that humans share musical universals not only with people in other cultures, but also with
animals.

The musical example illustrates that elementary clarity judgements are very deeply rooted in our physiological make-up. Clear
musical intervals are characterized by simple frequency ratios.
These simple ratios—like $\frac{1}{2}, \frac{2}{3} \frac{3}{4}$ for the octave, the fifth, and the
fourth—are simple not only in the sense that they just happen to
appear simple in the decimal number system: they also have a
firm physical foundation in resonance frequencies that arise
naturally from the harmonics of any sound, independently of
the number system chosen. This suggests that notions of simplicity of fractions are not mere arbitrary conventions. Also, they
seem not to be attributable to some random aspects of biological
evolution; rather, they are ultimately grounded in the permanent
laws of physics.[1]

---

[1] I do not want to embark on this discussion here. It suffices to take the urge for
clarification as a given trait without specifying where it might come from. See Köhler
(1971) for some speculation on this.

The example of musical intervals illustrates that there exist clarity properties that are culture-invariant to the point of being related directly to the laws of physics. Other clarity properties, such as symmetry or focal colours, may be less directly grounded in physical realities, but are clearly culture-invariant as well. Thus, clarity cannot be fully reduced to a concept referring solely to culture-specific features.

Chapter 7

RULES AND SCHEMATA

7.1 *Customs and Rules*

A custom consists of a set of habitual, emotional, and cognitive regularities. These regularities may be described by rules which assign certain behavioural, emotional, and cognitive responses to emerging conditions. The processes by which a custom grows, stabilizes, or erodes can be characterized in terms of the evolution, stabilization, and dissolution of the underlying rule-systems. The formation, stabilization, and change of such rule-systems builds on spontaneous clarification processes, as introduced and discussed in the previous chapter.

It will be argued that the concept of a 'rule' itself presupposes that the human mind structures the world in a particular way. This structuring is fundamental for all kinds of perception, learning, and memorizing. It pertains, in particular, to the perception, learning, and memorizing of the rules of custom and generates phenomena such as rigidity and hysteresis on a purely cognitive level.

7.2 *A Game of Cards*

In order to understand the nature of rule formation, consider a very simple example, the game of cards called Eleusis, which illustrates the pertinent problems.[1] It is played as follows. One of the players, the 'regulator', invents a rule for possible sequences of cards, such as alternating between 'red' and 'black' cards, and secretly writes it on a sheet of paper. The deck of cards is distributed among the remaining players. The players try to form a card sequence conforming to the secret rule. Each of them in turn adds a card to the cards already in the middle of the table, in the hope that the new card will fit the rule. If not, the card is rejected by the regulator and must be kept by the player. Each of the active players tries to get rid of as many cards as possible in order to earn points. The regulator tries to maximize the discrepancy between the players' outcomes by selecting a rule that is neither too complicated nor too easy, as his points are calculated according to this difference. The game is, thus, essentially concerned with rule detection.

To illustrate the processes occurring here, consider the sequence of cards depicted in Fig. 7.1. This sequence is certainly compatible with many rules, such as:

Rule 1: Play always *club, diamond, spade, heart* in sequence.

Rule 2: Alternate between black and red.

Rule 3: Alternate between playing up and down at each court-card.

Rule 4: After a king, play even; after a queen, play odd.

Rule 5: After a king, play up; after a queen, play down.

These are just a few of a very large number of possible rules. The typical way the game is played is that each player develops several hypotheses and tries to place cards that simultaneously conform to *all* of those hypotheses. This usually leads to much more restricted sequences than the original rule would permit. For instance, some may initially suspect that rule 1 is true even though the regulator has selected rule 2; they place their cards accordingly, and the cards are accepted because the stricter rule 1 is subsumed within the softer rule 2. This will make the strict rule 1 very dominant,

---

[1] The game was invented by Robert Abbott (1975: 66–75).

Figure 7.1
How Should this Sequence of Cards Continue?

and all players will tend to use this rule as long as they can, hoping that the others will have to deviate and thereby generate new information.

Further, if a certain hypothesis works very well for a long time, but fails to do so in one instance, a player will usually not discard it altogether but will look for a better hypothesis that is also compatible with his information. Until he finds this better alternative, he will stick to his own rule even if he knows that it is wrong in some cases—it is, after all, better than playing randomly.

The game of Eleusis exemplifies in a paradigmatic way several features of rule formation, rule detection, and inference. The following sections will deal with some pertinent problems.

7.3 *'Random Rules' and History*

Consider first the problem of rule inference under the assumption that the set of feasible rules is completely unstructured. The regulator might have selected one of the conceivable rules by chance. This is the case of 'random rules'. The number of these possible rules is very large indeed.[1]

It is easy to determine the optimal strategy for each player in this case. Everybody may play what he likes. Every card is equally likely to be wrong or right. The sequence of cards on the table will not contain any information about permissible sequels, because each sequel is equally likely.[2]

There is, thus, no way of improving future performance by looking at the past. Eleusis could equally well be played blindfolded. In the case of 'random rules', history will contain no useful information, and learning will not be possible.

This holds true not only for that particular game, but for all kinds of extrapolation and interpolation in all fields of knowledge. In order to extrapolate, it does not suffice to assume that there is some regularity linking the past and the future. As long as it is assumed that all conceivable regularities are possible, the past will contain no information about the future. The assumption of constancy alone will not help. It does not carry any information. In Eleusis, any 'random rule' may be fixed and remain constant once

---

[1] There are $52! = 8.066.10^{67}$ possible sequences of 52 cards. An impression about the incredible size of this number may be obtained if we imagine a cube spanned by edges having the length of one light-year. The number of square millimetres contained in this cube is $8.46.10^{53}$. This number is well below the number giving the possible sequences of cards. Each 'rule' may be defined as a set of such sequences, which are usually described with reference to classes of cards (such as red cards − black cards, or cards with odd numbers). There are, therefore, far more rules than sequences. In addition, there are many rules that do not exhaust all the 52 cards ('always play black', for instance). So the number of possibilities is enormous. Simply assuming rule-guided behaviour without constraining the set of possible rules any further amounts, therefore, to saying nothing. There is, of course, no chance for the individual to learn any such rule in a behaviourist manner by 'operand conditioning'. There will be no chance to try each single rule at least once during an entire lifetime. Arguments such as those proposed by Hayek (1952: 48–78), which try to develop Gestalt principles from associations and elementary sensory impulses, face the same difficulty.

[2] In some more detail, the argument runs as follows. A rule will give, for any sequence of cards on the table, the set of cards that are permissible sequels. This set is formed from the remaining cards, and a 'random rule' would select one of the possible sets randomly with equal probability. As the set of possible sets—the 'power set'—is determined by the set of remaining cards, independently of the particular sequence of cards lying on the table, the sequence does not contain any useful information about permissible sequels. Further, the power set treats all remaining cards symmetrically, and so each card has the same chance of being a permissible sequel to the sequence of cards on the table.

it has been determined; but, in spite of this constancy, no clues for permissible cards can be obtained by looking at the past.

With respect to legal criticism, the same insight has been formulated as follows: 'But elementary logic teaches us that every legal decision and every finite set of decisions can be subsumed under an infinite number of general rules, just as an infinite number of different curves may be traced through any point or finite collection of points.'[1] Just as with 'random rules' in Eleusis, pure logical reasoning can never indicate how to continue a given sequence of observations in the future, and past observations do not carry implications for the future. Learning, in the sense of extracting information about the future from past observations, cannot flow from unaided logical reasoning.

Learning is possible only in so far as the past does contain information about the future. This excludes 'random rules'. It must be assumed *a priori* that some rules are more probable than others. If some 'unreasonable' rules can be excluded from the beginning, and only a few 'reasonable' rules are considered, this narrows the set of alternatives drastically and permits learning. Past observations may rule out some of the reasonable rules. In this way, learning can take place.

In Eleusis, such a distinction between reasonable and unreasonable rules appears natural because the regulator has an incentive to select rules that the players consider plausible. In order for them to play well, he makes use of shared psychological knowledge about simplicity and clarity of different conceivable rules.

In other fields, a similar appeal to simplicity and clarity must be made, although such an assumption seems often less reasonable than in the game of Eleusis. In science, the relevant assumption is termed the 'principle of parsimony', according to which the value of an explanation depends on its simplicity. There is, of course, no reason to assume that the laws of Nature should care about human ideas of simplicity. Yet without the principle of parsimony

---

[1] Cohen (1933: 33).

no conclusions could be drawn.[1] So the principle is widely used. Somewhat surprisingly, it works well in the natural sciences. This is in itself a remarkable phenomenon. The human psychological concepts of simplicity and clarity, which render learning possible, seem to find their counterparts in the laws of Nature. The biologist Konrad Lorenz has linked this 'coincidence' to biological evolution,[2] but, whatever the explanation for this remarkable parallelism may be, it stresses the universalistic nature of clarity judgements from another angle.

7.4 *Categorization*

Another feature that can be observed in the game of Eleusis is the role that categorizations play. It is not possible to learn from repetition of individual card sequences, because each card is unique. Once it lies on the table, it cannot be played again. As a consequence, there can never be any kind of strict repetition. Rules build on forming classes of 'similar' cards and detecting regularities spanning these classes. The rule 'black–red–black–red' builds on classifying according to colour. All elements of one class are taken as perfect substitutes for another. The rule 'play first up, then down' relies on forming classes of cards with a certain count and considering their members as substitutes. In this way, repetition in terms of class elements becomes possible, and learning by repetition can occur.

This is, again, a fairly universal phenomenon related to learning. Even the most elementary associationist accounts of learning must assume that each instance of a certain reward is an element of the class of similar rewards. In animal experiments, no grain

---

[1] On the role of simplicity in statistical inference, see Harrod (1956: ch. vi) and Jeffreys (1961: 4–5, 47). By the way, Harrod's argument is not convincing. He maintains that we prefer simple hypotheses because their probability of being correct is smaller than that of complex hypotheses; so they can be refuted more easily. This is an argument in favour of singular hypotheses, but they need not be simple. Instead of looking at linear relationships, we could equally well concentrate on singular complicated hypotheses, such as polynomials of the nth degree with identical coefficients for each term, for instance. [2] Lorenz (1993).

will taste exactly like another, no electroshock will feel exactly like the previous one. Individual animals must be assumed to classify them as similar in order to perceive repetition and establish a connection between an action and its consequence. This is actually the case. 'Similar' stimuli generate 'similar' responses. The phenomenon is known as 'stimulus generalization'.[1] In this sense, categorization processes must be presupposed for all kinds of learning. These processes may be spontaneous or deliberate, but they are essential. Rule-learning is very intimately connected with categorization processes.

Categorization is of fundamental importance for all kinds of knowledge. Modern botany became possible, for instance, once Linné had introduced a new classification system for plants. Earlier systems grouped together plants that were similar in outward appearance, even if biologically they were very different. In contrast, Linné's classification was based on functional aspects and grouped functionally similar plants together. This was the first step to finding stable regularities within these categories.

7.5 *Good Continuity*

Once a categorization has been made in Eleusis, a rule must be devised to describe permissible moves. Suppose that the regulator has decided to take the suits as his categories and to treat all cards within the same suit alike. (This would be a very simple and natural categorization.) Regarding possible rules based on these categories, consider first the case of 'random rules'. Assume that the regulator has randomly selected one rule from the set of all possible rules that build exclusively on the four suits and that disregard other distinctions. There is now a sequence of cards lying on the table, and the question is, what might a permissible sequel be? The answer is simple again, and for the same reason discussed above. Each player may play what he likes.[2] The set of possible sequels is determined by the set of remaining cards alone.

---

[1] Hilgard *et al.* (1971: 194).   [2] See S. 7.3.

So the cards on the table will contain only the information that these cards have been played already and fit the rule. They will contain no information about permissible sequels.

Rule inference is, thus, not possible under the assumption that all rules are equally probable *a priori*. In order to form rules, the players must presume that not all conceivable patterns are equally likely. They know, and the regulator knows, that not all patterns can be detected and understood with equal ease. This psychological knowledge is common knowledge, and it would be unreasonable to ignore it. In the end, the players must rely on finding recurrent patterns and forming judgements about good continuity. They must rely on clarity.

A similar assumption has been made tacitly in the discussion of conservatism and conformity.[1] Conservatism maintains the patterns that have emerged in the past. People follow these patterns, just as the players of Eleusis did. They face the same problems. In order to extrapolate, they must resort to simplicity. Similarly, conformity maintains the pattern appearing in the environment. If a person observes a group forming a circle, he may join in order to conform, and may enlarge the circle thereby. This gives better continuity to the prevailing pattern than standing aside and leaving the circle unchanged. All this is a matter of pattern recognition, just as in Eleusis, and pattern recognition is governed by clarity.

7.6 *Rule Formation in Social Interaction*

The game of Eleusis illustrates how people learn rules in a social context. In the social sphere, nothing repeats itself in a strict sense. In Eleusis, each card can be played only once, and this excludes strict repetition. In the social world, repetition is precluded by incessant and pervasive change. The continuous flux in the social world prevents strict and permanent repetition. In both cases, the individuals must rely on forming categories and detect-

---

[1] S. 1.3–1.4.

ing regularities in order to succeed. These regularities can be found only on an abstract level, where categories are formed and rules are built but the underlying elements are constantly changing.

Real life differs from the game, however, in that there is usually no regulator who secretly scribbles on a sheet of paper a rule that must then be detected. Rather, people perceive or suspect some rules and behave accordingly. They may do so for reasons of conservatism or conformity, or they may pursue their own advantage by building on these rules (like in Eleusis). All this creates regularity and may lead to the establishment of social structure. The individuals *assume* regularity in social interaction, and this *creates* regularity in social interaction. The entire process builds on spontaneous clarity judgements.

7.7 *Clarity and Rationality*

Up to now any mention of rationality has been avoided. At the present stage of the argument, however, it must be pointed out that no contradiction to rationality is involved in recognizing the significance of clarity considerations. The players of Eleusis try to play as rationally as possible, and it is perfectly reasonable to use clarity judgements in order to win.

Thomas Schelling has brought this to the fore. In particular, he has stressed the communication aspect of clarity and has emphasized its immense strategic importance. It is remarkable that this line of thought has been so much neglected by game theory.[1]

The dominant view seems to be that clarity judgements are too vague. At the same time, it is routinely assumed that preferences are less vague. This view seems to be paradigm-driven rather than

---

[1] Schelling (1980: 107) writes, for instance: 'Without full communication, one's ability to convey . . . a pattern of intentions is dependent . . . on the capacity of the other player to recognize the formula (Gestalt) of retaliation when he sees a sample of it.' It is only recently that clarity has been used as a device for equilibrium selection (Sugden 1986). But the impact of clarity goes much further. Game-theoretical approaches to rule formation, such as Lewis' (1969) and Schotter's (1981), must tacitly presuppose that people perceive certain patterns rather than others.

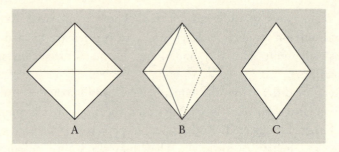

Figure 7.2
A Rotating Octahedron

founded on empirical regularities.[1] It will often be the case that information about clarity judgements is more readily available than information about tastes, because clarity judgements are more widely shared than tastes. The argument, if taken seriously, would then point in the opposite direction.

7.8 *Clarity, Singularity, and Stability*

Figure 7.2 depicts three views of a three-dimensional object, an octahedron. The changes in view may be conceived as being generated by continuous rotation. If A and C are considered in isolation, they appear two-dimensional, whereas B appears three-dimensional. Thinking in terms of rotation, there are the two prominent constellations, A and C. All intermediate constellations are less clear. In this sense, clear constellations are singular. A position between two clear constellations is usually less clear.

This is a fairly universal feature of clear phenomena. They lie apart and are singular in a neighbourhood. It has been noted earlier that prominent numbers lie apart on the range of numbers, that focal colours lie apart on the spectrum, or that clear musical intervals lie apart in terms of frequency. The term 'singularity' refers to this type of local uniqueness.

The singularity of clear configurations is a pervasive feature of

---

[1] See S. A.8 in App. A.

psychological organization. One way of thinking about it is as follows. Consider a point of maximum clarity in a neighbourhood. All changes away from this point must decrease clarity. So all neighbouring states must be less clear, and there cannot be another point of maximum clarity close to the first one. Thus, all local maxima will be isolated maxima. They will be singular in the sense of being separated.

Another way of thinking about singularity relates to stability. If a certain state of psychological organization is stable, there should be a tendency to correct deviations. Any stable state must, therefore, be surrounded by unstable states, where forces push towards the stable state. As a consequence, stable psychological configurations must be singular. If stability is achieved through clarification processes, the stability argument merges with the clarification argument.[1]

It will be assumed in the following that all clear configurations are singular in the above-mentioned sense. Such an assumption is implicit in most parts of cognitive psychology. In making the singularity assumption, a feature is captured that is typical for a host of psychological phenomena. This does not rule out exceptions.

7.9 *Schemata*

Consider the sequence of numbers

$$1, 2, 3, 4, 5, 6, 7, 9, 10, 11, 12, 13, 14, 15, 16.$$

This will be perceived as an arithmetic series ranging from 1 to 16, with the 8 'missing'. (The reader may have overlooked the missing number.) This illustrates a fairly general feature of perception. Conceptualizing proceeds by relating an event to an adjacent clear case, and by noting the exceptions. Psychologists use the term

---

[1] A further related argument is that social rules must be 'communicatively stable', in the sense of withstanding erosion by transmission errors (Schlicht 1979).

'*schema*' for the implied clear case and describe the way in which an event is related to the implied schema by 'assimilation'.[1]

Instances illustrating this psychological regularity abound. An ellipse may be described as a compressed circle, but a circle is not described as a fully symmetric ellipse. Stockholm may be described as the Venice of the Baltic, but Venice will not be described as the Stockholm of the Adriatic (not even by persons who know Stockholm better than Venice). In *Roget's Thesaurus* there is an entry for 'brownness' which includes the word 'henna'; there is no entry for 'hennaness' which mentions brown.

In a similar vein, a swan may be described as a bird with a long neck. Such a description refers implicitly to a typical 'bird' (which may sing and sit in a tree) and picks up the exceptions. The reader may experience a similar phenomenon when recalling the story about the 'War of the Ghosts'.[2]

In the social sphere, concepts are formed in the same manner. Individual observations are linked to categories. A person may be described as a 'somewhat chaotic law professor', but another law professor will not be referred to as a 'somewhat orderly law professor'—the adjective here would refer to something typical for law professors and it would, therefore, be redundant. Similarly, a co-determined firm may be described as an intermediate case between a capitalist firm and a labour-managed firm, rather than being considered as a schema in its own right. This example shows also that social categories are fairly rigid and do not necessarily reflect frequent exposure, since this way of categorizing firms may be encountered also in Germany. All large firms in Germany are co-determined and labour management is rare. It has been shown that social categories (mother, father, nurse, driver) exhibit the same regularities as natural categories (bird, tree, blue). Both

---

[1] The assimilation - accommodation terminology is due to Piaget (1967). Psychologists distinguish between '*prototype*' and '*schema*', but I do not want to introduce this distinction. The prototype is a typical case that may actually exist, and a schema is a prototype with certain features unspecified. The arithmetic series would thus be the prototype for the series given above, whereas 'bird' would refer to a schema since features like colouring are left open.   [2] See page 73 S. 6.5.

types of category exhibit the inflexibility that is brought about by
the singularity of clear cases.[1]

This way of perceiving and remembering the world creates
fuzziness in borderline cases. While people agree that an apple is
a fruit, they are uncertain how to classify a *pumpkin*.[2] This
fuzziness translates into the fuzziness of scope and renders custom
malleable. This reinforces the case that has been argued earlier.[3]

7.10 *Change and Schema Switches*

The reference to clear cases can also be observed in the game of
Eleusis. When considering a rule, the clearest cases are considered
first. Some simple hypotheses are developed that build only on
colours or only on numbers; more elaborate hypotheses can be
formed by combining the elementary hypotheses. In this way, a
complicated rule may be developed from a combination of simple
patterns.

Consider now what happens if a change occurs. In Eleusis, a
player may hold a certain hypothesis and play accordingly. He is
successful for a while, but suddenly one of his cards is rejected.
Others may play cards that do not fit this particular player's
hypothesis, yet they are accepted. So his hypothesis was wrong.
However, he will not discard his hypothesis until he has found a
better one. He will continue to use his rule because this is better
than playing randomly. While playing, he will try to figure out a
better rule.

There are two ways of finding a better hypothesis. The first is to
look for a refinement of the previous hypothesis by discovering
what explains the incidence of the exceptions. The other way is to
find an entirely different rule. This is illustrated by the series of
shapes in Fig. 7.3. Here, A will be perceived as a triangle, D as a
square. Now think about a continuous transformation from A to
D that passes through stages B and C. Between stages A and B, the

---

[1] Dahlgren(1985); see also S. 6.9 above.
[2] M.E. McCloskey and Glucksberg (1978).   [3] See Ch. 5.

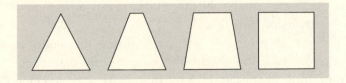

Figure 7.3
A Continuous Sequence of Figures
Involving a Discontinuous Switch in the Schema

figures may be easily conceptualized as modified triangles, i.e. triangles with dissected peaks. Closer to D, however, a triangle will not serve as a good schema any more: rather, these shapes will be conceived as distorted squares. Somewhere in between, the schema has switched from triangle to square (perhaps in several steps, i.e. from triangle to trapezium to square).

In this way, a continuous change may at a certain point lead to a switch in the schema adopted.[1] Ambiguous figures play on the double meaning of intermediate cases where two schemata can be used equally well (Fig. 7.4).

7.11 *Learning*

The process described in this abstract manner is typical for many learning processes. The theory of learning proposed by Jean Piaget describes learning in such terms. According to Piaget, new knowledge is first integrated into a prevailing schema by means of refinements. This is termed 'assimilation'. If the necessary refinements become too complicated, a new schema is established. This constitutes an 'accommodation'. The formation of concepts of number, mass, volume, and so forth in early childhood has been

---

[1] Schemata switches have been discussed in the literature under various names including 'reorganization' (Koffka 1935: 506), 'accommodation' (Piaget 1967: 243), 'revolution' (Kuhn 1970), 'Gestalt switch' (Groeben 1975; Schlicht 1979), 'code switching' (Glason 1973), and 'paradigm shifts' (Margolis 1987).

Figure 7.4
A Goblet with David Hume's Profile

studied in this framework. Later on it turned out that the overall
pattern was fairly general.[1]

Collective learning follows similar patterns. Thomas Kuhn has
described the growth of knowledge in physics as alternating
between refining and developing a schema (a 'paradigm') and
switching to a new one. Problems are tackled first within the
received theoretical framework. If such problems become insur-
mountable, a profound change in the overall structure of knowledge takes place. Examples are the Copernican and the
Einsteinian revolutions in physics.

Individual problem solving and all kinds of learning that
depend on insight may also be characterized in terms of assimilation and accommodation.[2] Consider the problem of how to form a
single circle of twelve links out of four pieces of chain, each three
links in length, where, in order to accomplish this task, at most

---

[1] Kohlberg (1983), for instance, has explained moral development along these lines.
[2] Wertheimer (1959) has described this. He also analysed Galileo's and Einstein's
discoveries in psychological terms and in this way related the collective processes
described by Kuhn to individual discoveries.

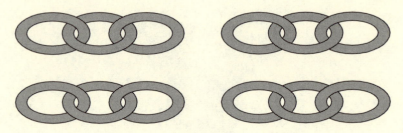

Figure 7.5
**Open and Close only Three Links
to Form a Circle with Twelve Links**

three links may be opened and closed (Fig. 7.5).[1] If the solution is not obvious, a simpler problem, depicted in Fig. 7.6, may be considered first: form a circle of six links out of three pieces that are each two links in length, by opening two links at most. Now the problem given in Fig. 7.5 should be easily solvable.[2] Once the schema is grasped, it is easy to solve an entire set of similar problems, such as forming a ring out of five chains with four links each while opening/closing just four links.

A difficulty in solving the original problem may arise because the symmetrical setting of the problem suggests another schema, namely, to treat all chains symmetrically and open just one link in each chain. The solution requires us to abandon the idea of symmetry and to switch to another schema. The problem would have been easier if it had first been posed in an asymmetrical setting, such as starting with one chain of three links and three chains of nine links. This feature illustrates the 'situational forces' that will play a role later.[3]

The example illustrates that there are two schemata that may be used alternatively for the purpose of forming a necklace. One schema is to treat all pieces of chain symmetrically and attach each piece of chain to the next one. The other schema is to

---

[1] This is the 'cheap necklace problem' used by Silveira (1971) to study incubation effects in problem solving.
[2] To solve the problem given in Fig. 7.5, open all three links in one chain and use the three open links to connect the three remaining chains.   [3] See Ch. 8.

Figure 7.6

**Open and Close only Two Links
to Form a Circle with Six Links**

decompose one piece of chain into its links and to use these links to connect the remaining pieces of chain. A problem is solved by starting with one or the other schema. Both may be used alternatively. If one schema is used routinely but becomes inappropriate for extraneous reasons, modifications will be introduced, and the prevailing schema will be weakened and eventually replaced by another schema.

An example taken from traffic regulations illustrates such schema switches. In the 1960s, a left turn was permitted in Germany only after oncoming traffic had passed (Fig. 7.7); the 'American' way was illegal unless indicated by painted lines on the surface of the street, or by appropriate signs. In the course of time, the streets became wider and the American way of turning more widespread, both formally, with explicit signs mandating it, and informally, i.e. against the law. In view of this development, the law was adapted. In the 1970s both ways of turning were permitted. Today, the law mandates the American turn, and the old turn is illegal. Practice has thus changed in a smooth manner, but the schema has altered discontinuously. Note that there are no clear intermediate cases. Thus, the evolution of traffic rules followed the patterns described by Piaget for learning, and by Kuhn for the development of the natural sciences.

Schema switches will occur because schemata feature particular clarity. Clear cases are singular, and so are schemata. All this

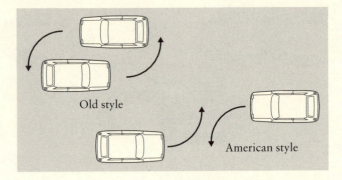

Figure 7.7
The Old Style and the American Style of Turning Left

implies that schema switches are discontinuous in nature, although they may be induced by smoothly changing circumstances.

7.12 *Hysteresis*

If change engenders schemata switches, hysteresis will occur. The reason is different from, albeit related to, those that have been discussed under the critical mass heading.[1] If circumstances change, people will try to apply the previous set of rules. If this fails, they will try to develop refinements to the basic schema. When the refinements no longer work, or the underlying pattern becomes buried under a heap of exceptions, another schema will be adopted. In this way, the incumbent schema will have a tendency to remain, even beyond the point where it becomes inappropriate. This may be illustrated also by means of Fig. 7.3, depicting a continuous change from triangle to square. Comparing a movement from A to D with a movement from D to A, the first will have a switching point farther to the right.

This 'psychological' hysteresis is immune to the arguments about erosion and adaptation made earlier.[2] It creates

---

[1] See S. 3.3, 3.6–3.8.   [2] See S. 5.3–5.5.

psychological discontinuity in an objectively continuous environment. The singularity of clear cases thus induces a kind of discontinuity that prevails even under conditions of fuzziness. Just as prominent numbers punctuate the ray of numbers, schemata lie apart, and the earlier observations about rounding generalize, in this sense, to the entire social sphere. This opens an avenue for understanding the rigidity of rules as a phenomenon of cognition. It does not, however, explain why people may wish to behave according to these rules. The next chapter turns, therefore, to motivation.

Chapter 8

RULE PREFERENCE

8.1 *Overall Clarity*

Entitlements and obligations are the backbone of market processes and other kinds of social interaction.[1] They emerge from customary regularities. Such regularities have been related to underlying processes of perception and memory in rule formation.[2] Up to now, the discussion has focused on cognitive issues. Restricting the argument to cognitive aspects eased the task of elucidating clarification processes that generate rules and schemata, organize perception and memory, and induce context dependency.

This view will be broadened in what follows. There is no reason to assume that clarification processes are constrained to the cognitive sphere. They integrate all kinds of psychological processes, independently of human terminological choices. Psychological organization aims at overall clarity and coherence. This ties emotions and cognitions together, shapes motivation and action, and introduces context dependency in a broad sense.

The present chapter discusses behaviours that flow from a desire to maintain regularities—from 'rule preference'.[3] This rule

---

[1] See Ch. 2.   [2] See Ch. 6. and 7.
[3] I will introduce various psychological theories by mentioning just one typical experimental setting. This is intended to describe, rather than prove, the effect in question. All the theories and effects to be discussed have been widely tested and refer to robust phenomena. There is a literature on each of the topics that the interested reader may consult. A good survey is provided by Zimbardo and Leippe (1991).

preference relates directly to the workings of custom. It underlies conservatism and conformity but influences many other phenomena as well. The term 'rule preference' refers, of course, not to 'random rules' but to psychologically meaningful, or clear, rules.[1]

While considering aspects of behaviour and taste formation with respect to custom in this and the following chapter, it should be kept in mind that the overall clarification processes do not shape psychological regularities in isolation, but integrate cognitions, motivations, and actions. As has been remarked repeatedly, it is the mutual reinforcement of received habits, legitimizing views, emotions, and motivations that renders custom effective and powerful. The force and stability of custom derives mainly from its texture, rather than from its single elements. This force evaporates if single aspects are treated in isolation.

8.2 *Commitment*

One relevant set of phenomena relates to the behavioural impact of commitment. It was noted earlier that a promise will increase the probability of an individual's acting in the promised way.[2] Consider some cases.

If somebody leaves his place at the beach and asks his neighbour to keep an eye on the radio on the blanket, this will induce the neighbour to feel responsible. In field experiments, subjects tried to stop thieves not only with words, but also by chasing and grabbing them. Asking for a match rather than asking the neighbour to keep an eye on the radio produced quite different behaviour:[3] subjects were then much less inclined to try to prevent the thefts. Phenomena of this kind can be understood as arising from the commitment generated by the request of the owner, and the affirming reaction of the person approached.

---

[1] On 'random rules', see S. 7.3. The idea of rule preference pursued here is somewhat different from Buchanan's (1994: 127–8) postulate of a preference for moral rules, in that it refers to rules quite independently of their 'morality'.

[2] See S. 2.10 on contracting.

[3] This has been studied by Moriarty (1975) at a New York beach(!).

Commitment also arises, however, without any kind of request and without explicit agreement. The mere fact that a decision has been made will induce a strong tendency to maintain whatever course of action or thought has been decided. If somebody has agreed to buy an item for a low price, and it turns out that the commodity can be delivered only at a higher price—the salesman might say 'because the cheap offer is not available anymore'—then the customer will be more willing to pay the higher price than he would have been if confronted with the higher price at the outset.[1] Similar phenomena arise whenever someone 'has made up his mind'. A decision to behave differently would require a change of the accepted pattern. It is essential, however, that the decision was reached freely, in the sense that reasonable alternatives were available. Without a choice between relevant alternatives, the commitment effect will be much weaker.

A related phenomenon is that people have a strong inclination to complete briefly interrupted tasks, such as solving a crossword puzzle.[2] A further phenomenon of commitment is exploited by the 'foot in the door technique' of salesmen. Gaining compliance with a small request, like being allowed to come in, increases the chances of obtaining compliance with a larger request.[3]

All these commitment phenomena may be understood as arising from a preference of individuals to maintain a pattern of behaviour once they have adopted it. This is not necessarily a matter of deliberation. Rather, commitment phenomena are particularly pronounced in situations that do not allow careful thinking.[4]

---

[1] See Zimbardo and Leippe (1991: 80–3) for a delightful account of related research.
[2] This is known as the 'Zeigarnik effect'; see Koffka (1935: 334–42) for a description of the classic studies.
[3] See Zimbardo and Leippe (1991: 81–2) for a brief survey.
[4] Cialdini (1988: ch. 3).

8.3 *Obedience and Authority*

The commitment effect can be very strong. This is illustrated by a set of experiments conducted by Stanley Milgram on obedience and authority.[1]

A typical experiment runs as follows. Subjects are recruited by means of a newspaper advertisement requesting participation in an experiment on memory and learning. A subject appears at the designated place and meets an experimenter in a white coat and another subject who has responded to the advertisement as well. The experimenter explains that this experiment is about the effect of punishment on learning. The purpose is to develop a way of helping people to improve their memory. One of the subjects will be the 'teacher', the other the 'learner'. The subjects are assigned to the roles by drawing slips of paper from a hat. The teacher is to read word pairs to the learner and then test the learner's memory by giving the first word of each pair and asking for the word that belongs to it. Incorrect answers are to be punished with an electric shock that is administered by pushing the button of a 'shock generator'. The teacher is advised to punish each error with a shock of increasing voltage, starting with a mild 15 volts, and going up to 450 volts in stages. The buttons in the 195–240 volt range are labelled with 'very strong shock', in the 375–420 volt range with 'danger: very severe shock', and in the 435–50 volt range simply with 'XXX'.

The 'learner', a sympathetic, middle-aged man, is strapped to a chair. His skin is treated with an electrode paste to avoid blisters and burns, and an electrode is attached. The experiment starts. Upon the first mistake, the teacher administers a shock. At the next error, a more severe shock is administered, and so forth. At 75 volts, the learner is starting to moan; at 150 volts he starts to protest and demands discontinuing the experiment; and so on. Above 300 volts, he screams in agony, and above 330 volts he reacts no longer.

[1] The following is a brief account of the classical Milgram (1974) experiments. See also Zimbardo and Leippe (1991: 65–76) for an excellent discussion.

The majority of the 'teachers' were prepared to escalate punishment up to the maximum shock. The 'teachers' themselves were, of course, the true subjects of the experiments. The learner was a lay actor, and no real shocks were administered. The actor was, however, very convincing. The teachers had dreadful dreams after the experience. During the experiment, they exhibited many signs of stress. When requesting to stop the experiment, however, they obtained standard answers from the experimenter, such as 'It is absolutely necessary that you continue', or 'You have no other choice, you must go on.' The subjects were objectively perfectly free to leave the experiment, and a minority decided to do this. A majority felt compelled to stay.

This experiment has used several psychological mechanisms to enforce compliance through situational channels. One of the most important was commitment. People initially agreed to participate in the experiment. They committed themselves to obey the experimenter, and this led them to do things that they would otherwise have refrained from doing freely. They were not forced to perform by the threat of sanctions. Another important situational force was related to the bit-by-bit increase. This made it difficult to determine a critical point for triggering disobedience. Further, the teacher was unable to predict whether the next question would be answered correctly or wrongly. So he could hope not to be forced to induce a shock when asking a single further question. By asking a further question, the teacher entered an implicit commitment to administer a shock in response to a wrong answer.

The Milgram experiment illustrates the strong force of situational factors in determining individual behaviour. These effects go far beyond what would be attributable to conventional incentives. It illustrates further that the influence of psychological motives is not confined to ambiguous cases where clear high-powered incentives are absent. Obedience in this instance was seen to override straightforward utility-maximizing behaviour.

Before continuing this topic, it must be pointed out that commitment mechanisms and related situational determinants of behaviour are not necessarily negative and detrimental. If people are committed to helping others, this will be very beneficial. Acts that flow from such motivation spring from the most sublime features of human nature. The authority experiments illustrate the negative side. Commitment mechanisms can be severely misused. Commitment phenomena, as well as other features of human nature, must be taken as factual givens. They enable humans to perform tasks that they would otherwise not be able to perform, for the good or the bad. The noblest features of human nature—such as making a commitment to the well-being of others—and the most appalling features—such as torturing others—flow from the same source.

8.4 *Status Quo Preference and the Endowment Effect*

The commitment effect helps us to understand the relevance of behavioural patterns that have been 'adopted'. A custom may prescribe such a behavioural pattern. In this way, a custom may influence action. It is not, however, necessary for commitment effects to rely on explicit 'adoption'. Adoption may well be implicit. This implicit adoption is obviously of great relevance for the behavioural effect of custom.

The implicit adoption of certain behavioural patterns can be illustrated by '*status quo* preference' which gives rise to the 'endowment effect'. This effect is an example of rule preference. It is very similar to the commitment effect but works without any explicit 'commitment'.

The endowment effect is illustrated by relating the following experiment.[1] Subjects were offered a choice between a decorated mug, worth about $6 at the university bookstore, and a sum of money. First, a group of subjects answered a series of questions to determine the valuation of the mugs in terms of money. After finishing the questionnaire, they were offered a choice between a mug and a certain amount of money. A second group of subjects were then each given a mug; they answered similar questions to

---

[1] Kahneman *et al.* (1990); see also Kahneman (1994: 24) for further references.

determine their valuation of the mug. Thereafter, they were offered that amount of money for their mug, which they either accepted or rejected. The choosers in the first group objectively faced the same options as the owners in the second group. The choice was, in both cases, to leave the experiment with either a new mug or some extra money. Yet the average cash value of the mug was much higher for the owners than for the choosers, e.g. $7.12 against $3.50.

The experiment illustrates a general regularity. The price demanded for selling a commodity exceeds the willingness to pay. People prefer the *status quo*. If they are given a mug, they value the mug more highly than they would if it did not belong to them.[1] This effect is noted in many different experimental settings.

One interpretation of the endowment effect runs in terms of rule preference and good continuity. The term '*status quo* prefer-ence' suggests such an interpretation. If the individuals have a desire to maintain established regularities, and an aversion to disrupt them, *status quo* preference prevails, and the endowment effect results.

With regard to custom, the behavioural impact of tacit commit-ment to perceived regularities seems very significant, because cus-toms will usually be adopted in such a tacit manner.

8.5 *Loss Aversion versus Rule Preference*

The endowment effect has usually been interpreted differently. It may be brought about by a general feature of evaluative processes that stress losses more than gains. This interpretation of the endowment effect in terms of 'loss aversion', as proposed by Kahneman and others, involves two assumptions:[2]

---

[1] The above discussion omits several fine points. It must, for example, be assumed that money is not subject to the endowment effect. Further, shopkeepers should not become emotionally attached to the goods they want to sell. See Kahneman *et al.* (1990) for more detail.   [2] See Kahneman *et al.* (1990).

1. Individuals make their decisions by starting from a reference point, typically provided by the *status quo*. The reference point 'frames' the decision in the sense that alternatives are evaluated by comparing them with the reference point. Deteriorations with respect to the reference point are considered as losses, and improvements as gains.
2. Losses loom larger than gains. A loss is weighted substantially more than an objectively commensurate gain. This is the assumption of loss aversion.

Because gains and losses are defined in terms of deviations from the reference point, changes in the reference point induce changes in gains and losses in cases where the set of alternatives remains objectively unaltered.

The mug experiment described in the previous section offers an example for such induced changes in evaluation. It can be interpreted as follows. The *status quo* serves as a reference point for the owners as well as for the choosers. The owners of a mug consider the selling a loss, the choosers consider the acquisition a gain. As a consequence of loss aversion, the sellers reveal a higher evaluation of the mug than the buyers.

This interpretation is somewhat different from the interpretation in terms of rule preference proposed earlier. The interpretation in terms of rule preference, however, offers the following advantages.

First, the rule preference assumption can formally account for all phenomena of loss aversion. If the move from one alternative to the other is considered a gain, and the reverse movement a loss, the hypothesis of loss aversion asserts that the evaluation of the loss is larger than that of the gain. This result is also implied by rule preference in the sense of *status quo* preference. The bias can be introduced formally by saying that any evaluation of a utility difference between two alternatives has two components. The first is the 'objective' utility difference, evaluated independently of the *status quo*. (This utility difference may be determined by judging the two alternatives from the point of view of another quite unrelated *status quo*.) The other component is the utility of maintaining the *status quo* as such. Moving from a bad alternative to a good one involves the 'objective' gain minus the costs from departing from the *status quo*. Moving from a good to a bad alternative involves the 'objective' loss plus the loss of departing from the *status quo*. If the 'objective' gain equals the 'objective' loss, the total loss incurred by moving from the good to the bad alternative must exceed the total gain obtainable from moving from the bad to the good alternative. In this way, a *status quo* preference will account for all phenomena of loss aversion without invoking loss aversion as such.[1] Loss aversion is implied by rule preference.

Second, the assumption of rule preference accounts for a class of phenomena that are not covered by straightforward loss aversion. These relate to the distinction between legitimate and illegitimate possession. From the point of view of the endowment effect, the valuation of an item should not be affected by the way in which it has been obtained. Yet it makes a big difference to the owner whether an object has been obtained rightfully or not. Rule preference would account for such observations, because the illegitimate possession of the item involves a rule violation, but the legitimate possession does not.

Third, rule preference accounts for the fact that rule violations induce emotional responses, but no active involvement would flow from the idea of loss aversion, as it is concerned with evaluations only. Assume for instance that someone has been given a mug with the understanding that he may trade it for some money. Unexpect-

---

[1] Consider three alternatives, A, B, and C. The alternatives A and B are to be compared. Alternative C serves as another possible *status quo*. If the *status quo* is A, the utility difference between A and B is evaluated as a ; if the *status quo* is B, the utility difference between A and B is evaluated as b ; if the *status quo* is C, the utility difference between A and B is evaluated as c. *Status quo* preference entails that all comparisons are biased in favour of the *status quo*. This implies $a > b$. It implies further $a > c$ and $b < c$, and the *status quo* preference may be construed as equal to $a-c$ for the *status quo* A and $c-b$ for the *status quo* B. The phenomenon of loss aversion can be subsumed here as special case of *status quo* preference, where a and b are both positive; i.e. alternative A is unambiguously better than alternative B. If the *status quo* is A, a change from A to B is evaluated as a loss of size a. If the *status quo* is B, a change from B to A is evaluated as a gain b. The loss b looms larger than the gain a. *Status quo* preference accounts formally for phenomena of loss aversion.

edly, the experimenter changes his mind and takes the mug back in order to offer a choice between money and mug right away. From the perspective of loss aversion, the endowment effect should be weakened by his taking the mug away.[1] This would not explain the subject's indignation, however. The subject may even reveal an increased willingness to pay in order to obtain the mug.[2]

Fourth, the rule preference assumption integrates the phenomenon of *status quo* preference into a much wider class of phenomena. The idea of loss aversion applies only to a restricted class of phenomena. Commitment to promises, obedience to authority, or compliance with entitlements may be interpreted as having been brought about by rule preference, but these are not covered by loss aversion. This suggests an interpretation in terms of rule preference.

8.6 Reciprocity and Retribution

The scope of rule preference also covers phenomena of reciprocity and retribution which are central to large segments of social theory. People tend to return favours or to reciprocate the help of others. They try to match whatever they have received by appropriate action. This behavioural pattern affects economic and social interaction significantly.[3]

Reciprocity and retribution have been interpreted as flowing

---

[1] See Loewenstein and Adler (1993).

[2] This would follow from Brehm's (1966) theory of 'psychological reactance'.

[3] An empirical case is analysed in Platteau and Abraham (1987); theoretical consequences (for game theory) are pointed out in, e.g., Rabin (1993). Güth and Tietz (1990) survey experiments in ultimatum games, and Fehr et al. (1996) provide further strong experimental evidence for the behavioural importance of patterns of reciprocity and retribution. The behavioural importance of reciprocity is amply documented by the powerful sales techniques based on this behavioural tendency; see Cialdini (1984: ch. 2). Reciprocity is, of course, incompatible with conventional concepts of rational behaviour although it may be used rationally in a different sense. The following statement by the sociologist Coleman (1990: 309–10) epitomizes this: 'A rational, self-interested person may attempt to prevent others from doing favors for him . . . because the call for his services may come at an inconvenient time (when re-paying the obligation would be costly).' While this observation correctly describes how people normally behave, it contradicts the assumption of strict rationality because it would seem even more preferable to obtain a favour while withholding the return favour.

from a universal 'norm', which is shared by all human beings.[1] Yet the perspective of rule preference suggests another interpretation. Rather than viewing reciprocity as an irreducible behavioural disposition, it may be conceived as a straightforward consequence of rule preference. Such a treatment seems more adequate, for two reasons.

First, the equity norm underlying reciprocity is quite indeterminate. It posits that favours and return favours—or, more technically, 'inputs' and 'outputs'—tend to be equalized. The inputs and outputs are, however, gauged by entitlements.[2] An individual will perceive something he receives as a 'favour' only if it surpasses his entitlements. He will then reciprocate by giving more than the other party is entitled to obtain. Reciprocity and retribution, moreover, arise when individuals attempt to offset rule violations and, in this way they reconfirm the original regularity.[3] This may actually imply entirely unequal outcomes. It has been shown that, 'under the right conditions, both exploiters and their victims are capable of convincing themselves that the most unbalanced of exchanges is in fact perfectly fair'.[4]

8.7 *Conformity*

Conformity may be understood directly in terms of rule preference. It could be described as a force that tries to maintain a pattern that has been perceived in a group. The forces of conformity are again very strong. In a series of experiments, Asch tried to demonstrate that previously established effects of conformity

[1] Gouldner (1960). This kind of behaviour is basic to equity theory (Adams 1963) and social exchange theory (Blau 1955; Homans 1961), and is an important consequence of balance theory (F. Heider 1958).

[2] In an experiment about division of gains, Selten and Berg (1970) have shown that different presentations of the same division problem induce quite different allocations of gains in experiments. This 'presentation effect' witnesses the behavioural importance of 'framing'.

[3] F. Heider's (1958: 265–75) classical treatment of 'retribution' takes this perspective. For an interpretation of reciprocity in terms of gestalt theory, see also Kubon-Gilke (1995).

[4] Austin and Hatfield (1980: 80). See also F. Heider (1958: 264). 'Equity theory' may, thus, be a misleading term.

would disappear in unambiguous settings. Yet his results turned his attempt into a classical confirmation of the forces of conformity.[1]

In experiments involving six to eight collaborators of the experimenter and one subject, the subject was asked to tell which of three lines of evidently different length was equal to a fourth line. In one-third of the experiments, the subjects followed the majority in giving wrong answers, while in two-thirds they maintained their independent judgement. Both the yielding and the independent subjects showed signs of tension and uneasiness.

Thus, group opinion played a strong role in the individual's judgements and publicly stated opinions. This should not be seen, however, as a merely negative trait of human nature. It springs from rule preference and, thus, from the same source that engenders commitment to the most valuable goals. It confirms also that people do not underestimate the opinions of others and do not overestimate the soundness of their own judgement. Thus, these experiments should not be perceived as revealing a basic irrationality and foolishness of human judgement. Rather, each subject was made to assume that the others had arrived at their judgements under just the same conditions as he himself, and it is not unreasonable to take this as an important piece of information that can be used to check the individual's judgement. If a set of mathematical calculations had to be performed, and a large majority reached a certain conclusion while one individual arrived at a different result, it would not be unreasonable for the dissident to doubt his own reasoning.

8.8 *Rule Preference, Custom, and Clarity*

The phenomena of obedience, *status quo* preference, reciprocity, and conformity are all instances of an overall rule preference on the side of the individuals. In this, they tie action to rule forma-

---

[1] Asch (1952: 450–501).

tion. Custom establishes rules, and these rules have an impact on individual action, because the individuals prefer regularity.

Rule preference is a manifestation of a desire for clarity. This desire is related to current concepts of 'rationality', but it goes further. Current concepts of rationality relate to attaining goals in the most efficient manner. The goals themselves are a-rational or even irrational. In contrast, the desire for clarity may be interpreted as a desire on the side of the individuals to pursue not arbitrary goals, but goals that fit a perceived pattern. Goals can then be justified by pointing to these patterns. Such justification depends on the fit between the goals and the perceived patterns— or, in other words, on clarity.[1]

---

[1] The various 'rationality' postulates encountered in the choice-theoretic literature, such as transitivity, independence of irrelevant alternatives, and so forth, witness the desire to introduce 'rationality' assumptions on the level of individual preferences in a theoretical framework that insists on the a-rational nature of preferences. In this sense, choice theory is driven by a desire to achieve 'rationality' even on the level of preferences, although this possibility is theoretically negated. The desire to introduce these considerations into choice theory seems closely related to the ideas about justification in terms of regularities and matching patterns mentioned above.

Chapter 9

ATTRIBUTION AND MOTIVATION

9.1 *Clarity and Motivation*

The previous chapters established the importance of clarification processes in rule-perception and rule-formation, and described the way in which rule perception influences action. But custom is not confined to merely moulding the behavioural rules that direct action. It shapes convictions and creates tastes and motives. The present chapter will illustrate how such motivational influences can be understood as another consequence of basal clarification processes. Psychological mechanisms of attribution, discounting, and overjustification fashion strong motives and convictions in diffuse contexts. In this manner, the diffuse and multifarious customary patterns engender motives and convictions. National and social stereotypes regarding tastes and habits provide examples.

9.2 *Attribution and Discounting*

If an individual notes that his guest at the breakfast table is choosing the brown rather than the white bread from a basket containing both, he will infer that his guest prefers the taste of brown bread. This is a 'causal attribution'. Such inferences are typically not unique, however. There may be many other reasons for the guest to select brown bread rather than white. Brown bread may be considered more nutritious or better for the teeth; his guest may have followed the advice of his physician; he may have promised his wife that he would try brown bread in order to fight his prejudice against it; or he may select brown bread in order not to disappoint his host who is known to have a serious interest in good health. There are many possible causes for any action, just as there are many possible sequels to any given sequence of cards on the table.[1]

The principles that have been identified by psychologists as guiding attributions are principles of clarity. Fundamental aspects of clarity include simplicity, salience, and consistency.[2]

Simple explanations are preferred to complicated accounts. If there are two sufficient causes to explain an action, it suffices to select one of them and disregard the other: this will simplify the explanation, and simpler explanations are preferred. Brown bread may be favoured for both its taste and its healthiness. Each of these reasons may be sufficient to explain the guest's choice. Therefore it will, be sufficient to focus on one motive while neglecting the other, even if both are of similar importance. The preference for simple explanations tends to produce over simplified accounts. This psychological regularity is known as the 'discounting principle': hypotheses involving as few causes as possible are preferred to more complicated accounts. The discounting principle is the scientist's 'principle of parsimony' in a different guise.

Regarding *salience*, the more obvious, more visible, and more solid explanation is generally preferred. If a musician obtains

---

[1] Cf. the discussion of the induction problem in the context of the game of Eleusis in S. 7.2.

[2] See Zimbardo and Leippe (1991: 89–107) for a good survey. Attribution theory goes back to F. Heider (1958) and Kelley (1967;1973). The centrepieces of attribution theory may already be found in Hume (1740*a*: 479; 1777*b*: 314): 'Actions are at first only consider'd as signs of motives.' 'To ascribe any single effect to the combination of several causes, is not surely a natural and obvious supposition.'

money for playing, the salient attribution of the money motive will supersede on attribution based on a possible intrinsic motivation to play for fun; money is clearly visible and more tangible than the joy of playing.

If, however, on other occasions the musician is observed playing without being paid, an attribution based on intrinsic motivation will be preferred. This is obviously a clearer hypothesis than the assumption that the musician plays for money whenever he gets paid, and plays for fun on other occasions.[1] The attribution of playing because of an intrinsic motivation rather than for monetary reward is '*consistent*' in the sense of being applicable to a wider range of observations.

The phenomena of discounting, simplicity, and consistency can be summarized by saying that clear explanations are preferred to others. This psychological tendency pre-selects among the possible explanations and renders learning possible, just as the principle of parsimony permits inferences in science.[2] On the other hand, the preference for clarity comprises the danger of over-simplification. Clarification processes entail both good and bad consequences.

9.3 *Self-Attribution and Over-Justification*

Individuals infer the causes or motives of their actions from observing their own behaviour. This is similar to the way other causal attributions are made. If a person usually takes brown bread for breakfast, he will tend to attribute this to his preferring brown bread. It has been shown that such self-attributions induce systematic changes in preferences, motives, and convictions. This is known as the 'over-justification effect'. Having been induced to eat brown bread with no single apparent reason, a person will attribute his eating brown bread to his taste and will develop a preference for brown bread. The underlying mechanism is as

[1] The psychologists' account is somewhat more detailed. The last example conjoins consistency and covariance arguments. The more detailed account can, however, also be justified by the clarity postulate in a straightforward way.   [2] See S. 7.3.

follows. There may be many reasons for selecting brown bread, including taste, health, convenience, politeness, and habit. Although several of these reasons may apply simultaneously, the individual selects only one of them to generate a parsimonious self-attribution. The interpretation in terms of preference appears straightforward and is accepted. A further change of preferences favouring brown bread sharpens and tightens the selected interpretation. In this way, preference changes are brought about that generate a clear picture.

The spontaneous nature of the processes of self-attribution and over-justification is illustrated nicely by the following experiment. Subjects were asked to participate in a 'stereo headphone test'. The headphones played a mixture of music, interrupted by a short message announcing an increase in fees at the subject's university. One group of subjects were asked to nod at certain occasions to 'test the comfort of the earphones', another group were required to shake their heads at similar instances. After the experiment, the subjects' changes in opinion about tuition increases were evaluated. It turned out that those who nodded were significantly more likely to be in agreement with the contents of the message, and those who shook their heads tended to disagree with the increase in tuition. Subjects were not aware of this connection. Furthermore, the self-attribution 'I nod, therefore I agree' arose spontaneously, unintentionally and subliminally.[1]

It must be mentioned, again, that these phenomena have been studied mostly with reference to unwarranted or surprising distortions. They depend typically on deliberately misleading the subjects. This does not imply that clarification processes are always distortive. In general this is not the case. The striving of the human mind for clarity and coherence provides the basis for thinking and feeling, and it would be unwise to discredit the clarification process on the grounds that it is sometimes conducive to distortive results, while neglecting the many other cases where such processes work in an acceptable fashion. The conclusion 'I

---

[1] Wells and Petty (1980); Zimbardo and Leippe (1991: 275–6).

nod, therefore I agree' is usually quite appropriate, and it would be unreasonable to disregard the information embedded in such associations.

9.4 *Cognitive Dissonance and Forced Compliance*

While attribution processes seek to simplify explanations of behaviour, the theory of cognitive dissonance deals with conflicting cognitions, motives, emotions, and actions.[1] Whenever such conflicts arise, there is a tendency to remove them by aligning cognitions, motives, and emotions with one another. The following experiment illustrates the processes occurring here.

If someone has agreed to make a public political statement that conflicts with his privately held political views, he will find himself in a state of conflict: how can he justify making such a statement in public? There seems to be no way other than by changing his political views in favour of the public statement. This is what has been observed.[2] This 'forced compliance' phenomenon may be understood as arising from a desire for self-justification. The only way to justify the action is to change the opinion in such a way as to justify the action. The action cannot be changed after the fact.

The forced compliance phenomenon fits well with the phenomena of self-attribution and over-justification. While self-attribution shapes preferences in diffuse situations, it does not do so if adequate reasons are provided that account for a person's past behaviour. If money were paid for eating brown bread, this would provide an adequate reason for eating brown bread: there would then be no reason to look for another explanation, such as taste or healthiness. The individual would not develop a preference for brown bread in order to explain the choice in a simple way, because the payment provides an adequate reason. As

---

[1] The account given here neglects many fine points relating to differences between attribution and cognitive dissonance approaches. For a more detailed account, see Zibardo and Leippe (1991: 87–126).   [2] Festinger and Carlsmith (1959).

a consequence, preference changes favouring brown bread should be less pronounced when monetary incentives are attached to the choice. Such a regularity has been reconfirmed experimentally in a variety of settings.

The general framework for studying these forced compliance phenomena is best explained as, follows. Two groups of subjects are induced to engage in the same type of activity. One of the groups is provided with minimal and diffuse incentives, the other is rewarded by means of strong incentives. After this procedure, attitude changes or preference changes with regard to the activity are evaluated. It turns out that the minimal incentive setting produces stronger changes in favour of the activity than the strong incentive situation. For example, people who were induced to make public political statements with minimal and diffuse incentives changed their political views significantly, whereas those who were given money for making such statements changed their views only slightly; individuals who were made to eat fried grasshoppers with minimal and diffuse incentives started to like them better than those who were given strong incentives for eating the animals; and so forth.[1]

9.5 *The Miasma of Reward*

The over-justification effect is induced by the psychological striving for clarity. The individual selects a simple and straightforward reason for action. This reason is further stressed by attaching more weight to it; preferences or convictions may, for instance, be adjusted such that the reasoning becomes even more convincing.

At the same time, other possible causes are discounted or disregarded. This is also strengthened by corresponding changes in preferences or convictions. By striving for clarification, some

---

[1] Festinger and Carlsmith (1959); Zimbardo *et al.* (1969). Zimbardo (1969) contains a number of studies in diverse fields, such as physiological hunger indicators and classical reflexes that can be shaped by the forced compliance.

salient motives are confirmed and other less salient motives are abated. The more salient motives oust the less perspicuous ones.

Such a supersession of an imperspicuous motive by a more prominent one is of particular relevance for the maintenance of 'intrinsic motivation', *viz.* a preference for engaging in certain tasks without any further external inducement. Such intrinsic motivation is, as a rule, less perspicuous and less tangible than clearly discernible external rewards. As a consequence, it can be destroyed if such a reward is offered. The effect has been referred to as 'the hidden costs of reward' and by the saying 'extrinsic motivation destroys intrinsic motivation'.[1]

The effect may be described as follows. Consider an activity that is pursued spontaneously, or is 'intrinsically motivated'. If external rewards are attached to the activity, an 'extrinsic motive' is added. Such an extrinsic motive may be provided by offering money, for instance. Once the extrinsic reward is introduced, the activity may be pursued more intensely, but when the money reward is withdrawn the spontaneous activity level declines below the previous spontaneous level. Several experiments have reconfirmed such regularities.

The argument rests on self-attribution and discounting. If the person obtains money, the payment will be perceived as a salient cause. The intrinsic motive—the joy of performing the task for its own sake—is less apparent and less tangible. Self-attribution will select the extrinsic money reward as the motive, rather than the less obvious intrinsic inclination. Preferences and convictions will adapt to strengthen the self-attribution to the money motive. Any additional cause, such as a preference for the activity, would blur the picture; this complication is avoided by attenuating the intrinsic preference. Eventually, the extrinsic (i.e. money) motive attenuates the intrinsic motivation to engage in the task.

The detrimental effect of extrinsic incentives on intrinsic motivation is of some economic significance, as it offers an explanation

---

[1] See Deci (1971), Lepper and Greene (1978), and Frey (1995). This discussion has, by the way, another dimension, related to the difference between 'task orientation' and 'ego-orientation'; see Asch (1952: 302–10). This is often disregarded.

for the conspicuous absence of high-powered incentives in certain labour contracts. Recent theorizing has ascertained that such 'incomplete' contracts sometimes create severe market-clearing problems, but the reasons for this incompleteness have hitherto remained enigmatic. A possible reason may relate to the negative motivational impact of such incentives, which flow from psychological clarification processes.[1]

9.6 *Conservatism, Conformity, Consistency*

The striving for clarity and consistency is an important psychological force underlying conservatism and conformity. If an individual has behaved in a certain manner in the past, a change of behaviour poses problems. In order to justify a change of behaviour, the person will have to provide reasons about why it is better to behave differently in the future, and why it was appropriate to behave differently in the past. With unchanged behaviour, all these explanations would be unnecessary. The self-attribution processes discussed above will further stabilize and ingrain conservatism.

In a similar way, the striving for consistency generates conformity. If a person behaves differently from others acting under similar conditions, he feels impelled to justify his deviation and provide reasons why the others are wrong and he is right, or why his situation actually differs from that of the others. Self-attribution will reconfirm conformity on a cognitive, emotional, and motivational level.

---

[1] The problem is the central issue in the exchange between Shapiro and Stiglitz (1984, 1985) and Carmichael (1985) and has been reviewed in Stiglitz (1987, 29–30). The motivational aspects mentioned above are stressed in Schlicht (1985*b*; 1990*b*), Kubon-Gilke (1990: 156–85), Brandes and Weise (1995). The detrimental effect of reward was first introduced into the economic literature by Frey and Stroebe (1980). Other applications may be found in Frey (1995).

9.7 *The Shaping of Motives by Custom*

The striving for clarity and coherence that manifests itself in attribution processes and processes of self-justification contributes to the shaping of motivation by custom in a tacit way. The situational forces generated by custom are often diffuse; they work through various channels, and are not clearly visible. In these cases, individuals tend to succumb to the 'fundamental attributional error' of discounting the situational forces. They stress motivational dispositions.[1] If somebody were told about one single trial in the Milgram experiment, he would attribute the act of torture to personality traits of the individual involved, rather than to sundry situational forces.[2] In a similar way, customary behaviour is attributed to individual motivation. This holds true for the individual's self-interpretation as well as for inferences about the motivations of others.

Actions that are prompted by diffuse and multifarious external causes will be attributed to preferences and other internal causes. This shapes motives. An Englishman prefers cricket, while an American prefers baseball; in the same vein, a Bavarian prefers beer and a Frenchman prefers wine. Such preferences and consumption patterns must have been acquired in some way or other. They are not innate attributes of particular human genetic strains. Ultimately they cannot be explained in terms of inert preferences alone, because there was a time when other preferences prevailed. Some centuries ago wine was actually prevalent in Bavaria, for instance, and it was brought to France a few centuries earlier by the Romans. This illustrates that inertia alone cannot explain the prevalence of such stereotypical phenomena. Other factors, such as economic factors, contribute in constantly moulding and reshaping these preferences and consumption patterns. The Frenchman, for instance, will recall having repeatedly ordered wine rather than beer at functions where he had a free choice. His choice may have been prompted by conformity, but he will not have noticed. He perceived himself to have acted freely. This alone

---

[1] Ross (1977).   [2] See S. 8.3.

would generate the self-attribution of preferring wine. Further causes conjoin to produce that result—his French friends all prefer wine; French wine is affordable; the quality is excellent; French cooking is geared to being accompanied by wine. In short, there is a multitude of possible causes. The preference for simple explanations will lead him to select the most salient account. The host of diffuse causes will be discounted, even if each of them is a contributory cause to the behaviour, because each single cause is rather feeble. A salient cause, such as an intrinsic preference, will be selected or invented and will dominate self-perception. Self-attribution will then transform this self-perception into a true preference. In this way, a diffuse set of customary factors shape pronounced preferences. Such processes will also sharpen and stereotype features that have been prevalent in the group.[1]

The argument is not, however, confined to preferences. The psychological mechanisms of over-justification and attribution are very general. They influence pleasure, pain, guilt, and even physiological responses of the individual.[2] The overarching argument is that custom works through various diffuse situational channels and will not easily supply one single salient motive. This favours self-attributions based on individual dispositions and preferences and at the same time attenuates other reasons. In this way, national characters are moulded and appear as causes, rather than results, of cultural differences. They appear in this way both to the individuals concerned and to outside observers—all succumb to the same attribution error.

At the same time, the attribution argument enables us to understand why customs in one culture that look peculiar to members of other cultures appear nevertheless natural and sensible to its own members. Frequent action induces processes which align convictions and motives with the action. Just as nodding induces agreement in the headphone test, cultural practices lead to convictions supporting these practices.[3]

---

[1] The argument given in this section relates closely to Turner's (1987) 'self-categorisation theory'.
[2] See Zimbardo (1969)   [3] See S. 9.3.

Chapter 10

CUSTOM AND STYLE

10.1 Custom and the Human Mind

Custom presupposes a psychological propensity to form rules and to perceive regularities. This seems quite obvious and innocuous, to the point of appearing hardly worth mentioning. Yet an explicit acknowledgement of the psychological nature of rule formation entails a number of consequences.[1] Some of them have been described in the preceding chapters in the context of rule preference, commitment, and attribution.

One of the most important aspects of rule formation is that the human mind *cannot* be conceived merely as an amorphous *tabula rasa*, but must structure psychological phenomena quite actively. This runs against the grain of current views—adaptive, associative, behaviourist, or other—which portray the shaping of behavioural, emotional, and cognitive responses as a smoothly malleable process that yields indiscriminately to all kinds of influences but does not generate a psychological structure on its

---

[1] It is only recently that 'mental models' are receiving serious attention in economics; see North (1993) and North and Denzau (1994). Hayek (1952) has been one of the few earlier economists who have dealt with the underlying psychological issues explicitly, while modern approaches to custom and related phenomena tried to avoid these psychological issues, e.g. North (1990), Buchanan and Brennan (1985), Lewis (1969), Sugden (1986), Schotter (1981). Casson (1991) is very close to the present approach in stressing the moral and cultural underpinnings of cooperation, although he argues in part in game-theoretic terms that are criticized in this section.

own. Such malleability would effectually frustrate the possibility of learning because learning involves extrapolation, and extrapolation presupposes pattern recognition.[1] Learning is possible because the human mind structures impressions. The human mind is not merely a passive mirror. Rather, the process of rule formation requires an interaction of the human mind with its surroundings. Rule formation in general, and the formation of customs in particular, result from the specific way in which the human mind grasps reality and responds to external events. Custom is, in short, shaped both by circumstances and by the way in which the human mind acts upon them.

The structuring force of psychological processes has been related to clarification processes. Clarity requirements structure learning and constrain the set of possible rules and customs. Social interaction and social evolution must presuppose these psychological regularities. The resulting customs will thus reflect both psychological and factual influences.

The clarity view of custom proposed here, however, extends far beyond cognition. It maintains that rule perception and rule formation are complemented by rule preference, i.e. by an active desire to align reason and action. It maintains further that convictions, emotions, and actions are mutually adjusted to each other by clarification processes. The unifying force of these clarification processes will be stressed in the following sections by complementing the discussion with some observations on the nature of emotions. It will be explained how emotions interlink with cognitions through clarification processes and consistency requirements. As the set of customs adopted in a society is shaped by the overall clarification processes that take place in each individual's mind, processes of mutual adjustment generate an overall coherence of the set of customs adopted in a society, and a unity of style.

The clarity view can also be elucidated by contrasting it with the 'strategic' interpretation of custom which underlies many

---

[1] See S. 7.2–7.4.

current approaches to custom and related phenomena. This view seeks to explain the emergence of custom by emphasizing problems of strategic interaction and by discounting psychological factors. The subsequent critique of the strategic interpretation of custom will provide a starting point for the discussion of emotions.

10.2 *The Strategic Interpretation of Custom*

The strategic view of custom starts from the insight that costly conflicts and coordination failures can be avoided by adopting some coordination device. Psychological considerations enter at this point, in the sense that the set of 'plausible' coordination devices is determined by psychological considerations. Beyond this, psychological influences are discounted.

Once a coordination rule is selected for historical or other reasons, it can be sustained by the self-seeking behaviour of individuals without any reference to commitment or rule preference. A coordination rule will remain in place as long as it is advantageous for each individual to observe it, *provided* the others do the same. This explains persistence. A typical assumption would be that the *status quo*—the perceived pattern—serves as a focal point which can be used for coordination purposes. This generates a custom.[1] Any rule is better than no rule, and people select clear rules rather than unclear rules to serve as benchmarks for purposes of coordination. The rule is followed because it is advantageous to do so as long as the others do the same. Clarity aspects play a role for 'equilibrium selection', i.e. for settling cases where several mutually consistent self-seeking patterns of behaviour are possible. This is suggested by experiments where particularly simple strategies seem to dominate others without any conclusive theoretical reason.[2] According to the strategic interpretation of

---

[1] Schelling (1978), Lewis (1969) and Sugden (1986). This is also the starting point for David Hume (1740*a*: 490–8), who proceeds further, however, when talking about the motivations that emerge and stabilize the conventions so achieved.

[2] See Axelrod (1984).

custom, the position is as follows. Beyond its bearing of simplicity for equilibrium selection, the adoption of one rule rather than another one has no consequences regarding convictions, evaluations, or preferences of individuals. A central assumption of the strategic interpretation of custom is that the rules selected as coordination devices are used *in a purely instrumental manner*. All phenomena of rule obedience, commitment, etc., are assumed to be of only secondary importance and are disregarded theoretically. In contrast, the clarity view stresses the cognitive, emotional, and behavioural purport of customs through commitment, rule preference, obedience, and so forth.

The strategic interpretation of custom has the advantage of being parsimonious. This parsimony seems, however, unwarranted.[1] There are several problems emerging in connection with this approach. The first is a formal one. The idea of equilibrium selection according to clarity has the disadvantage of being not fully strategically rational. This problem arises because the knowledge that clear cases are used as coordination devices should lead people to exploit this knowledge strategically. If somebody chooses a simple rather than a complicated strategy, his opponent will learn this more easily. The terms of the game can, thus, be set more easily by the player with the simpler strategy. Therefore, adoption of a simple strategy may lead to a first-mover advantage, and full strategic rationality should take this and similar feedbacks into account. This would change the initial game by infusing psychological elements into it.

The strategic interpretation of custom must disregard, further, the possibility that phenomena of commitment, obedience, *status quo* preferences, and so forth may be exploited strategically. A person may, for example, leave his car at a particular spot in order to reconfirm his right to park in that spot, even if this involves some costs to him. Others will select their strategies by taking this into account. Once phenomena of obedience, commitment, and

---

[1] Some commentators dismiss the strategic interpretation of custom as yet another custom: 'To interpret one custom in terms of another one strikes me as slightly perverse' (Charles Th. Hecktik). I object strongly to this kind of easy aphorism.

rule preference are of importance, the logic of the strategic approach would seem to require incorporating these behaviours for purely strategic purposes.

Incidentally, the discounting of all phenomena related to rule preference, coherence, and clarity in the strategic approach are instances of the laws of attribution and discounting, as they have been described by psychologists. The conceptual simplicity and clarity of the strategic approach, which can be achieved by neglecting psychological aspects, is undoubtedly a strength. This strength results from clarity. A simple and clear interpretation is preferred to a complex and fuzzy one. Ironically, the preference for a strategic interpretation of human behaviour is prompted by the very clarity features that the approach neglects.

Although the strategic interpretation of custom discounts all phenomena related to rule preference and coherence, emotions can find a place, too. There are actually two ways of integrating emotions and motivations into a strategic interpretation of custom, but both appear somewhat inadequate.

The first is to view all kinds of psychological phenomena as emotional codings of optimal strategies. People will develop fairness norms, it is held, that encapsulate optimal strategic choices. This would justify the strategic interpretation of custom as an appropriate 'as if' construct.[1] This view sounds appealing in theory. It also finds some psychological support in that the emotional encoding of information is very common. Individuals remember particular persons in terms of good or bad impressions, but cannot necessarily recollect the reasons for those impressions. A certain situation prompts fear, but the reason for this reaction has been forgotten. All conditioning processes may be interpreted as encoding information in emotional terms. Although the 'as if' defence of the strategic interpretation contains, thus, a psychological grain of truth, it seems inappropriate because it makes assumptions that theoretically negate some obvious social

---

[1] Binmore and Samuelson (1994). On 'as if' theorizing, see also Schlicht (1990*a*).

phenomena such as the persistence of individually disadvantageous customs.[1]

The other way to incorporate emotions into a strategic picture
is to consider their strategic role.[2] To act emotionally and
'irrationally' may be of strategic advantage in certain situations,
especially if this reaction is known to others. If it is known, for
instance, that somebody reacts very aggressively if he feels
cheated, this will prevent others from trying to cheat him. This
approach would justify certain emotional dispositions in terms of
the strategic advantages that they engender. The problem here is
that the argument would seem to imply the typical emotional
response to be *optimal* from a strategic point of view. This,
however, has not been maintained in the discussion. It also
remains puzzling why the same type of emotion that generates
moralistic aggression should be of relevance for the formation of
private habits. As it stands, the arguments made amount to the
convincing point that 'irrationality' (from the point of view of the
abstract rationality assumption embraced by game theorists) may
be strategically beneficial and is important for the functioning of
society. This was the starting point for the earlier discussion of
entitlements and obligations.[3]

10.3 *Habitual Rules and Clarity*

The clarity view of custom is reconfirmed by looking at individual
habits that do not require any social interaction for their formation. There is a strong parallelism between the formation of
private habits and the evolution of social customs. As the strategic
interpretation deals solely with social customs, it must remain
silent about the formation of private habits. If social customs arise
solely from strategic interaction, private habits would have to

---

[1] See S. 5.6 for some examples. An extensive discussion of the issue may be found in
Schlicht (1995*a*).
[2] Frank (1988).   [3] See Ch. 2.

emerge for different reasons.[1] This poses the theoretical problem within the strategic view of how to defend the assumption that the tendencies active in the formation of habits play no role (beyond equilibrium selection) in the formation of social customs. The clarity view, on the other hand, accounts for the parallelism between customs and habits in a very natural way because both private habits and social customs are perceived as being brought about by the same clarification processes. The clarity view integrates phenomena of habit formation and custom quite naturally.

Examples of private habits abound. A person may have adopted the habit of dressing in a certain sequence, putting things in certain places, going for a walk in the afternoon, or parking the car at a certain spot in the carpark. All these habits clearly show the regularity that is also characteristic of social custom.

The phenomenon of habit formation can be understood in terms of rule preference, commitment, attribution, and so forth. A person may be prompted by various reasons to behave in a certain way. If he observes himself behaving in such a manner, he will attribute this behaviour to dispositional rather than diffuse situational factors and will develop a preference for this kind of behaviour.[2] This is based on rule preference, but it also has some purely functional advantages. If the car is always parked in a certain place, it will be easy to find, and will render it unnecessary to remember where the car has been left. Putting the key in a certain pocket renders it easier to retrieve it. Given fixed habits, routines can develop that help in solving rather complex tasks in a manner that is both efficient and automatic. Tacit knowledge is created by repeating certain patterns of behaviour, and the routines so developed work in the background without requiring attention.

---

[1] A theoretical possibility is that private habits arise from generalizations of strategically advantageous behavioural patterns to the private sphere—that social norms osmote to the private sphere. If such generalization processes occur, they must be assumed to occur also with social interaction. This would restrict the possibility of viewing strategies from a purely instrumental point of view.

[2] See the discussion of self-attribution in S. 9.3 and 9.7.

The argument about the appropriateness of individual rule-guided behaviour presupposes, again, that certain rules are selected rather than others. Selecting a 'random rule' would not be helpful.[1] Only a rule that simplifies and clarifies will be useful, i.e. a true rule in the psychological sense. A rule that entails putting the key each day of the week in a different pocket is as definite as any other rule, but it is psychologically less clear. The distinction between rule-guided and other kinds of behaviour refers implicitly to clarity and rule preference.

The example permits a digression on the nature of clarity, as the term is used here. In the discussion about establishing a rule as to where to store the key, clarity and simplicity are synonymous; the simplest rule will be the clearest one. In complex settings, however, simplicity carries connotations of inappropriate over-simplification. It will not necessarily be useful, for instance, to place the key of the car in the simplest place conceivable—the ignition, for instance. Rather, the key of the car may be stored together with all the other keys, and the bunch of keys may be stored in the place that is the most appropriate for their various uses as a whole. This will not necessarily be the simplest place for the individual key, and it may actually render it difficult for other people to find it. It would not amount to permanently optimizing the place where the keys are kept, since such an optimization would require reconsidering the problem with each new key that was added to the bunch. Rather, a fixed place will be selected, and this place will be reconsidered only if inconveniences arise. The pattern here is very similar to the pattern of rule-learning, and the persistence of an acquired habit provides just another instance of hysteresis.[2] The example of the bunch of keys may illustrate the sense in which clarity differs from straightforward simplicity. The terminological preference for 'clarity' over 'simplicity' is prompted by a concern with overall aspects, and with reducing the weight placed on the simplicity of individual features or items.

[1] See S. 7.3.   [2] See S. 3.8 and 7.12.

10.4 *Emotions*

The previous chapters have stressed the role of clarity in rule formation, rule following, and attribution processes that shape preferences and convictions. The earlier discussion of entitlements and obligations, however, has emphasized not only preferences and convictions, but also the role of emotions in social interaction. It has been argued, for instance, that entitlements are stabilized socially by moralistic aggression and by yielding on the individual level.[1] Thus, the important role of emotions needs some further elaboration. It is, of course, beyond the present scope to offer a full-fledged discussion of emotions here. The following remarks are intended to indicate only some general and broad aspects.[2]

Consider anger, which is an important element in the mechanism of moralistic aggression. People are prepared to defend their entitlements even if it does not seem sensible to do so. This action, i.e. the reaction to circumstances, is prompted by the emotion of anger. Anger thus plays an important part in the workings of custom.

Anger is, however, a much more general phenomenon. It arises from conflict and tension, independently of any strategic context. (Any exclusively strategic account of anger is, thus, misleading.) Anger may be provoked, for instance, if someone is induced to engage in an impossible task that appeared manageable initially, or if two contradictory statements are made at the same time.[3] Anger can appear also in an impersonal setting. A paper jam and subsequent computer breakdown that occurs during an urgent printout may be a cause for desperation to an author. Anger is a response to the same type of tension that induces cognitive dissonance.[4] It occurs if all ways of reducing the conflict are blocked, or are perceived to be blocked.

---

[1] See the discussion of the taxi ride in S. 2.6–2.7.
[2] See Asch (1952: 109–13) for a more detailed statement.
[3] The classical study is Dembo (1931). See also Koffka (1935: 407–10; 673) and Heider (1958: 142–4).   [4] See S. 9.4.

The action that flows from anger may be interpreted as the individual's response to that tension, and the state of anger may be conceived as an 'emotional coding' of that tension. In that sense, it may be understood, again, as arising from a desire for clarification. Sometimes, no action is possible to resolve the tension. This may produce quite distortive outcomes, such as looking for a culprit and seeking revenge. In experiments about anger that required subjects to perform nonsensical tasks, strong desires for revenge were induced, to be wreaked on the experimenter.[1]

Anger is particularly pronounced close to the goal, rather than far away.[2] A person may be angry if he missed winning the jackpot in a lottery by just one number, or if he lost a close contest, but he will take things more calmly if it was not such a near-miss. This relates again to clarity. It will be percieved to be more pressing to remove a single item disturbing an otherwise clear picture, than to attempt to clarify a messy situation containing many unclear elements. Reactions to infringements of customs are often quite similar in nature.

Anger illustrates in a very straightforward way the nature of emotions. They emerge as signals that indicate the fate of the individual's goals. Consider another example of an emotion; fear. If something is dangerous, the individual will be frightened. His fear is the emotional representation of the impulse to cope with danger. Escaping danger by a hair's breadth is sometimes traumatic. Proximity to the danger thus sharpens its intensity, as in the case of anger. Other emotions relate, again, in a very definite way to the perception of the surroundings. A graceful act may cause delight, an unexpected event will prompt surprise, an unaccountable phenomenon will puzzle, and so forth. In all these cases, the emotions relate systematically to cognitions; they are just aspects of cognitions. It may thus be said that cognitions generate emo-

[1] Koffka (1935: 673). I myself toyed with the idea of omitting the page number '100' in this book, and telling the reader that I deliberately did that in order to make him understand the emotional responses to infringements of order and entitlements. I dropped the idea, however, for fear that the experiment would work better than expected.   [2] F. Heider (1958: 141–4).

tions that belong to them. The fit between emotion and cognition may be interpreted as a clarity feature.

The categorical distinction between emotions and cognitions, as often drawn, seems inappropriate. If a solution to a mathematical problem is discovered, this is perceived as an emotion of insight; the problem is felt to be understood. In this sense, cognitions *are* emotions. It is usually concluded from such observations that cognitions are *just* emotions. The suggestion implicit in such a parlance is that cognitions are as arbitrary as emotions. A good deal of behaviourism is nourished by taking this position as a starting point. An equally valid conclusion would be to take emotions as *forms of cognition*. They represent the way individuals perceive themselves in relation to their surroundings. This phrasing implies that emotions are as lawful as cognitions, and valuations may be considered as having the same objective status as cognitions. The recent findings in cognitive psychology lend some support to this view. In any case, the clarity view proposed here takes this as its starting point.[1] This does not exclude the possibility that some emotions may indeed be volatile, vague, and unfounded, but this holds true for thoughts as well as emotions.

10.5 *Action*

Emotions are related to action. Action may quite generally be understood as a response of the individual to reduce a state of tension.[2] An individual will try to soothe his hunger by eating

---

[1] The view is actually quite old. Truth, beauty, and the good have been portrayed together quite often. Wertheimer (1934;1935) has developed this position with regard to psychology, and so have Gestalt psychologists like Asch (1952: 109–13,357–8) and Köhler (1938), but modern psychology has accepted the superficial dichotomy of cognitive and emotional processes. This leads to some strange and entirely artificial problems. Behaviourists have objected to cognitivists that it does not suffice to explain rules: we must also explain why people observe rules. In order to do that, they propose to revert to ideas about conditioning (Reese 1989: 35; see also H. J. Eysenck 1976). They are, of course, right, given their premises. But the argument depends entirely on drawing that unwarranted distinction between different kinds of psychological events, termed 'emotions' and 'cognitions'. Nature seems, however, not to care about these man-made distinctions and treats the entire set of psychological events as a whole.

[2] Other descriptions speak of 'drive reduction' or 'stress reduction': see e.g. Hilgard *et al.* (1971: 206–7); Koffka (1935: 342).

something, he will try reduce his longing for a certain commodity by buying it, he will try to get rid of his uneasiness by moving around. It is to be noted also that the attempt to reduce tension will not always succeed. Some actions may be inadequate, some desires addictive.

Action, however, cannot be described merely with reference to prevailing tensions alone. Quite often, action is undertaken in order to *avoid* tensions rather than reduce them. For instance, an individual will avoid touching a hot stove in order to avoid burning himself; he will keep a promise because he wants to avoid the tension involved in breaking his word; or he may avoid the side of the street where a beggar implores the passers-by. Actions may thus be understood as aiming at tension reduction in a wider sense, which includes avoidance of anticipated tensions.

This may be rephrased in terms of clarity. Tension results from imbalance and unclarity. This manifests itself in emotions. Clarification processes work to reduce tension. The success is accompanied by other emotions that signal that success. From this perspective, actions are just specific instances of clarification processes, and the individual may be viewed as governed by a tendency towards overall clarity. This tendency manifests itself in balancing cognitions, emotions, motivations, and actions.[1]

This balancing may cut both ways. A person witnesses the theft of a radio at the beach.[2] This will induce tension. The person may try to resolve the tension by taking action, but action is costly; it involves risking conflict with the thief. There is, thus, also a reason to avoid taking action. The person will be less inclined to risk such a conflict if he does not feel responsible. Yet, with inaction, the tension will persist. It can be reduced by supplying reasons for inaction, such as exaggerating the danger of intervention, or minimizing responsibility by arguing that everyone is equally respon-

---

[1] Walker (1980: 1) has stated this principle as follows: 'Psychological events nearest optimum complexity are preferred.' The economist may note that the principle is also a maximization principle, like the one used in economics. It differs in that psychological structure is taken into account and preferences are taken as being shaped rather than given.

[2] See the discussion of this incident in the context of commitment in S. 8.2.

sible and that the theft had to be expected anyhow, sooner or later, with such careless action on behalf of the owner of the radio. In the end, the victim will be blamed. The tension may, however, induce another action: the witness may leave his place on the beach, thereby avoiding the need for explanations and further tension.

The episode illustrates that clarification processes work both by engendering action and emotion, and by changing cognitions. Actions and evaluative changes are often substitutes in stress reduction, and they interact quite strongly. This is another instance of the strong interdependence of cognitions, emotions, and actions and the tendency of the human mind to integrate them.

10.6 *The Emergence of Entitlements and Obligations*

The way in which entitlements and obligations are generated may be illustrated by means of an example. There is a parking spot in front of a house, which a tenant uses to park his car. Two cases may be compared. In the first case the car is parked at this spot regularly; in the second case the spot is used only occasionally. In the first instance, the tenant will feel a stronger entitlement to park his car in that particular place. Others will tend to agree and will be inclined to respect the claim more easily than if he used the space only occasionally. The tenant will also be prepared to defend his entitlement to some extent. He may for instance park in such a way that the person who has infringed his right experiences some difficulty in pulling out, and he will feel entitled to use such impolite measures. The tenant may also leave the car at the spot even if this is inconvenient for him. He will do this in order to reconfirm his 'right'.

This episode illustrates the way in which entitlements emerge. They are induced by a confluence of various influences. The ownership effect creates a preference for parking at a particular spot. The first occupier will feel the strongest entitlement. Conservatism

establishes an adherence to the *status quo*, and conformity reconfirms the behaviour: everybody else behaves in a similar manner.
The emotional responses to be expected from infringing the established pattern thus prevent others from interfering. The entire
arrangement is further stabilized by self-attribution processes
and habit formation. The argument rests on the perception of a
regularity and on the behavioural and emotional impact of this
perception.

In a way, the emergence of entitlements is very similar to the
endowment effect.[1] A perceived regularity works like an endowment. Just as the endowment effect will increase the preference for
keeping an object, a regularity generates the perception of an
entitlement, and the desire to defend this right and to execute it.
The perception of having obtained an entitlement is induced by
observing a pattern, and by relying on that pattern.

Compliance with perceived entitlements may be understood as
emerging from clarification processes. This involves reversing the
arguments that have been made regarding the motivational impact
of entitlements for those who hold them. Just as the endowment
effect generates attachment, it implies that attachment will be less
for things that are not owned. Similarly, a preference for the *status
quo* works both ways, and the acceptance of entitlements held by
others entails respecting these entitlements. Further, the anticipa-
tion of moralistic aggression by those who perceive themselves
entitled to certain actions will strengthen the tendency to yield
to those demands.

This simple episode illustrates some crucial features of the
formation of property rights, and how they relate to clarification
processes. The clarity view of property, as it flows from the
clarity view of custom, will be further developed in the next
chapter. Before entering this discussion, however, some general
remarks on overall clarification processes would seem to be in
order.

---

[1] See S. 8.4.

10.7 *Custom and Social Approval*

Group processes will reinforce the regularities of custom formation in many ways. This important mechanism links the individual's self-interest to the interest of others. Adam Smith has
described in a classical way how virtuous behaviour springs
from pride:

It is not the love of our neighbour, it is not the love of mankind, which
upon many occasions prompts us to the practice of those divine virtues. It
is a stronger love, a more powerful affection, which generally takes place
upon such occasions; the love of what is honourable and noble, of the
grandeur, and dignity and superiority of our own characters. . . Our
continual observations upon the conduct of others, insensibly lead us
to form to ourselves certain general rules concerning what is fit and
proper either to be done or to be avoided. Some of their actions shock
all our natural sentiments. We hear everybody about us express the like
detestation against them. This still further confirms, and even exaspe-
rates our natural sense of their deformity. It satisfies us that we view them
in the proper light, when we see other people view them in the same light.
We resolve never to be guilty of the like, nor ever, upon any account, to
render ourselves in this manner the objects of universal disapprobation.
We thus naturally lay down to ourselves a general rule, that all such
actions are to be avoided, as tending to render us odious, contemptible,
or punishable, the objects of all those sentiments for which we have the
greatest dread and aversion. Other actions, on the contrary, call forth our
approbation, and we hear everybody around us express the same favourable opinion concerning them. Everybody is eager to honour and reward
them. The excite all of those sentiments for which we have by nature the
strongest desire; the love, the gratitude, the admiration of mankind. We
become ambitious of performing the like; and thus naturally lay down to
ourselves a rule of another kind, that every opportunity of acting in this
manner is carefully sought after.[1]

By the shared desire for mutual approval, all impulses that work
on the individual level are strengthened by reciprocal reinforcement. Such processes would work on all social phenomena, not
only on those that Smith envisaged in the above passage. They
apply also to vices and hatred. They magnify the tendencies that

[1] Smith (1759: 137, 159).

work on the individual level.[1] Because the others approve each individual's sticking with the custom and not breaking the rules, he will be even more inclined to conform.

Yet the quest for social approval alone will not shape any kind of specific behaviour. Adam Smith saw this clearly. He introduced the idea of 'sympathy' with others as the ultimate driving force. That 'feeble spark of benevolence which Nature has lighted up in the human heart' is magnified by the mechanism of social approval to align self-interest with collective imperatives.[2] Whatever tendencies may work in the human heart, or in the human mind, they will be magnified by the mechanism of social approval in the same way as the weak impulses of sympathy are magnified by pride. Clarification processes are strengthened collectively in the same way.

10.8 *Interlocking Customs*

If it is customary to raise one's hat in greeting, this requires the associated custom of wearing a hat (rather than a turban, for instance). The one custom presupposes the other. In this way, many customs interlock and form a complex of some solidity. The solidity springs from the interaction of each custom, while each single element may be rather flexible. Some decades ago, it was indeed customary to raise one's hat. If one was not wearing a hat, one would greet by making a certain gesture, raising the hand to the brow, but avoiding any kind of military salute. (Militarism was not welcome in postwar Germany.) In this way, the overall pattern of greeting was maintained by using that substitute gesture.

The rule was certainly supported by the custom of wearing a hat. However, with the spread of the motor car, or perhaps for other reasons, hats became outdated and were worn less

---

[1] In Hume's (1740a: 424) words: 'Custom increases all *active* habits but diminishes *passive*.'

[2] Smith (1759: 137). See also Schlicht (1984b) for a critique of this particular argument.

frequently. The somewhat ridiculous substitute gesture for greeting vanished as well, giving rise to less clumsy gestures, like waving the hand.

On the other hand, the custom of greeting by hat-lifting certainly helped to stabilize the wearing of hats in a minor but discernible way. It made it possible to greet someone in a formally correct manner, and to avoid the air of embarrassment accompanying the substitute gesture. The custom was also stabilized in many other ways. Each restaurant had a proper hat-stand, whereas nowadays one expects one's hat to be returned in a rather poor shape after a concert performance. Interlocking thus occurs in many diffuse ways.

Another example would be the rule of driving on the left-hand side of the road. In countries with left-hand traffic, pedestrians on the pavements follow this rule as well. The staircases in Australia mostly turn left; in Germany they mostly turn right.[1] The supermarkets are mostly organized clockwise in Australia, but counterclockwise in Germany, and so forth. The generalization of one rule to another, and the mutual adjustment of various rules and regulations, instances the tendency towards overall clarification.

10.9 *Style*

The entire set of customs may be conceived as forming an interlocking system, just like the different branches of physics interlock. Such a system will appear fairly elastic in various dimensions and can be adapted to new discoveries and exigencies, but the basic structure, the underlying schema, is invariant. If it does not fit, exceptions will have to be introduced. This will weaken the schema but will not change it. The schema is rigid, but its operation is not. Custom guides individual events on an elastic band, so to speak. It creates a tendency towards coherence and clarity and in this way

---

[1] Exceptions reconfirm this. The central staircase of the Baillieu Library (University of Melbourne) turns right. Interestingly, there you also find some conspicuous signs telling you 'please keep to the right'.

engenders that particular unity of style and appearance within cultures that bewitched Lévi-Strauss (but led him to conclusions different from ours):

> The customs of a community, taken as a whole, always have a particular style and are reducible to systems. I am of the opinion that the number of such systems is not unlimited and that—in their games, dreams, or wild imaginations—human societies, like individuals, never create absolutely, but merely choose certain combinations from an ideal repertoire that it should be possible to define. By making an inventory of recorded customs, of all those imagined in myths or suggested in children's games or in adult games, or in the dreams of healthy or sick individuals or in psycho-pathological behaviour, one could arrive at a sort of table, like that of the chemical elements, in which all actual or hypothetical customs would be grouped in families, so that one could see at a glance which customs a particular society had in fact adopted.[1]

The position taken in this book tries to account theoretically for this remarkable unity of style in universalist rather than culturalist terms. Lévi-Strauss's classificatory frenzy seems, however, as hopeless as it is enchanting. There seems no reason for supposing that the number of possible cultures or complexes of custom is limited, even if they are discrete. It would also be implausible to assume that the number of possible machines is finite in any practical sense, even if the laws of Nature could be reduced to two or three fundamental principles, and even if each machine had to form a functional unit of some sort. Even if the set of possible systems were strictly finite, moreover, there would be no reason to suppose that they involve fewer possibilities than the game of Eleusis.[2] This is prohibitive. It does not, therefore, seem necessary to start from an exhaustive inventory, just as it is not necessary in mechanics to start from an exhaustive inventory of machinery in order to deduce the laws of mechanics. It seems more promising to study the basic laws that make it possible to build a machine or understand a custom, and to proceed by figuring out other ways in which these laws may combine, forming entirely new machines or entirely new customs.

---

[1] Lévi-Strauss (1955: 178).   [2] See S. 7.2.

Proceeding further on a purely analytical level, however, would involve the danger of losing contact with actual phenomena. Therefore, it seems appropriate to check the fruitfulness of the clarity approach by applying it to some areas of social and economic interaction where custom plays an important part. The subsequent chapters will, therefore, discuss how the forces of custom contribute in shaping property, the law, the firm, and market organization.

Part II

CUSTOM IN ACTION

Chapter 11

PROPERTY

11.1 A Tension

The system of property rights is, in any society, fundamental for economic and social interaction. Property rights are rooted in custom. Modern societies have, moreover, added separate legal systems that shape and reshape property rights in a centralist manner, somewhat independent of custom.

The focus in this chapter is on those aspects of property that emerge from custom, and on how this relates to the market process. It will be seen that the modern theory of property rights will gain in definiteness if the influence of indispensable psychological elements is recognized.

The same clarification processes that mould custom shape property rights, and in a similar manner. They render the system of rights responsive to outside influences, such as economic incentives and the forces of competition. At the same time, they constrain the set of feasible arrangements. Accordingly, a consideration of the psychological aspects of property formation will sharpen the insights that can be obtained from the approaches pursued in the new institutional economics. It will help us better to understand the limits of competitive forces in shaping and redefining property rights.

The largely instrumental view of property entertained in

economics has been repeatedly challenged by authors who stress self-developmental aspects, morality, the cultural significance, and the political aspect of property.[1] The tension between moral and instrumental views of property has indeed always been there. It crops up in public opinion as well as in learned writings. It ignites the hottest debates. Heat, however, is not light. Thus, we see that the parties are mainly engaged in simply restating their own positions.[2]

The debate may be approached in a constructive way by exploring how systems of property rights emerge, and why they entail such conflicting convictions. It will be argued that the conflicting convictions are brought about by the same human tendencies that contribute to the formation and stabilization of property rights in the first place.

11.2   *Unravelling Hume's Theory of Property*

The clarity view of property may be understood as a straightforward elaboration of David Hume's chapter on property in the *Treatise of Human Nature*.[3] This makes it convenient to follow Hume closely and to inject, at some critical junctures of the argument, doses of 'clarity' and elements of minor disagreement.

There are several reasons for couching the argument in Hume's own words. The first is that Hume expresses his central ideas in a way that can hardly be surpassed in eloquence. His description of pertinent clarification processes is presented in a mode entirely

---

[1] Ryan (1984), Waltzer (1983).

[2] Ryan (1984), in a book devoted exclusively to property, does not touch on the economics of property rights and declares, under the entry of 'Property' in the authoritative *New Palgrave*: 'The least abashed intellectual heirs of the 18th and 19th-century utilitarianism are the defenders of the so-called "economic theory of property rights"' (Ryan 1987: 1031). In the subsequent—and otherwise most penetrating—entry 'Property rights', Alchian (1987: 1032) mentions that issues about social acceptability are due to a misunderstanding of the market process.

[3] Hume (1740*a*). Hume's theory of property builds on earlier writings, particularly those by Grotius. With regard to the origin of Hume's ideas, see N. K. Smith (1941), Mossner (1980), and Flew (1986). The following draws in part on Kubon-Gilke and Schlicht (1993).

different from mine; hence his perspective will add another dimension to the discussion.

The second reason for citing Hume extensively is that the parallelism of psychological and instrumental considerations, which is a major innovation of Hume and is of central importance for the social sciences, is not immediately suggested by reading the Treatise. This is due to the fact that the instrumental argument is developed largely in the main text, whereas the psychological argument is expanded in a sequence of accompanying footnotes; moreover, the subdivision of the footnote argument into a number of separate notes destroys the perception of unity and continuity in the footnote text. The strictly parallel presentation of Hume's two lines of reasoning offered in this chapter thus provides a new interpretation of Hume's theory of property.[1]

Hume's theory of property has been largely neglected, perhaps because of having been presented largely in footnotes.[2] The theory, if unravelled, reveals the staggering fact that one of the great classical economists, the father of British associationism and grandfather of utilitarianism, could equally well pass as the father of Gestalt ideas, or the grandfather of modern cognitivism. However, this aspect, implicit in what follows, will not be explicitly elaborated in this book.

11.3　Hume's Counterpoint

Hume offers two separate lines of argument in order to establish the principles that govern ownership. The first is instrumental; it

---

[1] In this, the present chapter is akin to Reisman's (1987) reconstruction of Alfred Marshall's unwritten sequels to the Principles.

[2] Rotwein (1987), in his authoritative article about Hume as an economist, does not even mention Hume's theory of property and adds: 'In the literature Hume's economic writings have typically been treated as an entirely self-contained aspect of his work. This is not surprising, since in his economic essays he does not allude to his other writings, and subsequent disciplinary specialization has not encouraged consideration of the interrelationships between the two' (Rotwein 1987: 692). Obviously, the Treatise, which contains Hume's theory of property, is not counted as belonging to the economic writings.

seeks to understand property by looking at its contribution to individual advantage and social welfare, or 'publick utility'. The other is psychological; it takes the phenomenon of property as arising from 'imagination'. Because of this duality, Hume's chapter on property is structured like the counterpoint in a piece of music. The theme is introduced in the instrumental mode in the main text. Its development is then submerged in a psychological argument, which is expanded and intensely elaborated in a sequence of footnotes.

Hume is quite explicit about pursuing two parallel lines of reasoning at once. He suspects that the psychological laws are of prime importance, but offers a free choice to the reader:

No questions about philosophy are more difficult, than when a number of causes present themselves for the same phænomenon, to determine which is the principal and predominant . . . Thus, in the present case, there are, no doubt, motives of public interest for most of the rules, which determine property; but still I suspect, that these rules are principally fix'd by the imagination, or the more frivolous properties of our thought and conception. I shall continue to explain these causes, leaving it to the reader's choice, whether he will prefer those derived from publick utility, or those deriv'd from the imagination.[1]

Hume thus offers two parallel lines of argumentation, one instrumental, the other psychological. In his actual presentation, he mixes these freely. This is appropriate. Observation suggests, and without any preconceptions, that both aspects are of relevance. Indeed, the 'clarity' view taken here suggests that both 'imagination' and instrumental considerations interact closely. As long as they work in the same direction, there would be no need to opt for one or the other alternative, save for a preference for simplification and monocausal explanation.[2] By choosing to acknowledge both lines of thought *at once*, the possibility is offered of understanding strains and contradictions such as the tension between instrumental and moral aspects of property men-

---

[1] Hume (1740a: 504n).
[2] That such a preference may lead one astray, and that non-instrumental aspects of behaviour are of great economic significance, has been stressed by Hirschman (1985).

tioned above. Furthermore, the conjoint emergence of instrumental and moral considerations can be understood from such a perspective. It shows how they act at the same time and often reinforce each other, while at other times working in opposite directions. Regarding the overall project, the counterpoint argument integrates phenomena of property into an overall view of custom.

11.4 *Stability*

The starting point for Hume is an instrumental view of property. The first thing he considers is the *stability of possessions*:[1]

I first consider men in their savage and solitary condition; and suppose, that being sensible of the misery of that state, and foreseeing the advantages that would result from society, they seek each other's company, and make an offer of mutual protection and assistance. I also suppose, that they are endow'd with such sagacity as immediately to perceive, that the chief impediment to this project of society and partnership lies in the avidity and selfishness of their natural temper; to remedy which, they enter into a convention for the stability of possession, and for mutual restraint and forbearance.[2]

It is, in short, in everyone's interest to accept the principle of the stability of possessions. This explains the presence of a 'convention about stability'. The hypothetical nature of this approach is defended as follows:

I am sensible that this method of proceeding is not altogether natural; but besides that I here only suppose those reflexions to be form'd at once, which in fact arise insensibly and by degrees; besides this, I say, 'tis very possible, that several persons, being by different accidents separated from the societies, to which they formerly belong'd, may be oblig'd to form a new society among themselves; in which case they are entirely in the situation above-mention'd.[3]

---

[1] The principles discussed in this and the subsequent sections go in part back to Grotius (1625), but Hume's treatment is much more penetrating.
[2] Hume (1740a: 502–3).   [3] Hume (1740a: 503).

Thus, no sovereign is needed to enforce the stability of posses-sions.[1] Stability of possessions is required in order to avoid conflict. Property emerges gradually and naturally because it turns out to be advantageous.

11.5 *Symmetry*

Yet, the principle of stability of possession is not enough. It is too general. Property rights must be specified more closely:

Tho' the establishment of the rule, concerning the stability of possession, be not only useful, but even absolutely necessary to human society, it can never serve any purpose, while it remains in such general terms. Some method must be shewn, by which we may distinguish what particular goods are to be assign'd to each particular person, while the rest of mankind are excluded from their possession and enjoyment. Our next business, then, must be to discover the reasons which modify this general rule, and fit it to the common use and practice of the world.[2]

An obvious way would be to design a rule that maximizes utility at any instant, but this is not feasible:

'Tis obvious, that those reasons are not deriv'd from any utility or advantage, which either the particular person or the public may reap from his enjoyment of any particular goods, beyond what would result from the possession of them by any other person. 'Twere better, no doubt, that every one were possess'd of what is most suitable to him, and proper for his use: But besides, that this relation of fitness may be common to several at once, 'tis liable to so many controversies, and men are so partial and passionate in judging one of these controver-sies, that such a loose and uncertain rule wou'd be absolutely incom-patible with peace of human society. The convention concerning the stability of possession is enter'd into, in order to cut off all occasions of discord and contention; and this end wou'd never be attain'd, were we allow'd to apply this rule differently in every particular case, according to every particular utility, which might be discover'd in such an application.[3]

---

[1] This contrasts with Hobbes (1651).   [2] Hume (1740*a*: 501–2).
[3] Hume (1740*a*: 502). All emphases—here and elsewhere—in the original.

A utilitarianism that maximizes instant by instant entails conflict because it gives no clear guiding principle.[1] In order to minimize conflict, a clear rule must be found. Thus, the instrumental view is modified by introducing psychological clarity considerations.

Hume does not dwell on this problem. Instead, he moves directly to the conclusion that the rules must be general because, as a matter of fact, justice is general:

Justice, in her decisions, never regards the fitness or unfitness of objects to particular persons, but conducts herself by more extensive views. Whether a man be generous, or a miser, he is equally well receiv'd by her, and obtains with the same facility a decision in his favour, even for what is entirely useless to him. It follows, therefore, that the general rule, *that possessions must be stable*, is not apply'd by particular judgements, but by other general rules, which must extend to the whole society, and must be inflexible either by spite or favour.[2]

Hume enlarges on the important issue of general and inflexible rules in the *Enquiry Concerning Human Understanding* in a particularly outspoken way:

All the laws of nature, which regulate property, as well as all civil laws, are general, and regard alone some essential circumstances to the case, without taking into consideration the characters, situations, and connexions of the person concerned, or any particular consequences which may result from the determination of these laws in any particular case which offers. They deprive, without scruple, a beneficent man of all his possessions, if acquired by mistake, without a good title; in order to bestow them on a selfish miser, who has already heaped up immense stores of superfluous riches. Public utility requires that property should be regulated by general inflexible rules; and though such rules are adopted as best serve the same end of public utility, it is impossible to prevent all particular hardships, or make beneficial consequences result from every individual case. It is sufficient, if the whole plan or scheme be necessary to the support of civil society, and if the balance of good, in the main, do thereby preponderate much above that of evil. Even the general laws of the universe, though planned by infinite wisdom, cannot exclude all evil or inconvenience in every particular operation.[3]

---

[1] See also Hume (1740*a*: 532), where he speaks about the 'confusion' that would otherwise arise.

[2] Hume (1740*a*: 502).   [3] Hume (1777*a*: 305–6).

Thus, the viewpoint taken by Hume is that pointwise optimization is not feasible because there are no clear principles that could be used to achieve this end. In order to avoid conflict, the primary concern must be to establish clear principles. Among competing clear principles, those should be selected that give the highest 'publick utility'.

This perspective is shared by modern 'rule-utilitarianism'.[1] While 'act-utilitarianism' would require the maximization of utility at all times, rule-utilitarianism requires acting according to the appropriate rule. The selection of the rule reflects a desire to produce, on average, the highest utility possible from among all the conceivable rules.

The distinction between rule-utilitarianism and act-utilitarianism can, however, be maintained only if the 'best' rule requires that the agent on certain occasions acts in a non-maximizing manner. This would be incomprehensible from a strict utilitarian point of view, since an amended rule could be devised that would be identical to the old one with the single exception of prescribing maximizing behaviour in cases where the old rule did not.[2]

As a consequence, rule-governed behaviour implies either deliberate inefficiencies (which would destroy all utility-related arguments for the rule) or a rule preference.[3] Such a preference would apply not to 'random rules', and not to the amended rule with some inefficiencies ironed out, but to true psychological rules that are clear and intelligible.[4]

The rule 'Never tell a lie' is, in this sense, preferable to the rule

---

[1] See Mackie (1977: 136–8) and Hardin (1988: 14–18) for modern philosophical expositions. The book by Buchanan and Brennan (1985), entitled *The Reason of Rules*, develops the position taken in 'constitutional economics'. It is characteristic that it does not contain any hint about features that might distinguish a rule from a non-rule. It seems, thus, that the argument must presuppose a psychology of rule formation. See also Buchanan (1994) for a recent restatement, and Schlicht (1994) for criticism. Many accounts of rules in the social sciences share the feature of using the term as a primitive concept while providing no hint or characterization regarding the psychological or other nature of rules, e.g. Ellickson (1991: 128–36), North (1990: 48).

[2] See also Basu (1994: 8), Mackie (1977: 136–8), Schlicht (1994), and Smart (1973: 9–12). [3] See Ch. 8.

[4] See the discussion of 'true rules' versus 'random rules' in S. 7.3.

'Never tell a lie if it can be detected; otherwise select the best alternative.' Yet the second rule is certainly better with regard to individual outcomes (i.e. if the individually best alternative is chosen) or collective outcomes (i.e. if the collectively best alternative is chosen). Settling for the clear rule can, it seems, be understood only with reference to some underlying rule preference—a preference for the rule *itself*. The rule 'Never tell a lie if it can be detected; otherwise select the best alternative' should always be preferable from a purely instrumental point of view. However, the rule is not clear and does not appear convincing. This must then be the reason why it is 'ethically' unappealing.

Following Hume, then, a rule preference must be stipulated. Rule-governed behaviour must be preferred to other types of behaviour purely because it is rule-governed. As Hume writes, 'For there is a principle in human nature, which we have frequently taken notice of, that men are mightily addicted to general rules, and that we often carry our maxims beyond those reasons, which first induc'd us to establish them.'[1]

The impartiality of the rules must be presupposed very much in the same vein as symmetry can be understood as an aspect of clarity. It is a purely formal feature which cannot be derived in any useful instrumentalist way.[2] Utilitarian defences presuppose symmetry in the problem–setting in order to derive symmetry in the result.[3] Philosophical approaches to politics start with assumptions about 'equal citizenship' or similar symmetry assumptions, rather than derive them from more fundamental sources.

It should also be noted that this formal symmetry does not say very much about equal treatment. Slaves will not be citizens, and equality before the law is very different from equality of possessions. Symmetry applies to elements of a category. It is a very formal concept, related to clarity aspects of categorization.[4] The entire argument comes down to saying that the stability of possessions requires the implementation of clear rules. As it happens,

---

[1] Hume (1740a: 551).   [2] See S. 6.7–6.12.
[3] e.g. Sen (1973).   [4] See S. 6.4–6.9 and 7.4.

this is also the way in which custom works. From a planning perspective, it may be of interest to find that system of rules among the feasible rules that yields the highest 'publick benefit'. From a positive perspective, it may be inquired which rule-system among the feasible systems ultimately emerges.

11.6 *Status Quo Preference*

The rules that govern property must be specified more closely. Hume argues that the initial rule will maintain the *status quo*. He argues as follows:

For when men . . . have observ'd, that the principal disturbance in society arises from those goods, which we call external, and from their looseness and easy transition from one person to another; they must seek a remedy, by putting these goods, as far as possible, on the same footing with the fixe'd and constant advantages of mind and body.[1]

Thus, the external things—movable and immovable objects—are assimilated to personal features. In this way, a concept of 'property' is formed. The term still retains this double meaning.

Once this is established, the rules that govern property must be specified further:

'Tis evident, then, that their first difficulty, in this situation, after the general convention for the establishment of society, and for the constancy of possession, is, how to separate their possessions, and assign to each his particular portion, which he must for the future inalterably enjoy. This difficulty will not detain them long; but it must immediately occur to them, as the most natural expedient, that every one continue to enjoy what he is at present master of, and that property or constant possession be conjoin'd to the immediate possession.[2]

According to Hume, it is 'natural' that the *status quo* serves as a reference point. The reason given by Hume relates directly to the 'endowment effect' discussed earlier:[3]

---

[1] Hume (1740*a*: 489).   [2] Hume (1740*a*: 503).   [3] See S. 8.4.

Such is the effect of custom, that it not only reconciles us to any thing we have long enjoy'd, but even gives us an affection for it, and makes us prefer it to other objects, which may be more valuable, but are less known to us. What has long lain under our eye, and has often been employ'd to our advantage, that we are always the most unwilling to part with; but can easily live without possessions, which we never have enjoy'd, and are not accustom'd to. 'Tis evident, therefore, that men wou'd easily acquiesce in this expedient, that every one continue to enjoy what he is at present possess'd of; and this is the reason, why they wou'd so naturally agree on preferring it.[1]

This argument confounds instrumentalist and psychological arguments. It is *because of the psychological inclination to maintain the status quo* that it is instrumentally expedient to maintain it. Hume also offers a further argument, which is couched entirely in terms of continuity and clarity:

'Tis a quality, which I have already observ'd in human nature, that when two objects appear in close relation to each other, the mind is apt to ascribe to them an additional relation, in order to compleat the union; and this inclination is so strong, as often to make us run into errors. And as property forms a relation betwixt a person and an object, 'tis natural to found it on some preceding relation; and as property is nothing but a constant possession, secur'd by the laws of society, 'tis natural to add it to the present possession, which is a relation that resembles it. For this also has its influence. If it be natural to conjoin all sorts of relations, 'tis more so, to conjoin such relations as are resembling, and are related together.[2]

There is, thus, at this level no contradiction between the two lines of argumentation; rather, the instrumental view builds on the psychological, and both work together.

11.7 *Occupation*

Once the initial possessions have been determined, there is a need to cope with change:

But we may observe, that tho' the rule of the assignment of property to

---

[1] Hume (1740*a*: 503–4); paragraph break added.   [2] Hume (1740*a*: 504–5 n.).

the present possessor be natural, and by that means useful, yet its utility extends not beyond the first formation of society; nor wou'd any thing be more pernicious, than the constant observance of it; by which restitution wou'd be excluded and every injustice wou'd be authoriz'd and rewarded. We must, therefore, seek for some other circumstance, that may give rise to property after society is once establish'd . . .

The possession of all eternal goods is changeable and uncertain; which is one of the most considerable impediments to the establishment of society, and is the reason why, by universal agreement, express or tacite, men restrain themselves by what we now call the rules of justice and equity. The misery of the condition, which precedes this restraint, is the cause why they submit to that remedy as quickly as possible; and this affords us any reason, why we annex the idea of property to the first possession, or to occupation. Men are unwilling to leave property in suspence, even for the shortest time, or open the door to violence and disorder. To which we may add, that the first possession always engages the attention most; and did they neglect it, there wou'd be no colour of reason for assigning property to any succeeding possession.[1]

Again, an instrumentalist and a psychological argument are employed conjointly. It would obviously be inefficient to leave resources idle. The first person to find something becomes its owner. This reduces possible inefficiencies from idleness. The psychological argument relates directly to the psychological salience of first possession. It is to be noted that the efficiency argument for the occupation rule is not entirely convincing. It may produce 'search externalities' if two individuals each try to be the first to reach an object.[2] Random allocation would be better in this case. Furthermore, the first occupant may actually not use an object immediately, but may still establish his claim, while another may have an immediate use. To give the right to the second person in these cases would be preferable from the point of view of reducing idleness of the resource.

Without a clarity requirement, quite different rules would be expected to emerge for different cases. The clarity requirement restricts such tendencies; yet they are not entirely eliminated from practical life. Custom would induce you to offer your seat to an

---

[1] Hume (1740a: 505).   [2] Sugden (1989: 85–6).

old person. Occupation sometimes works, however, in a very subtle way:

And I farther observe, that a sensible relation, without any present power, is sometimes sufficient to give a title to any object. The sight of a thing is seldom a considerable relation, and is only regarded as such, when the object is hidden, or very obscure: in which case we find, that the view alone conveys a property, according to the maxim, *that even a hole continent belongs to the nation, which first discover'd it.* 'Tis however remarkable, that both in the case of discovery and that of possession, the first discoverer and possessor must join to the relation an intention of rendering himself proprietor, otherwise the relation will not have its effect; and that because the connexion in our fancy betwixt the property and the relation is not so great, but that it requires to be help'd by such an intention.[1]

This may be restated by saying that it is the clearest case (relatively speaking) that dominates, even in an unclear setting. The clearest connection between a person and an object is sharpened, and other connections are discounted. However, it seems that the intention of the discoverer or possessor can assist understanding only if it is expressed in a way that can be perceived—in a clear way. Otherwise the intention will not help to establish property.[2]

The problem of occupancy is in the end entirely related to 'our fancy', up to a point where issues become really inextricable:

Two *Graecian* colonies, leaving their native country, in search for new seats, were inform'd that a city near them was deserted by its inhabitants. To know the truth of this report, they dispatch'd at once two messengers, one from each colony; who finding on their approach, that their information was true, began to race together with an intention to take possession of the city, each of them for his countrymen. One of these messengers, finding that he was not an equal match for the other, launch'd his spear at the gates of the city, and was so fortunate as to fix it there before the arrival of his companion. This produc'd a dispute betwixt the two colonies, which of them was the proprietor of the empty city; and this dispute still subsists among philosophers.[3]

---

[1] Hume (1740*a*: 507 n.).   [2] Hume(1777*a*: 199 n.).
[3] Hume (1740*a*: 507–8 n.).

Hume comments on this as follows:

I find the dispute impossible to be decided, and that because the whole question hangs upon the fancy, which is in this case not possess'd of any precise and determinate standard, upon which it can give sentence. To make this evident, let us consider, that if these two persons had been simply members of the colonies, and not messengers or deputies, their actions wou'd not have been of any consequence; since in that case their relation to the colonies wou'd have been feeble and imperfect. Add to this, that nothing determin'd them to run to the gates rather than the walls, or any other part of the city, but that the gates, being the most obvious and remarkable part, satisfy the fancy best in taking them for the whole. . . . Besides we may consider, that the touch or contact of one messenger is not properly possession, no more than the piercing the gates with a spear; but only forms a relation. . . . Which of these relations, then, conveys a right of property. . . I leave to the decision of such as are wiser than myself.[1]

Thus, the rule of occupation rests on the strength of the 'connection' between each colony and its messenger, and on the strength of the connection between each messenger and the city. The problem would have been easier to solve if one of these chains, rather than both, had been weakened. If one of the two persons had been a messenger of one colony, and the other simply a member of the other colony but if both had behaved physically just as described before, then Hume would probably have given the town to the messenger's colony.[2]

11.8 *Prescription*

Another important rule described by Hume is that long-standing possession creates property rights. This is the rule of 'prescription':

But it often happens, that the title of first possession becomes obscure thro' time; and that 'tis impossible to determine many controversies, which may arise concerning it. In that case long possession or *prescription* naturally takes place, and gives a person a sufficient property in any

---

[1] Hume (1740a: 508 n.).
[2] This is in direct analogy to the earlier observation that entitlements rest entirely in the cognitive domain; see S. 2.7.

thing he enjoys. . . . A man's title, that is clear and certain at present, will seem obscure and doubtful fifty years hence, even tho' the facts, on which it is founded, shou'd be prov'd with the greatest evidence and certainty. The same facts have not the same influence over so long an interval of time. . . . Possession over a long tract of time conveys a title to any object. But as 'tis certain, however every thing be produc'd in time, there is nothing real, that is produc'd by time: it follows, that property being produc'd by time, is not any thing real in the objects, but is the offspring of the sentiments, on which alone time is found to have any influence.[1]

Long and uninterrupted possession generates property rights that supersede other rights. Hume explains the phenomenon as follows:

Present possession is plainly a relation betwixt a person and an object; but is not sufficient to counter-balance the relation of first possession, unless the former be long and uninterrupted: In which case the relation is encreas'd on the side of the present possession, by the distance. This change in the relation produces a consequent change in the property.[2]

Thus, the prescription works very much like attribution processes in general.[3] The most prominent relation is selected and strengthened, and other relations are discounted. Long and uninterrupted possession creates a 'strong relation' that supersedes other relations.

11.9 *Accession*

The rule of accession describes how the property in one object implies property rights in other related objects. This is known as the right of *usu fructus*—the right to the fruits of the property. Hume sees this in a much more fundamental way. The right of accession for him is established by any kind of 'relation' between a person and an object. This is a matter of 'imagination' and builds on the 'strength of relations', i.e. on clarity:

---

[1] Hume (1740*a*: 508–9).   [2] Hume (1740*a*: 509 n.).   [3] See S. 9.2.

We acquire the property of objects by accession, when they are connected in an intimate manner with objects that are already our property, and at the same time are inferior to them. Thus the fruits of our garden, the offspring of our cattle, and the work of our slaves, are all of them esteem'd our property, even before possession. Where objects are connected together in the imagination, they are apt to be put on the same footing, and are commonly suppos'd to be endow'd with the same qualities. We readily pass from one to the other, and make no difference in our judgement concerning them; especially if the latter be inferior to the former.[1]

The way in which accession works—in which property in one object entails property in another related object—is, according to Hume, based entirely on psychological propensities of man concerning grouping and concept formation. 'This source of property can never be explain'd but from the imaginations; and one may affirm, that the causes here are unmix'd.'[2] Hume thus sees no instrumental reasons here. Moreover, some peculiarities of the formation of property point to the importance of psychological considerations:

the ascribing of property to accession is nothing but an effect of the relations of ideas, and of the smooth transition of the imagination. . . . The empire of Great Britain seems to draw along with it the dominion of the Orkneys, the Hebrides, the Isle of Man, and the Isle of Wight; but the authority over these lesser islands does not naturally imply any title to Great Britain. In short, a small object naturally follows a great one as its accession; but a great one is never suppos'd to belong to the proprietor of a small one related to it, merely on account of that property and relation. . . .

When we attribute to a person a property in two objects, we do not always pass from the person to one object, and from that to the other related to it. The objects being here to be consider'd as the property of the person, we are apt to join them together, and place them in the same light. Suppose therefore, a great object and a small object to be related together; if a person be strongly related to the great object, he will likewise be strongly related to both the objects, consider'd together, because he is related to the most considerable part. On the contrary, if he be only related to the small object, he will not be strongly related to

[1] Hume (1740a: 509). [2] Hume (1740a: 509 n.).

both, consider'd together, since his relation lies only with the most trivial part, which is not apt to strike us in any degree, when we consider the whole. And this is the reason, why small objects become accessions to great ones, and not great to small.[1]

Further examples of the importance of psychological regularities in the formation of property by accession provided by Hume relate to property in rivers and bays. Recent history provides many further examples reconfirming Hume's thesis. The rules relating to the ownership of islands, shelves, or uninhabited regions like Antarctica belong to this category. A conspicuous example of a conflict between the rules of occupation and accession is provided by the ongoing dispute between Great Britain and Argentina over the Falkland Islands. This group of islands belongs to Great Britain by occupation; accession, however, would entitle Argentina to the ownership, since the Falklands are closer to Argentina than to any other country, and also are much smaller than Argentina. Thus, there were conflicting rights emerging from Hume's principles—the rules of occupation and accession. This conflict erupted in a war.

11.10 *Succession*

Succession relates to the way in which property rights are allocated if the owner dies or disappears. Hume is very brief on that:

The right of succession is a very natural one, from the presum'd consent of the parent or near relation, and from the general interest of mankind, which requires, that men's possessions shou'd pass to those, who are dearest to them, in order to render them more industrious and frugal. Perhaps these causes are seconded by the influence of relation, or the association of ideas, by which we are naturally directed to consider the son after the parent's decease, and ascribe him a title to his father's possessions. Those goods must become property of some body: But of whom is the question. Here 'tis evident the persons children naturally present themselves to the mind; and being already connected to those

---

[1] Hume (1740*a*: 510–11 n.).

possessions by means of their decease'd parent, we are apt to connect them still farther by the relation of property.[1]

Thus, the rule of succession is explained with reference to 'connections which naturally present themselves to the mind' between parents and children.

11.11 *The Workings of 'Imaginations'*

All these arguments relate mostly to the workings of 'imagination'. At this point in the *Treatise*, the instrumentalist theme is largely dropped. Hume's counterpoint—the parallel construction of causation discussed earlier—may of course be embellished by adding various instrumental reasons that reconfirm the principles of occupation, prescription, accession, and succession, but this will not be pursued here.[2] Whatever instrumental reasons might be, they cannot involve case-by-case optimization: they must be rule-bound, and this constrains the possibilities. This insight suffices for the moment. At a later stage, the instrumental theme will be resumed on a broad scale in the context of the theory of property rights.

Hume's argument about the workings of 'imagination' is summarized by him in a slightly more general fashion as follows:

It has been observ'd above, that the mind has a natural propensity to join relations, especially resembling ones, and finds a kind of fitness and uniformity in such a union. From this propensity are deriv'd these laws of nature, that upon the first formation of society, property always follows the present possession; and afterwards, *that it arises from first or from long possession*. Now we may easily observe, that relation is not confin'd merely to one degree; but that from an object which is related to us, we acquire a relation to every other object which is related to it, and so on, till the thought loses the chain by too long a progress. However the relation may weaken by each remove, 'tis not immediately destroy'd; but frequently connects two objects by means of an intermediate one, which

---

[1] Hume (1740*a*: 510–13). This passage consists of 14 lines scattered over four pages. The rest of those pages is devoted to 182 lines of footnotes in small print explaining the workings of imagination.   [2] On 'Hume's counterpoint', see S. 11.3.

is related to both. And this principle is of such force as to give rise to the right of *accession*, and causes us to acquire the property not only of such objects as we are immediately possess'd of, but also of such as are closely connected to them.

Suppose a *German*, a *Frenchman*, and a *Spaniard* to come into a room, where there are place'd upon the table three bottles of wine, *Rhenish, Burgundy*, and *Port*; and suppose they shou'd fall a quarrelling about the division of them; a person, who was chosen for umpire, wou'd naturally, to show his impartiality, give every one the product of his own country: And this from a principle, which, in some measure, is the source of those laws of nature, that ascribe property to occupation, prescription and accession.

In all these cases, and particularly that of accession, there is first a *natural* unity betwixt the idea of the person and that of the object, and afterwards a new and *moral* union produc'd by that right or property, which we ascribe to the person.[1]

In the terminology adopted previously, this can be restated by saying that the concept of property emerges from rule perception and from a desire to establish regularity. Once these rules are established, they shape morality:

the sense of morality in the observance of these rules follows *naturally*, and of itself; tho' 'tis certain, that it is also augmented by a new *artifice*, and that the public instructions of politicians, and the private education of parents, contribute to the giving us a sense of honour and duty in the strict regulation of our actions with regard to the properties of others.[2]

Morality in turn affects behaviour:

If morality had naturally no influence on human passions and actions, 'twere in vain to take such pains to inculcate it.[3]

The 'sense of morality' that establishes this connection, is 'natural'.[4]

Thus, the argument is straightforward. It goes from pattern perception to action. The link is obtained by postulating a moral sense that engenders a preference to rule-following. Therefore,

---

[1] Hume (1740*a*: 509–10 n.).   [2] Hume (1740*a*: 533–4).
[3] Hume (1740*a*: 457).   [4] Hume (1740*a*: 619).

Hume's theory of property may be understood as a special instance of customary rule formation, as outlined in this book.

11.12 *Universality*

The theory of property as expounded by Hume is intended to be universalist. Even if his idea of justice is 'artificial' in a philosophical sense, he maintains that it is 'natural' in the sense of being 'inseparable from the species'.[1] The same universalistic stance is taken in the view of custom developed in the present book. Yet an obvious reaction to universalistic positions of this kind is that they inappropriately generalize the European experience of a few centuries to the whole of mankind, backwards to the Neanderthals, forwards to an indefinite future, and across all cultures around the globe. Such a position appears too strong to take. It may, therefore, be appropriate to consider the universalistic position with regard to the issue of property.

First, universalism is not entirely absurd. The statement that humans have two arms and two legs may go undisputed. Regarding clarity, rule perception, rule preference, etc., it has been argued earlier that the basic clarity principles are culture-invariant, but that clarification processes will generate framing effects of various kinds. This will allow for infinitely many cultures.[2] Hume's rules of property are actually encountered in many societies, but there are exceptions.[3] These exceptions are of particular interest since they tend to support, rather than undermine, Hume's fundamental position.

Regarding occupancy, Hume has argued that 'men are unwilling to leave property in suspence, even for the shortest time, or open the door to violence and disorder.'[4] There are however, tribes of hunters and gatherers who do not know private property in land. This seems at first sight to contradict Hume's principle of occu-

---

[1] Hume (1740*a*: 484).   [2] See S. 6.7–6.12.
[3] See Kubon-Gilke (1997), Hecker (1990), W. Schmidt (1939), Beaglehole (1931), Braeuer (1981), Reichard (1938: 377–404), Bunzel (1938: 333–404), Lips (1938: 494–5, 514–15), Nippold (1954).   [4] Hume (1740*a*: 505).

pancy. Yet the principle applies whenever there is a threat of violence and disorder. Such a threat would arise only from scarcity of land. Hume's principle must certainly be modified, but the thrust of the argument remains unaffected.

Regarding succession, Hume has postulated that property will pass from parents to their children because 'the persons children naturally present themselves to the mind; and being already connected to those possessions by means of their deceas'd parent, we are apt to connect them still farther by the relation of property'.[1] Yet in many cultures possessions are distributed among the clan according to customary rules. Here again Hume is wrong. Still, his argument can be maintained, as those societies are characterized by loose ties between parents and offspring.[2] Further, there are cases where private belongings are destroyed, burnt, or buried with the corpse. These practices can hardly be defended on the assumption that 'the goods *must* become property of some body'.[3] Yet the clarity view would suggest that a ritual like the burning of the personal belongings may help to re-establish clarity in the social pattern by destroying elements that may cause ambiguity and conflict.

Thus, it is easy to dismiss some of Hume's principles about property, although others—in particular on the stability of property, symmetry, prescription, and occupancy—appear more reliable. It is, however, less easy to refute the underlying clarity view. This view entails the perception of patterns that induce actions to complete these patterns or improve them. As it is difficult to demonstrate the universality of that view, it is only possible to hint at the psychological evidence that supports it. Another support can be obtained by looking at animal behaviour. The parallelism of traits shared by humans, chimpanzees, lizards, and cicadas is suggestive.

---

[1] Hume (1740*a*: 510–13).   [2] Kubon-Gilke (1997).   [3] Hume (1740*a*: 512).

11.13 *Property in Ethological Perspective*

The first man who fenced off a plot of land and said 'this is mine' was, according to Rousseau, the true founder of civil society.[1] This insight is a gem in the glorious tradition of hypothetical theorizing. It sounds as if Rousseau had never encountered a dog. Possessive behaviour is not unique to humans but is widespread among animals. Some insight concerning the foundations of possessive behaviour may be gained by considering some animal behaviour.

The most important form of possessive behaviour among animals is territoriality. The usual explanation given for the phenomenon of territoriality is that it has evolved because of beneficial effects for the survival of the individual and the species. If every individual defends a certain territory (i.e. its habitat) against other members of the same species, this will secure the necessary food supply for the individual. The result is to spread the species across space in such a way as to use the territory most efficiently. Friendliness would be unwarranted. It would be nice if you were prepared to share your territory with a newcomer, but the sharing would be an economic disaster. The food supply would not suffice to support two couples and their offspring, and the offspring would die. In this way, benevolent individuals are weeded out by evolution, and only the 'nasties' survive. This provides a socio-biological rationale for territoriality.

There are of course many animals that do not form territories. Some fish form schools but seem to have no definite home-turf that they defend. Other animals must travel from pasture to pasture. This does not contradict the argument about territoriality outlined above. Territoriality must be expected to occur only when it is conducive to survival. It should also be noted that man's closest relatives, the chimpanzees and the baboons, are territorial.

Let us consider the phenomenon of territoriality a little more closely before relating it to phenomena of property in human societies.[2]

---

[1] Rousseau (1754: 76).
[2] An introduction to the topic is provided by Eibl-Eibesfeld (1975: 340–71)

The first observation is that the establishment of a territory may involve some fighting, but once the territory has been established fighting will be rare. This is to be expected from an evolutionary perspective. There would be no great use to the individual in having a territory that must be defended by uninterrupted fighting, and it would be a disadvantage for the species to waste resources in this manner. Boundaries must be accepted. There may be possibilities of revision, and processes to revise them, but boundaries lose all their meaning if they are under permanent dispute. Territoriality requires that boundaries be respected. The 'nasties' should not be too nasty.

Thus, borders must have a direct behavioural impact, in much the same way as customs must carry entitlements. This is the case in the animal kingdom. There is a strong 'owner effect' to be observed in territorial animals, which is very closely related to the endowment effect.[1] If you put two male desert clickers in a territory 'owned' by one of them, the 'owner' will invariably win the fight.[2] This 'owner effect' is tied up with the way territories are defined and actually prevents fighting under normal circumstances.

Territories must be recognized and be recognizable. Natural landmarks often serve as territory boundaries. Domestic mice prefer large nearby objects as visual clues.[3] Territorial songs or scentmarks may mark territories. Ethologists *define* territories in terms of the residents' intolerance of intruders.[4]

Yet boundaries are not always respected. An animal may seek to take possession of a high-quality territory by invading it and attacking the incumbent owner. This is usually not successful, because owners of high-quality territories are normally in better physical shape than intruders or owners of low-quality territories, because they are better fed. This is not the determining cause, however, at least not among desert clickers: 'The occupation of

[1] See S. 8.4 on the endowment effect.
[2] Wang and Greenfield (1991). This regularity has been observed in many other animals, too; see e.g. Davies (1978), Riechert (1978), Franke Stevens (1988), Senar *et al.* (1989), Englund and Otto (1991), Eibl-Eibesfeld (1975: 348, Fig. 15–41).
[3] MacIntosh (1973).   [4] Eibl-Eibesfeld (1975: 344–5).

high-quality territories is primarily determined by early eclosion rather than by aggressive contests. Why late-eclosed males respect ownership by early-eclosed males is still an enigma.'[1]

Further, there is the possibility of enlarging one's own territory at one's neighbour's expense. The assumption usually made is that a border dispute will be settled by a fight, and that the winner will obtain ownership of the contested territory. Many biologists seem to have assumed that in an axiomatic way. Nature is, however, somewhat more complex, at least with regard to lizards.

As a lizard, you may use two strategies to enlarge your territory at your neighbour's expense.[2] One strategy is to invade the neighbour's territory and to chase him away if he objects; after a while, the territory will be yours. This works, however, only if you are stronger than your neighbour. If you are not, you can nevertheless succeed by sheer persistence. You may lose every fight, or may even find it advantageous to flee right away, but you return again and again. If you are persistent enough, you will become the owner. Might is not necessarily right, even among animals.

There exist quite refined systems of property rights in the animal kingdom: Many male cats can use the same area, but at different, well-established times. Each is only a temporal owner of the territory and retreats from it at other times.[3] It is also interesting that territorial species do not defend all areas they may visit against members of their own kind. Some areas are neutral and serve as commons.[4]

Turning to property in movable objects, quite astonishing features of possessive behaviour are reported with animals. Again, ownership must be recognizable and recognized. The ownership cues are quite different among different species. For example, proximity of the object to its owner, as well as the possibility of taking it away and moving it around, are ownership cues with the

---

[1] Wang and Greenfield (1991: 586).

[2] The following draws on Stamps and Krishnan (1995). The authors remark that field studies about territory formation are rare and that many existing studies assume that the winner of a fight has obtained the contested territory, instead of testing that independently.

[3] Eibl-Eibesfeld (1975: 344).   [4] Eibl-Eibesfeld (1975: 342).

macaques that inhibit non-owners.[1] In baboons, the mere *memory* of the owner's proximity can inhibit non-owners.[2]

These observations stress three interrelated features of property in a very general way. First, property must be recognizable. Second, property must have a behavioural impact, witnessed by the owner effect. Third, property must be able to emerge without any formal legal system.

In this way, property is tied up with the owner effect. This seems to be the core phenomenon. Individuals can develop special affinities with objects in their surroundings. These are just the 'connexions in imagination' that Hume emphasized. They form the foundation for property. On that basis, property can take many forms. The phenomenon may be compared to the faculty of having a language that must precede the learning of any single language itself among the many possible languages.

Ethology thus establishes that animals can form special psychological ties to territories, or to things. Such property is not necessarily a social phenomenon. An animal will form its territory even if no competitors are to be feared, just as Robinson Crusoe, lonely on his island, may form a special tie with his walking stick, in spite of being able to find many other pieces of wood that would serve the purpose just as well.[3] Property without society would be an entirely private affair, driven by rule preference like habit. It is not necessary to establish that humans must form certain specific ties to specific objects, although some ethnologists would argue along those lines. The mere unspecified possibility of forming ties is sufficient for the purposes of the present argument. The laws that underlie the formation of these ties may be said to constitute the ultimate source of property. They are assumed to be universal. The clarity view is even more daring in trying to conceptualize them as having been brought about by overarching clarification processes.

---

[1] Kummer and Cords (1991: 545–7).   [2] Sigg and Falett (1985).
[3] This aspect is usually neglected, e.g. by Hume (1740*a*: 501) and Demsetz (1967: 104).

11.14 *The Voluntary Transfer of Property*

Property, as has been shown, is not a uniquely human phenomenon. Man has, however, the possibility of transferring property voluntarily.[1] This is unique to humans, although rudiments of ownership transfers may be found in the case of apes.[2] Paraphrasing Adam Smith, it is not necessary to decide whether 'this propensity is one of those original principles in human nature, of which no further account can be given; or whether, as seems more probable, it be the necessary consequence of the faculties of reason and speech'.[3]

Smith referred, however, to the human 'propensity to truck, barter, and exchange one thing for another'.[4] This seems problematic. The statement mixes too many aspects and creates more confusion than is necessary. The problems with Smith's wording are as follows. First, it would be better to talk about a 'propensity to exchange common to all men' and drop 'truck' and 'barter'. Truck and barter derive from exchange, yet are not necessary aspects of exchange. 'Take it or leave it' offers are quite common in modern societies as well as in exchanges between alien tribes that share no common language ('silent trade').[5] The 'truck and barter' aspect is also unconvincing in other ways. Smith writes regarding truck and barter that 'nobody ever saw a dog make a fair and deliberate exchange of one bone for another with another dog'.[6] This statement adds the additional feature of fairness to exchanges. Such fairness has, however, no role to play in truck and barter, although it is important in the voluntary exchange of property.

[1] Ryan (1987: 1029) wrongly translates the Roman *ius utendi et abutendi* as meaning the right to use and the power to dispose and takes this as the definition of property. This is not my usage. I consider property as a particular bundle of rights, shaped by the same regularities as other rights. This comprises various cases of attenuated property rights. Often you cannot trade with gifts, or you are not allowed to misuse property or leave it idle. On the Trobriand Islands, property is related by lineage to mythical ancestors; as you cannot exchange your ancestors, you cannot exchange your property (Bell-Krannhals 1990: 104). Even the Roman 'right to use and to misuse' is too restrictive.   [2] Ellis (1985: 126).

[3] Smith (1776: 13).   [4] Smith (1776: 13).
[5] Basu *et al.* (1987).   [6] Smith (1776: 13).

Second, transfer of property takes place in various ways, and exchange is just a special case, i.e. a case that arises when one transfer is conditional on the other. It may be said that property may give rise to *quid pro quo* exchange, but only under certain conditions. There are societies, organized around principles of reciprocity, that rely on obligatory gift-giving without immediate equivalent returns; an approximate equivalence is achieved only in the longer term.[1] Modern societies maintain rudiments of reciprocity, such as the right to hospitality. Systems of public provision fall in this category, too.

It thus seems preferable to follow Hume and to consider the rule of 'transference of property by consent' as the stepping stone for the emergence of exchange:

However useful, or even necessary, the stability of possession may be to human society, 'tis attended with very considerable inconveniences. The relation of fitness or suitableness ought never to enter into consideration, in distributing the properties of mankind; but we must govern ourselves by rules, which are more general in their application, and more free from doubt and uncertainty. Of this kind, *present* possession upon the first establishment of society; and afterwards *occupation, prescription, accession*, and *succession*. As these depend very much on chance, they must frequently prove contradictory both to men's wants and desires; and persons and possessions must often be very ill adjusted. This is a grand inconvenience, which calls for a remedy. To apply one directly, and allow every man to seize by violence what he judges to be fit for him, wou'd destroy society; and therefore the rules of justice seek medium betwixt a rigid stability, and this changeable and uncertain adjustment. But there is no medium better than the obvious one, that possession and property shou'd always be stable, except when the proprietor consents to bestow them on some other person.[2]

This sounds convincing, and yet the right to transfer is far from universal. If, moreover, such rights do exist, they occasionally

---

[1] Mauss (1924). Lévi-Strauss (1949: 122) aptly terms this 'generalized exchange'. Smith's statement about the 'natural tendency to truck and barter' may suggest that markets are more 'natural' than other forms of social coordination. Reciprocity is, however, an equally 'natural' trait of human beings, and forms of social coordination building on reciprocity are, therefore, neither more 'natural' nor less 'natural' than markets. (See S. 8.6 on reciprocity.)   [2] Hume (1740*a*: 514).

appear quite different from the right described by Hume. However, the 'exceptions' tend again to reconfirm, rather than to invalidate, Hume's general view.

11.15 *The Theory of Property Rights*

An example is given by the system of property rights found among the Zuñis, an Indian tribe in New Mexico. Consider two Zuñis, named 'A' and 'B'. An anthropologist reports as follows about their property rights in land:

A has let his field go out of cultivation. If B wishes to plant in it, A cannot refuse. Although it still belongs to A, it would be 'mean'—and unavailing—to assert his claim so long as B is using it. It is perfectly clear to any Zuñi that B needs the field more than A. Isn't he using it? If A presses his claim, and he has the legal right to do so, B must offer another field in exchange. If he has no other field he can spare, this proves that he needs this one. So A compromises by offering a field in exchange. *B now has clear title to the second field.*[1]

This seems far away from any right of transfer as described by Hume. Yet the efficiency argument put forward by Hume may well apply here. The right to use uncultivated fields can certainly be defended on efficiency grounds. The same would hold true for the right to maintain the crop. If this were not assured, those who invest in cultivation could be exploited, and investment in cultivation would, rationally speaking, be suboptimal. In so far as the plants cannot be separated from the soil, the Zuñi system seems perfectly in accord with Hume's line of argument (if not with his result). Yet the Zuñi case violates one of the assumptions made by Hume, namely that property rights should disregard personal needs because this would lead to 'confusion'. In the Zuñi case, however, utility is objectified by cultivation. For that reason it is possible to attach general rules to cultivation. Because personal need can be objectified, it enters in the determination of property

---

[1] Bunzel (1938: 347).

rights. The Zuñi case thus reconfirms, rather than invalidates, Hume's general approach while conflicting with his conclusions.

The modern theory of property rights has centred around this type of argument.[1] The theory of the firm, to be discussed in a later chapter, draws extensively on such ideas. In the present context, however, it is useful to discuss yet another ownership phenomenon that seems to contradict Hume's conclusions but reconfirms his principles. This is communal property.

Communal property is a widespread phenomenon, but seems not to be covered by Hume's treatment.[2] A prominent example is the 'commons' in medieval England. This was communally owned pasture land. The institution of commons was widespread. It was maintained for more than a thousand years, and some parts survive to the present.[3] At first glance, this institution seems to carry all the known inefficiencies of public property with it. In particular, one would expect overgrazing. This was, however, reduced by communal regulations that restricted usage to members of the community and allotted quotas of cattle to them. So the 'overgrazing' inefficiency was checked by regulation.

Communal property in grazing land had considerable advantages.[4] The habit of cattle is such that they stray while eating. On a small pasture, the farmer cannot easily restrict the animal to a small part of that small field. A large herd, however, can be kept together on a certain part of a large field. This allows the rest of the grass to recuperate until the animals are allowed back on it. As a result, a large herd will make better usage of a large field than a small herd could on a correspondingly small field. Furthermore, the supervision of a herd of cattle, or a flock of sheep, involves

---

[1] The classical statement is Demsetz (1967). Important contributions include Alchian and Demsetz (1972) and Alchian (1984;1987).

[2] Hume (1740: 538) mentions joint property, however.

[3] The following draws on Dahlman (1980). See also Hoffmann (1975) and D. N. McCloskey (1975).

[4] I follow Dahlman (1980: 112–13) to illustrate the property rights argument. I do not, however, maintain that the account given by Dahlman is factually correct. It seems to have the weakness of neglecting political forces that may maintain economically inefficient states. Yet it serves to nicely illustrate the way in which property rights theory proceeds. See Hoffmann (1975) for a detailed historical account and references to the historical literature.

economies of scale. A communal shepherd with his dogs can easily supervise a large flock. The costs of fencing off individual plots can be saved.

Other advantages relate to more intricate features. Commons formed part of the 'open field system', which involved an elaborate mode of scattered strip farming, with fallows used for grazing and the animals fertilizing the fallows. Various complementarities between livestock and crops complicate the picture. It is not necessary to discuss this in detail. The overall argument is simply that a system of communal property rights may have efficiency advantages. In these cases, communal property should be expected to emerge.

A hypothetical story would be as follows. Starting from private property, people would transfer their rights to the community in exchange for grazing rights. They would be willing to set up such a system because it was perceived that everybody would benefit from it. This is, of course, hypothetical. The origin of communal pastures is obscure. It is likely that the system emerged historically from Germanic systems of communal property, and it certainly evolved 'insensibly and by degrees'.[1] It comes in many variants and shadings. A process of continuous trial and error may be imagined, for instance, whereby there would be an incessant re-arrangement of property rights until some stable pattern emerged. Subsequent variations would be reversed if they turned out to be disadvantageous, thereby stabilizing the pattern.

Or consider, as another hypothetical story, a community initially owning all property communally, but with potential advantages to be secured from switching to *private* property. In this case, there would be a continuous pressure to privatize. The members of the community would agree gradually to allot more rights to individuals, because this would benefit the whole of the group. Processes of this type do actually occur, such as the transformation of communal property that seems to be currently under way with the Hutterites, an Anabaptist group in North America.[2] The more dramatic developments of this kind—the dissolution of communal

[1] See Hoffmann (1975).   [2] Peter and Withaker (1981).

property in medieval England, the more recent collapse of the communist countries—cannot, however, be easily understood in this simple way. They involve explicit political power, rather than tacit and gradual social change.[1] While this topic will not be considered here, it should be noted that Hume offers a fruitful way of thinking about political power by analysing the origins of government and the nature of 'allegiance'.[2]

11.16 *Some Problems with Property Rights*

Once property rights are transferable, there will emerge a private incentive to rearrange them in such a way as to exhaust possible advantages. The modern contractual view takes this perspective. It sees institutions as being brought about by such a process of reshuffling property rights. Firms emerge in this manner, as do families, churches, states, and markets. The overarching view is that the various organizational forms will evolve from institutional competition; better institutional solutions will win out over inferior ones.[3]

---

[1] The dissolution of communal property in pasture is part of the 'enclosures' which have been discussed in the literature. It is beyond my scope to settle the controversial issues involved, but a brief indication of the problem is as follows. Dahlman (1980: 188–99) interprets the political processes that actually redefined property rights as being actuated by changes in relative prices, induced by changes in technology and demand; in other words, the system was changed in response to purely economic incentives. It was this that rendered enclosures profitable. Some would argue that a political power structure can prevail in spite of emerging inefficiencies, as long as it can be maintained by the interests of those in power, and that the systems of communal property can be viewed as having been retained in this manner. In certain instances, the dissolution of communal property was much more complex than a straightforward property rights approach would suggests. Property rights were not divisible, alienable, or transferable to begin with. Changes could be fostered by the lords if they were interested in promoting such changes, or they could be impeded by them if they saw dangers in the alternatives. The spread of markets and of long-distance trade induced them sometimes to act in ways that fostered, as unintended consequences, the further spread of markets and the dissolution of the traditional political structure. For instance, the lords were prompted to replace the personal services they were entitled to receive from their followers by cash rents. This process led to the dissolution of feudal bonds and the further spread of market transactions and privatization. This is the 'bauble thesis' advanced by E. L. Jones (1981: 85–7), following Smith (1776: 385–94). It goes far beyond the boundaries of any straightforward property rights approach.

[2] Hume (1740a: 534–67).   [3] Alchian (1984), O. E. Williamson (1985).

Yet this approach has some difficulties. The first is the *efficiency problem*. The approach cannot easily explain inefficiencies, in the sense of wasted resources, from the point of view of the members of a whole group or whole society. There would be no reason to expect that such arrangement could be perpetuated. There would be an incentive to change it. The benefits of so doing would outweigh the costs, and the losers could be fully compensated by the gains, leaving some surplus to be distributed. This would allow for optimization step by step, rather than the weaker form of optimization through the selection of appropriate rules. In other words, the approach does not take into account all the psychological forces that constrain possible rules, and therefore possible institutions.

Property rights theorists start from the assumption that the most efficient practices are the most likely to survive. The argument should carry over to all types of social arrangement, institution, and technique. This stands in contrast to the many inefficiencies that are said to be observed in any culture. From a property rights perspective, these alleged inefficiencies may be understood as ultimately serving some hidden and unintended purpose, but this seems largely a matter of unfounded faith. It seems to be better to try to understand the reasons for the inefficiencies rather than complacently to assume them away. Consider, as an illustration, the following account, which relates to the persistence of an inefficient tool:

A good example for the persistence of an unimpressive design is the Oldowan hand axe. . . . It consists of a waterworn pebble about the size of a fist, from one end of which a few chips were knocked off to produce a rough edge that could be used for hacking, mashing, scraping, grubbing for roots, and breaking bones to extract the marrow. This tool remained in use for at least two million years until the development of the Acheulian hand axe, made of flint, which gave a sharper edge.

To argue that the Oldowan hand axe persisted for so long because it was marvellously adapted is clearly absurd: as a piece of technology it was crude in the extreme, and very far from the most efficient use that could have been made of stone even at that time, as subsequent developments in the later Palaeolithic and the Neolithic showed very clearly.[1]

Such 'survival of the mediocre' over millennia, as Hallpike describes it, is a conundrum for all theoretical approaches that put exclusive stress on instrumental considerations.[2] The theory of property rights is one of these approaches.

The second problem relates to the *unspecified set of alternatives*. Because of this difficulty, the property rights approach is not able to explain very much. It can explain why one institution is selected from a given set of feasible alternatives, but it does not say anything about the set itself. This renders the set arbitrary. By introducing some further alternatives, the theorist may change the result of the analysis. This has not gone unnoticed. Dahlman, in his discussion of the open field system, is quite explicit about the issue:

> The argument . . . will emphatically not be that the open field system was 'the best of all possible worlds'. Since the set of 'all possible worlds' is impossible to define in any relevant manner . . . we can only make use of a more limited notion of efficiency. The argument presented here will, therefore, only be that the open field system with its specific property rights mixture was efficient relative to the modern system of farming with one man, one owner, one decisionmaker; that is, relative to enclosed farms.[3]

Analogues to the putting-out system, or the factory system, are not discussed. It is certainly not possible to consider all feasible alternatives. A property rights explanation of an institution thus boils down to two assertions: that the institution can maintain itself, and that it is superior to any other institution considered. This seems not to be a very daring position. Its grip depends entirely on the set of alternatives considered. There is no constraint on the range of possibilities that can be entertained.

The third difficulty relates to the *relevance of property rights*. It is not clear why the specific nature of property rights (whether

---

[1] Hallpike (1986: 114). The book contains many other references of this kind.
[2] I thank Eric Jones for stressing this and providing the reference.
[3] Dahlman (1980: 99).

private, communal, or other) should matter at all. It may be sufficient that property rights are well specified.[1] Consider again the institution of the commons and compare it to a system of private property rights in tracts of pasture. If communal use were better, with private ownership prevailing, the owners of the patches could join together and employ a shepherd to facilitate the common use of the pasture. There would thus be no need to introduce communal property. Conversely, in the case of inefficiencies arising from communal property, plots of land could be rented out to individual farmers, and a kind of market socialism could then emerge. Quite generally and abstractly, all regulations that can be made in the one system could be introduced in the other.[2] There is, again, some vagueness here.

11.17 *Rituals*

Yet, despite these theoretical difficulties, the right to transfer property by consent has great advantages. It enables individuals to capture the benefits arising from comparative advantage and the division of labour. Hume describes this as follows:

> This rule can have no ill consequence, in occasioning war and dissentions; since the proprietor's consent, who alone is concern'd, is taken along in the alienation: And it may serve to many good purposes in adjusting property to persons. Different parts of the earth produce different commodities; and not only so, but different men both are by nature fitted for different employments, and attain greater perfection in any one, when they confine themselves to it alone. All this requires mutual exchange and commerce; for which reason the translation of property by consent is founded on a law of nature, as well as its stability without such consent.[3]

In spite of all the benefits that arise from having property transferable, the moral aspect creates difficulties:

> The property of an object, when taken for something real, without any reference to morality, or the sentiments of the mind, is a quality perfectly

---

[1] The following is a variation on Coase's (1960) ideas.
[2] This has been stressed in particular by Cheung (1969).   [3] Hume (1740*a*: 514).

insensible, and even inconceivable; nor can we form any distinct notion, either of its stability or translation. This imperfection of our ideas is less sensibly felt with regard to its stability, as it engages less our attention, and is easily past over by the mind, without any scrupulous examination. But as translation of property from one person to another is a more remarkable event, the defect of our ideas becomes more sensible on that occasion, and obliges us to turn ourselves on every side in search of some remedy.[1]

This search for remedies give rise to various rituals, and lawyers and moralists help in augmenting the inventory:

Now as nothing more enlivens any idea than a present impression, and a relation betwixt that impression and the idea; 'tis natural for us to seek some false light from this quarter. In order to aid the imagination in conceiving the transference of property, we take the sensible object, and actually transfer its possession to the person, on whom we wou'd bestow the property. The suppos'd resemblance of the actions, and the presence of this sensible delivery, deceive our mind, and make it fancy, that it conceives the mysterious transition of property. And that this explication of the matter is just, appears hence, that men have invented *symbolical* delivery, to satisfy the fancy, where the real one is impracticable. Thus the giving of the keys of the granary is understood to be the delivery of the corn contain'd in it: The giving of stone and earth represents the delivery of the manor. This is a kind of superstitious practice in civil laws, and in the laws of nature, resembling the *Roman catholic* superstitions in religion. As the *Roman catholics* represent the inconceivable mysteries of the *Christian* religion, and render them more present to the mind, by a taper, or habit, or grimace, which is suppos'd to resemble them; so lawyers and moralists have run into like inventions for the same reason, and have endeavour'd by those means to satisfy themselves concerning the transference of property by consent.[2]

Thus, Hume returned in the end to his counterpoint. Instrumental considerations suggest transfers that cannot easily be maintained psychologically. As a remedy, rituals may help to stabilize transactions on a 'moral' plane that cannot easily be grasped by the moral sense unless 'help'd' in this way. The actions serve a purpose and are beneficial. The rituals that underpin them are, therefore, defensible on purely utilitarian grounds. The often-encountered

---

[1] Hume (1740a: 515).   [2] Hume (1740a: 515–16).

problem of explaining costly and time-consuming rituals as arising from rational behaviour disappears. Rituals may well be an
integral part of general economic equilibrium. Their function may
well be that of reconfirming property rights.

11.18 *Moral Forces*

Transfers, divisions, and refinements of property rights that are
instrumentally useful need a ritual or legal underpinning. That
underpinning serves to satisfy the moral sense and to generate the
ownership effect in cases where it would not occur spontaneously.
This may be costly. The costs may loosely be described as 'moral
costs'.[1]

Moral costs are 'transaction costs', i.e. costs that are necessary
to run and maintain a certain institution. These costs must be
included when evaluating the efficiency of institutions.[2] If this is
done, the vagueness of the property rights approach will be
reduced in several ways. The cost terminology, however, has, the
drawback that the moral *costs* of one institution, compared with
another, are also moral *benefits* when the comparison is reversed.
It seems preferable to speak about moral forces that are shaped by
property rights and rituals. The difficulties of the property rights
approach, as mentioned above, relate to the explanation of persisting inefficiencies and to the unspecified set of alternatives.
Those difficulties appear less disturbing once the impact of these
moral forces is taken into account.

Regarding the *efficiency problem*, Hume has already made the
point that rituals that seem a waste of resources may be important

---

[1] On the ownership effect, see S. 8.4 above, and Kubon-Gilke (1997).

[2] Casson (1991: 3) has stated this as follows: 'Overall economic performance
depends on transaction costs, and these mainly reflect the level of trust in an economy.
The level of trust depends in turn on culture. An effective culture has a strong moral
content.' While Casson is concerned mainly with generating trust through moral
leadership, the present considerations focus on the behavioural, or possibly 'moral',
implications of alternative institutions. In contrast to Casson, guilt is seen as caused
not so much by a leader's manipulation of the individuals, as by their own perception of
rule violations.

in establishing property rights. Thus, many apparent inefficiencies disappear. Even the enigma of massive and persistent inefficiencies may be explained in this way. Examples will be provided in the context of long-term contracting in the following section.

Regarding the *unspecified set of alternatives*, the introduction of psychological considerations restricts, in principle, the set of feasible alternatives. This would not be of much use if the set of alternatives were left unspecified. Yet the earlier considerations about rule formation stress the *principle of good continuity*. New rules and regulations build on the prevailing set of rules. The process of evolution is rather like the process of learning. Hence, only local alternatives to a given institution need be considered, and they can be generated by starting from the prevailing schema. This drastically reduces the set of alternatives. Correspondingly, it sharpens the thrust of the theoretical approach. The alternatives would involve gradual change if new problems could be solved by adapting prevailing practice. They would also entail drastic change if new developments required a switch to an adjacent schema of organization.[1]

Regarding the *relevance of property rights*, it seems clear that those forms of organization that can do with as little ritual as possible are economically preferable. In this sense, communal ownership of the commons is preferable, because this does not require the extra transfer of rights from individuals to the community and the corresponding rituals. Conversely, private plots are owned privately because this does not require the transfer of rights from the community to the individuals and the corresponding rituals. Further, social organization should exploit ownership effects in the most appropriate way, but this affects issues of responsibility, to be discussed elsewhere.

Hume's counterpoint may in this way help to reduce ambiguities in institutional analysis. The following words suggest that conclusion in a different way. The allocation of property rights affects

---

[1] See S. 7.10 on schema switches. A hypothetical example of this type of change is discussed in somewhat more detail in Schlicht (1979).

behaviour; otherwise it would be irrelevant to consider them. The sources for this behavioural effect must be taken into account when thinking about reshuffling property rights. The first of these sentences generates a hypothesis in terms of a revealed preference argument that is applied to property rights theory; the second sentence draws the conclusion.

11.19   Long-Term Contracts and Emergent Entitlements

A prominent political scientist asserts: 'One can conceive of a society in which haircuts took on such central social significance that communal provision would be morally required.'[1] This seems superficial and misleading. It is superficial in the sense that one can conceive of anything if one disregards important features of reality. It is misleading because it suggests that ignorance is a sufficient reason for cultural relativism. A more precise formulation would be: 'We do not have a theory that would explain how social significance emerges'.

Yet the topic is important. It seems that market systems generate systematic tensions in the sense that moral and instrumental considerations point in different directions. Hume's counterpoint could help to approach these problems in a serious way. Hume's argument about rituals suggests that problems may emerge. Rituals exist because they support the acceptance of certain property rights on a moral plane; as a consequence, problems of legitimization would arise in the absence of these rituals. The reshuffling of property rights is not unproblematic.

The idea may even be pushed a little further. Consider the opposition between prescription and the transfer of rights. It has been argued above that long and uninterrupted possession creates property rights, and that these may override previous rights of ownership. Hence a transfer of property for long periods will create property rights that may be incompatible with the underlying legal ownership arrangements. This is precisely what has

[1] Waltzer (1983: 88 n.).

happened in the German tenancy market. The general perception of tenancy as something quite different from a simple exchange contract found articulation in extensive legislation to protect the tenant (rent control and protection against eviction, for example). By a recent ruling of the German supreme Court (Verfassungs- gericht), the tenancy 'rights' that have emerged in this manner are protected by the clause in the constitution that protects property in general. Custom overrides black-letter law.

Labour legislation abounds with examples of this kind. A worker in Germany has a right to his job in the sense that the employer cannot replace him without good reason. Incumbent workers have a right to be considered first for vacancies when they arise.

It may appear that the politicizing of those markets is due to their 'social' importance. This is true. The 'social importance' does not derive, however, from the intrinsic importance of the transactions in question. It is just another way of stating that the market creates customary rights that contradict the formal prop- erty rights structure. This tends to bend the law. It is not related to the importance of the commodities. Cars are in many ways as important as work and housing. The price of most cars exceeds six months' salary; yet the car market is not controlled. Food is certainly as important as housing; yet the market for food is not controlled in favour of the customers.[1]

Hume's counterpoint makes it possible to understand some of the moral dilemmas that seem systematically to emerge in market systems. These may give rise to severe inefficiencies. A flourishing tenancy market may be destroyed by such legislation. Rented property is increasingly being transformed into owner-occupied property in Germany. Similarly, the establishment of property rights in jobs may create problems of unemployment for the economy as a whole (whether or not they are actually beneficial at the firm level).[2] Yet the establishment of property rights in jobs

---

[1] It is true that the market for food is strongly politicized and regulated in the European Community, but this regulation works deliberately to exploit rather than protect consumers and favour the farmers—a minuscule part of the population.

[2] This is, however, a somewhat complex issue; see Schlicht (1995*a*).

would become unavoidable if repetitive tasks became automated and the remaining tasks involved much firm-specific knowledge. The market response would be to create contracts that tie workers to firms, for efficiency reasons. The moral tension generated by emerging entitlements would follow suit. These examples illustrate that Hume's counterpoint permits *massive* inefficiencies, such as the suppression of entire markets.

A political response could be to invest more in rituals, or actively to create a property rights structure that induces less difficulty in legitimization while maintaining efficiency. A wrong response, however, would be the moralistic one of condemning the foolishness of the people. The same tendencies of human nature that create moral problems in long-term contracting provide the moral and behavioural foundations for the institution of property. Neither can exist without the other; or, in Hume's words: 'Tis impossible to separate the good from the ill.'[1]

---

[1] Hume (1740*a*: 497)

Chapter 12

THE LAW

12.1 *The Law and Custom*

Law and custom are closely related. Common law has even been identified with general custom. This overstates the case.[1] Even if the law were concerned solely with codifying prevailing customs, the urge to codify would constitute a deeper element warranting explanation. But the law goes beyond that. It may influence custom. Law and custom interact, and neither can be fully reduced to the other. This chapter will deal with some aspects of the interaction. It will be argued in particular that the clarity view expounded in Chapters 6–10 offers a natural perspective for approaching the issue.

An attempt to survey current theories about the sources of law would exceed the present compass.[2] The purpose of the following sections is confined, therefore, to describing some implications of the clarity view for jurisprudence and to establishing what the view implies for the interaction between law and custom. Conflicting views will be criticized not so much in order to refute them (which would often require a much more elaborate analysis), but to isolate the clarity view by means of contrast.

[1] Paton and Derham (1972: 194).
[2] See Paton and Derham (1972: 188–269) for a review of the most important issues; and Fuller (1968: 43–119) for a brilliant restatement.

12.2   *A Blind Spot*

'When men talk or think about law, they talk and think about *rules*.' Thus writes the lawyer Karl Llewellyn; and he adds: 'This is traditional.'[1] The 'rule of law' amounts in this formulation to the 'rule of rules'. The first question to ask therefore is what might constitute a 'rule'. Yet any characterization of the nature and sources of rules is conspicuously absent in legal writing. Distinctions between different kinds of rules, such as principles, precepts, rights, legal entitlements, abstract versus end-connected rules, etc., beg the question of the nature of rules. This is a question that must be resolved before we start. In a similar way, the discussion about the origin of law—whether ultimately deriving from fiat or from natural law—presupposes, rather than clarifies, the distinction between rules and non-rules.[2]

The nature of rules remains a blind spot in jurisprudence, in spite of its central importance for legal thought. This inattention seems to flow from a deep-rooted inhibition against considering the nature of the human mind as the ultimate foothold for analysis, perhaps out of a fear of subjectivity and arbitrariness.[3] Many disciplines manifest the same inhibition. It is ingrained in current thought. Economics stresses the ostensibly arbitrary quality of *all* preferences and valuations. The same can be said for large parts of philosophy.[4] Psychoanalysis and behaviourism, although antithetical in many other ways, both insist that human nature is fundamentally irrational. Current experimental psychology tends to highlight distortions, erroneous judgements, and misperceptions while failing to mention the immense functional value (and beauty) of the underlying psychological tendencies that give rise

---

[1] Llewellyn (1962: 6).

[2] The same can be said with regard to the insistence that a rule-free characterization of rules is not possible; see Field (1984).

[3] There are, however, important exceptions, such as Fuller (1967). The aversion to psychology in economics is a rather recent phenomenon. Economists like Jevons and Edgeworth considered that they belonged to the 'psychological school'.

[4] See Appendix C on 'Hume's Law'.

to the most astonishing faculties of thinking, perceiving, and acting. It is not only economics that looks at man with an evil eye.

Such debasement of human nature renders odious all attempts to take the human mind as a starting point for social analysis. Yet such an abhorrence is quite unreasonable. As has been argued before, rules cannot be defined in any 'objective' sense, if 'objective' is held to imply independence from cognitive processes. That approach entails a misleading idea of objectivity, as it would mean the conceiving of all kinds of patterns, numbers, laws of nature, language, and even truth as 'subjective'.[1] Rules may, indeed, be conceived as entirely objective in the sense of being brought about by universal human tendencies.[2] The clarity view posits that the distinction between rules and non-rules is rooted in an objective way in the nature of the human mind. Rules are conceived as being shaped by clarification processes that are not further reducible to rational or adaptive learning. Rather, these processes are the ones that render learning and extrapolation possible. The game of Eleusis has been used to illustrate the point.[3]

The nature of rules emanates from the regularities of cognition and rule perception. These regularities can be studied objectively. They cannot be changed by fiat. Legal positivism is constrained by these laws. Human nature must be viewed as one of the fundamental sources of law, since this is the ultimate source of 'rules'. Regarding the law as alien to human nature, and as merely constraining action from the outside, cannot be sustained. Elements of natural law must enter once it is conceded that rules are psychological entities. As rules rely on clarity, so the law must rely on clarity too.

---

[1] Asch (1952: 245). Contrary to the appearance of extreme subjectivism, Hume's position on this issue is very similar to the position defended here. Resemblance, contiguity, and causation are mentioned by Hume as the fundamental principles of association, being 'the only links that bind the parts of the universe together, or connect us with any person or object exterior to ourselves . . . and as these are the only ties of our thoughts, they are really *to us* the cement of the universe' (Hume 1740*b*: 32). As has been remarked before, Hume's associationism is not to be identified with any kind of prototypical modern associationism, as it contains important traits of Gestalt psychology. 'Resemblance', for example, is central to Hume's thought, being a precondition for, rather than a result of, association (Hume 1740*a*: 11).

[2] Cf. Ss. 6.7–6.12.   [3] S. 7.2.

12.3 *Law and Reason*

The rule of law has also been identified with the rule of reason, as opposed to the rule of force.[1] This relates to the way in which legal arguments are developed, and to the overall coherence of legal doctrine.

If a case is to be decided, by precedent or by law, this involves a process of abstraction and classification from the outset. The given concrete case is to be identified as belonging to a certain class of cases, or as being similar to certain other cases in important ways. The question, 'Does rule X *or* rule Y govern the set of established facts?' can hardly be answered in a strictly logical way. It may nevertheless be settled by convincing reasoning.[2]

Reasoning may proceed here in various ways. By pointing out similarities and analogies with other clear cases, an argument may be provided for using one rule rather than another. Fictitious examples may be employed to stress certain features and discount others by driving particular arguments to absurdity. The reasoning may be absolutely straightforward and compelling, and yet not be logically deducible from first principles in a 'geometric' way. Reason manifests itself as *elegantia iuris*.

The way in which such reasoning proceeds may be illustrated by means of the game Eleusis.[3] Consider a sequence of cards that has been placed on the table, when the regulator—the person knowing the true rules—is no longer present. The players want nevertheless to continue the sequence on the table and ask a judge to decide whether an additional card is correct or has to be withdrawn. The judge will look at the cards on the table and will try to reconstruct the cases where previous cards had been rejected. As a result, he will come up with a set of possible rules. To decide which one is correct, the judge will think of other arguments. He will consider which of the possible rules fits the interests of the original regulator best. This will eliminate rules that are too complicated, or too equitable, or would make for a boring game. In this way, he

---

[1] Fuller (1968: 3).   [2] This follows Derham *et al.* (1971: 172–8).
[3] See S. 7.2.

may decide the case in a reasonable way. When a further card is added, and a new judge is consulted, he will proceed like the first one but will refine the judgment. The judgment can now be based on a longer run of observations. As a result, more and more of the remaining ambiguities will be removed. Ultimately, a rule will emerge in the game. The game, however, is played with definite cards. Reality, on the other hand, produces an incessant sequence of ever-changing problems. It proposes, so to speak, entirely new cards all the time that must be fitted into the sequence.

The law develops, furthermore, not as single rules in isolation, but as a large set of rules all at once. Analogies tie the various rules together. Initially, case A may have been decided in a certain way. A similar case B has later to be decided on the analogy of case A. Assume now that new developments occur that favour deciding case A in a different way. In spite of these new requirements, the analogy between case A and case B will have been established and will work back from B to A. As a result, the arguments for deciding A in a new and functionally better way will have to be quite strong to overrule the analogy; without case B, weaker reasons would be sufficient to tip the balance.[1] The extensive use of analogies and other modes of reasoning that interrelate various decisions and rules expand the possibilities for settling disputes by reasoning and reduce subjective arbitrariness. They do not, however, necessarily reduce *ex ante* uncertainty.

Reason, so conceived, lines the various rules together and adjusts them mutually to one another. New problems are decided by analogy with known cases, and old rules are invalidated if the underlying reasons cease to apply. As a result, 'the law is not a mere collection of detailed rules, but an organic body of principles with an inherent power of growth and adaptation to new circumstances'.[2]

However, if the question is asked, what are the principles that guide such adjustment, growth, and decay, the answer will point to

---

[1] In other words, hysteresis occurs; see S. 3.8.

[2] Paton and Derham (1972: 199), writing about the Australian state of Victoria.

the same principles that govern the growth and decay of custom. These are the principles of similarity, symmetry, contiguity, and good continuity that underlie classification and rule formation in all realms of human life. In short, *elegantia iuris* is a matter of clarity.[1]

12.4   *The Law as Transformation of Custom*

One approach to law formation consists of viewing the law as a codification of custom. Law-making, so conceived, emerges to settle conflicts arising from conflicting entitlements. A simple and schematic account would be as follows.

There are 'spontaneous' rights, such as rights emerging from occupancy, contiguity, habit, and custom, that relate directly to psychological processes. These spontaneous rights may conflict with each other in certain instances. The conflict between occupancy and prescription envisaged by Hume may serve as an example.[2] The first occupier may have obtained ownership by occupancy. Another person may have obtained ownership of the same thing by long and uninterrupted possession ('prescription', 'adverse possession'). So the 'spontaneous' rights of occupancy and prescription can conflict in some cases. The conflict may be resolved by creating 'artificial' rights, like the rules governing adverse possession. 'So a person who takes possession of something in Victoria, for example, without the permission of its owner, and who retains such possession—for fifteen years in the case of land, or six years in the case of other things than land—will be able to resist a claim to recover that property instituted by the owner after those periods of time have passed.'[3]

The right of adverse possession may delimit the scope of the 'spontaneous' rights of occupancy and prescription. Although the

---

[1] Fuller (1967: 111) is quite explicit in recognizing the laws of the mind and the 'inveterate hang of the human mind toward an organized simplicity' as central to jurisprudence. He refers to Hume, Gestalt psychology, and clarification processes governing memory and recall (Fuller 1967: 103 and 111 n.).
[2] See S. 11.8.   [3] Derham *et al.* (1971: 93–4)

delimiting rule by itself is, thus, quite arbitrary, it becomes an integral part of the overall system of principles that govern entitlements. Without the delimiting principle, the prevailing rules would come into conflict.

Although a certain delimiting principle may be artificial and unintelligible if considered in isolation, its validity rests in its function of confining the spontaneous rights that gave birth to the delimiting principle. Its 'reason' rests in the way it is tied up with similar apparently arbitrary principles that are used to delimit other entitlements. Other rights, such as personal obligations, may be attenuated in similar ways after a certain number of years. The required spans of inaction that invalidate rights reflect the relative importance and fixity of the stale claims. Similar cases are treated similarly, even if the resemblance is rather faint. The system of the 'artificial' rights must thus exhibit an overall coherence that reduces, or even removes, the arbitrariness of each single artificial rule.

One source of law-making springs, therefore, from a desire to create clarity in cases where conflicting entitlements emerge. Lawmaking, so induced, serves to codify custom. It formalizes, confines, and codifies entitlements that have been developed for other reasons. By looking for reasonable principles, conflicts can be removed in a non-arbitrary way. The sources for these principles are very comprehensive. They 'include anything that may be drawn into the process of creation. Thus an English judge may adopt a principle from an ancient Roman text or a modern American case, from a text-book of law or a custom of the community.'[1]

The 'artificial' rights, so established, acquire a life of their own. If the 'spontaneous' right of occupancy is limited by an 'artificial' prescription period to fifteen years, this modifies the previous right of occupancy by making it more definite, strengthening it for the first fifteen years and weakening it thereafter. Other issues may be solved by extending the regulation by means of analogy to other cases. Once these analogies have been established, they also work

---

[1] Paton and Derham (1972: 189).

in the other direction and reconfirm the previous regulation with reference to the other cases. In the end, there emerges an 'organic' system of rights which cannot easily be decomposed into 'spontaneous' or 'natural' components on the one hand, and 'artificial' or 'positive' components on the other.

The clarity view thus offers a perspective for dealing with the perennial conflict between natural law and positive law in the following way. There are 'natural' elements in law, emerging from the laws of perception, association, categorization, and rule-making, that give rise to 'spontaneous' entitlements and customs. Hume's discussion of 'imagination', as underlying property formation, exemplifies this. Man takes these natural tendencies as the raw material of the law. By applying his reason, he is able to transform and reshape these rights. The elements introduced here are 'artificial' in some sense. They may be dictated by functional considerations or somewhat arbitrary conventions, but the extensive use of analogy ties together all kinds of regulations, mutually adjusting them, and reducing arbitrariness. This mutual adjustment integrates the 'natural' and the 'positive' elements and tends to produce coherence overall—possibly without being able ever to achieve such perfection. Yet the 'spontaneous' principles that govern custom cannot be arbitrarily overruled by positive law. The law cannot detach itself from its sources. The problems associated with transferring property rights discussed by Hume illustrate the point.[1] Cases of customary law persistently contradicting formal law provide other examples.[2] The limits of positive law-making are also highlighted by the problem of revenge in criminal law:

It may be said—and it *has* been said many times—that we should start purging the law entirely of the notion that its function is to make the guilty man 'pay' for his crime. This justification for the criminal law has been castigated as brutal and primitive, as an anachronistic survival . . .

But the first question that must be faced is, *Can* it be eliminated? If there were no punishment of criminals it is reasonable to suppose that many acts now penalized by the state would become objects of private

[1] See S. 11.8.   [2] See S. 2.11.

revenge. An unregulated private vengeance would invariably degenerate into a war of reprisals and counter-reprisals. Such a condition is by no means unknown in primitive societies. One of the ancient roots of the modern criminal law can be discerned when social control was first asserted over acts of private vengeance and they were made subject to a kind of tariff of permitted, but limited retributions.

There is the famous remark . . . to the effect that the criminal law bears to the instinct of revenge the same relation that the institution of marriage bears to the sexual instinct. Both regularize and control a deep impulse of human nature that if not given legitimate expression is bound to find disruptive outlets.[1]

Criminal law must therefore serve to create deterrence as well as to organize revenge. In a similar way, most laws serve several ends at once. They have to incorporate ethical principles, take care of functional requirements, and embody ideas about human behaviour. The object of the law is, therefore, to tie many diverse demands together in a systematic way, such that *elegantia iuris* is achieved. The rule of reason expresses itself in aligning functional, ethical, and systematic requirements.

12.5 *The Customs of Lawyers*

The formal law depends in an important way on custom. Lawmaking is strongly affected by the specific customs prevailing in the lawyers' community:

Every trade has its mysteries. Lawyers' sense consists of the rules and conventions that are taken for granted, which 'everyone knows'. The young lawyer starts to absorb them in his first year of study; he picks up more at lunch tables, legal conferences, general conversations over a drink—and naturally by sitting in court. Sometimes he learns by stern reminders from his senior colleagues.

The legal profession often has strong ideas on the substantive law. Judges may favour a precedent as having 'always been approved by the profession'. Of some proposed change it may be argued 'the profession is against it'. Sometimes the profession has been right in these matters—speaking sagely from long experience; at other times it has stolidly opposed the most valuable reforms . . .

[1] Fuller (1968: 27).

But, for good or ill, the sense of the craft is powerful. A chain of reasoning that is acceptable and accepted with a casual nod by an audience of trained lawyers will on occasion leave the ordinary man bewildered. It is not so much the way it is expressed as that the assumptions with which it begins and the consequences that follow from it are based upon special knowledge. In those critical situations, where the judge has to choose between valid competing principles, opposed rules, diverging analogies, he selects and combines his data with the expertise of many years of discussion, learning, knowledge of men and affairs to reach a decision that often only his fellow lawyers can appreciate. For his legal sense aids him in making a practical judgement. Admittedly, this requires making fine distinctions. But fine distinctions must be made in botany or mechanics or theology. The lawyer must not be afraid of them; though he must be prepared to justify them. To the question, 'Where to draw the line?', he must be able to say, 'Here, because . . .'[1]

If the reason supplied exhibits the clarity of *elegantia iuris*, it will be compelling.

As the law cannot be detached from law-making and the settling of disputes, it cannot be detached from the customs prevailing in the lawyers' community. Any full discussion of law must build on custom, if only for this reason.

12.6 *A Critique of Hayekian Evolutionism*

The nature of rules and rule obedience may be clarified by contrasting a widespread evolutionary view of the law and custom, as expounded by Hayek, with the clarity view. Hayek writes:

Man is as much a rule-following animal as a purpose-seeking animal. And he is successful not because he knows why he ought to observe the rules which he does observe, or is even capable of stating all these rules in words, but because his thinking and acting is governed by rules which have by a process of selection been evolved in the society in which he lives, and which are thus the product of the experience of generations.[2]

This quotation contains several interconnected assertions that are familiar but also partially wrong and severely distortive. Since the

---

[1] Derham *et al.* (1971: 176–77).   [2] Hayek (1973: 11).

clarity view bears some resemblance to the view embraced by Hayek, it is useful to highlight the points of disagreement in order to delineate the position defended here more sharply.

First, the functionalist bent in rule interpretation would require abandoning the concept of rule obedience altogether, since any rule that is inefficient in one instance can be superseded by another rule that is identical to the former one, but treats the particular case in a preferable way.[1] Such a process would substitute point-wise optimization for rule-guided behaviour. By leaving the concept of rules unspecified, and by neglecting the psychological exigencies that lead to rule formation in the first place, the argument cannot easily cope with inefficiencies.

Second, the Hayekian view shares the emphasis laid on human irrationality which is characteristic for contemporary thought. It is maintained that rules are obeyed because rule obedience has been successful. Any attempt to vindicate rules or to justify them by reason is explicitly denounced as 'constructivism' and 'rationalism'. The view has been aptly characterized as 'evolutionary agnosticism'.[2] This blind evolutionary view entirely neglects all aspects of insight, clarity, and coherence that are evidently pervasive characteristics of law-making. As a consequence, the Hayekian approach cannot deal successfully with issues of arbitration that must be adjudicated in the absence of definite rules but may nevertheless be accessible to reason. It is understandable that Hayek arrived at the conclusion that the case-by-case methods of common law are inconsistent with the ideal of the rule of law, and that 'social justice' is a meaningless expression.[3] While it is clearly possible to invent worlds where such statements are true, they are detached from human nature and social reality. In a way, Hayek seems to share with the socialists the view that human nature is an atavism that must be corrected.

By the same token, the Hayekian version of evolutionism

---

[1] In other words, the argument against act-utilitarianism put forward in S. 11.5 applies here, too.

[2] See Vanberg (1994), who tries to reconcile this with 'rational liberalism'.

[3] See Hayek (1955; 1976), Fuller (1981: 98–103).

excludes the typical way in which legal thought evolves. The use of analogy, similarity, and established standards of reasoning permits the law to evolve in response to new exigencies. This type of evolution has been stressed mainly by lawyers. It is quite remote from the trial-and-error process underlying Hayekian evolution. On occasion, such 'organic' evolution may be entirely dysfunctional. For instance, a law against wage discrimination may carry bad consequences for everyone on certain occasions. Yet such a law may be prompted by systematic reasons of an entirely legal nature, and it may require a deep readjustment of some parts of legal doctrine to remove the tension between functional and legal concerns in such cases.

12.7 *The Law and Behaviour*

A further question relates to the way in which the law affects behaviour. One way to approach the problem is to assume that human beings are pre-programmed rule-followers, who automatically obey all kinds of rules.[1] Such a view, stressed by some sociologists and evolutionists, cannot easily accommodate the observation that people are free to follow some rules rather than others. Nor can it account for the propensity to deviate by seeking new solutions to prevailing tensions between incompatible, competing prescriptions.[2] The 'automaton' view of human nature falls short of giving a sufficiently balanced account of rule preference and rule-following, as well as rule disobedience and innovation. It may also be criticized for neglecting aspects of overall coherence and clarity.

Although it is true that many laws are backed up by sanctions, everyday transactions are brought about by an interaction of entitlements and obligations, independently of sanctions.[3] The

---

[1] See Vanberg (1988: 151–2). Hayek (1973: 11;147–8) is not very clear about what he means when describing man as a 'rule-following animal', but seems to tend in this direction, too. The point made by Hodgson (1993: ch. 13) that 'real' choice excludes rule-following seems to be beside the point, as people may choose to follow rules because they prefer to do so.

[2] See S. 10.5 for an example.   [3] See Ch. 2.

law is able to affect action in a rather direct way. If a new law is passed that mandates the use of taximeters in taxi cabs, this will create entitlements on the side of the customers and corresponding obligations on the side of the taxi drivers. If it were merely customary to use taximeters, the result would be very similar. The law shapes explicit patterns that guide action, whereas custom merely provides implicit patterns. Yet the behavioural channels through which law and custom work are largely the same.

However, even if a law is enforced by means of sanctions, its enforcement must rely ultimately on custom, because the administration of sanctions depends critically on customary aspects of enforcement. As these sanctions are administered by the courts, the police, or the magistrate, their administration depends on the customs prevailing among the lawyers, police, or magistrates. The passing of a law must directly affect the behaviour of these enforcing agencies. It must shape perceptions of duty and entitlement in order to be of relevance for action. Law and custom are close siblings.

12.8 *The Law and Economics*

'It is hardly possible to discuss the functioning of a market without considering the nature of the property rights system, which determines what can be bought and sold and which, by influencing the costs of carrying out various kinds of market transactions, determines what is, in fact, bought and sold, and by whom.' So said the economist Ronald Coase.[1] Yet the dominant approach to the impact of the legal system on economic processes has largely confined itself to considering how the legal system provides economic incentives to behave in certain ways rather than in others. Behaviour is interpreted as being shaped exclusively by the interplay of preferences, sanctions, and rewards. A very simple (and crude) example of this type of 'economistic' reasoning is provided

---

[1] Coase (1977: 46).

by the economics of crime, where the 'supply' of criminal activity is seen as being brought about by the expected rewards of executing the offence successfully, the expected costs of being convicted, and the probability of conviction.[1] The view entails the further idea that the law is created by some law-making agency and is endowed with a system of sanctions, rewards, and remedies that ensure performance. This 'legal centralism' is obviously akin to legal positivism.[2]

As has been argued above, legal centralism is quite incompatible with important features of reality, in particular with the widespread use of non-enforceable contracts.[3] It neglects the informal (customary) ways of enforcement that rely on duties, obligations, and entitlements and on which a host of everyday market transactions depends. These cannot even be understood as being indirectly brought about by positive law, since important entitlements are stabilized that are *contrary* to the law.[4] Such instances appear rare, however, because the law tends to adapt in these cases.[5]

An economistic stance excludes from the outset the notion that people may actually attach importance to behaving rightly. But a person may go to court in order to test the validity of a claim he wishes to make. He may even be prepared to drop his claim if the judge, by a compelling argument, persuades him to the contrary. Just as the economistic view will not allow for any difference between legally and illegally acquired goods in terms of utility, it rules out any intrinsic demand for justice.

The clarity view, on the other hand, does allow for such a demand. As people act from principles, they are interested in the correctness of these principles and seek judgments in the courts in order to establish the validity of their reasoning. While the economistic view reduces the judge to a (rather expensive) random generator for delivering judgments and attaches no weight

[1] See e.g. Ehrlich (1973).
[2] See Ellickson (1991: 138–147) for a critical discussion of legal centralism.
[3] See S. 2.11 above and Witt (1986).   [4] Ellickson (1991: 110–120).
[5] See the example of traffic rules in S. 7.11.

to legal reasoning as such, the clarity view acknowledges that people have a demand for clarity which makes them interested in seeking judgments. They will be prepared to pay both for justice and for reasoning.

The economistic view holds that the sole reason for rule obedience derives from external incentives. It neglects the direct behavioural component which the law shares with custom. Thus, the economistic view would reduce the effect of private property to incentive aspects while neglecting 'ownership effects' and all kinds of psychological commitments that go with property.[1] Entitlements and obligations, which effectively stabilize ownership in informal ways, cannot be captured. The allocative effect of alternative property rights assignments is thereby reduced to practical unimportance. Whatever an initial property rights assignment might be, the economistic view would imply that all kinds of inefficiencies could be contracted away if it were worthwhile to do so. If the property rights were not sharply defined, and contracting possibilities were absent, there would then be strong incentives, in terms of mutual advantage, for everyone to define the rights and create the contracting possibilities. As a consequence, socialism ought to work as efficiently as capitalism, which is clearly not the case.[2] The economistic approach axiomatically rules out all behavioural aspects of ownership. This is unrealistic and conflicts with the truism that property rights must have behavioural implications in order to be of relevance for behaviour.

12.9 *The Law as an Integrating Force*

Custom provides the basis for the law. The law emanates from the same clarity requirements that shape custom. It transforms

---

[1] See S. 8.2 and 8.4.

[2] It is clear that the Soviet firm provided distorted incentives, and this induced severe inefficiencies (Furubotn and Richter 1997: S. 8.6). The question raised here concerns the rearrangement of property rights in order to avoid these inefficiencies. This must have been in the interest of everyone concerned, but it did not occur on a significant scale. See however Schlicht (1996) for a sceptical note on the 'Coase theorem', which underlies the argument about the rearrangement of property rights.

custom both by delimiting and sharpening customary entitlements and by creating new entitlements and obligations in response to functional or other (e.g. political) demands.

This transformation integrates three elements: the psychological requirements arising from contiguity, resemblance, and pattern perception; the requirements of systemic consistency, also ultimately rooted in psychology; and functional and other 'external' requirements.[1] As a consequence, the law typically serves many functions at once. In this sense, the purposes and reasons of the law are diffuse. In that it is again similar to custom.[2]

The formal law may be viewed as a kind of crystallized and systematized custom. The administration of law in the courts is brought about by the tacit knowledge, the routines, and the mysteries of the trade, as they have evolved among lawyers and judges. In this, the law is entirely a matter of custom.

---

[1] This contrasts with Eisenberg (1988: 43–50) who mentions the three 'standards for the common law': social congruence, systemic consistency, and doctrinal stability. The 'three elements' stressed here put the weights differently. Social congruence would be viewed as emerging from both psychological and external requirements, and doctrinal stability would be related to both psychological and functional requirements. This reflects the microanalytic view taken here which avoids starting from social norms as givens, instead trying to understand such norms as arising from individual entitlements; see S. 2.12.

[2] See S. 9.7, 10.3, and 10.8.

Chapter 13

THE FIRM

13.1 Islands of Custom

Anthropologists may travel from island to island and observe that each harbours people with a particular custom. It is not necessary to go that far away, however. In modern economies, each firm forms an island of custom in the ocean of the market. This chapter will explore the nature of the firm.

Firms are obviously of central importance for economic performance. It is hard to imagine a modern market economy with an extensive division of labour but no firms. It could be said that modern market economies rely on firms, and firms rely on the force of firm-specific customs.

In a sense, firms are creatures of the market. They have developed along with the rise of markets, evolving from organizational forms, such as the putting-out system, that were much closer to the market than modern firms. Their special structure—whether organized as capitalist firms, labour-managed firms, or partnerships—derives from market forces and competition. The growth and survival of firms in their various forms testifies to the competitive success of custom as a coordination device. This contrasts with the often-encountered view that customary arrangements are remnants of the past, to be eroded by modernization and competition.

This chapter relates the internal organization of firms to rule preference, custom, and clarity. The following three sections deal with some general observations relating to conceptual problems in institutional analysis. The subsequent sections turn to issues of internal organization and control.

It is argued that it is misleading to stress one single mode of control, such as authority or the administration of incentives, or one single feature, e.g. the suppression of internal markets, as the distinguishing mark of the firm. All these traits may be found associated with many firms, but no single trait suffices to identify a firm; any firm may lack one of these characteristics. Rather, a firm emerges if the various elements of control are tightly integrated and mutually adjusted to each other. It is the fit of the organizational elements, rather than the elements themselves, that characterizes a firm. Just as the quality of an orchestra performance cannot be adequately measured by the average quality of the performances achieved by the individual instruments, but depends crucially on the way the instruments are played together, so the productive value of a firm—as opposed to a set of individual contracting relationships—emerges from the quality that has been achieved through mutually adjusting the various activities that are carried on. It will be argued that integration is achieved by the same forces that shape custom. In a sense, the firm is characterized by a specific system of customs. This gives rise to its identity. The concern with 'corporate culture' and 'corporate identity' may be understood from this perspective.

13.2 *The Firm as an Institution*

The first question to be addressed is, however, of a more fundamental nature. It relates to the nature of social institutions. In which sense, it may be asked, can the firm be conceived as a social entity? Similar questions arise with regard to all kinds of social groups and institutions. The theory of the firm provides a stepping-stone for approaching these questions in a reasonably clear-cut way. The theory is to be seen in this double role. It is concerned with the nature of the firm as a question to be dealt with in its own right. The answers so obtained, however, are intended to serve as a foothold for approaching the wider issues concerning the nature of social institutions such as families, churches, government agencies and other associations. In this, the theory of the firm is social theory in a nutshell.

The theory of the firm deals with two theoretically separate issues at once. The first concerns *existence*: in which sense firms may be conceived as institutions that exert some influence on the individuals composing them, rather than merely reflecting their interests? The second concerns the *form* these institutions might take: how is the internal structure of the firm determined, and what modes of internal control and ownership exist? These questions, although theoretically different, will be addressed simultaneously.[1]

The discussion starts, counterfactually but in agreement with current economic theorizing, with the assumption that the term 'firm' is nothing more than a label for a set of contractual relations among individuals. The argument proceeds by discussing how such a set of contracts will give rise to a firm as a social institution that is not fully reducible to individual action but gains a life of its own. In other words, problems of form are discussed in order to answer the problem of existence. It will be argued that a stabilization of form gives rise to existence in much the same way, and in much the same manner, as a regularity gives rise to a custom.

13.3 *A Defence of Vagueness*

Before embarking on further discussion, the meaning of the term 'firm' needs to be clarified. The difficult problems involved here may lead to misunderstanding, or even to a total lack of comprehension. These difficulties are not specific to the theory of the

---

[1] A similar issue is addressed in App. C, where the problems *existence* and *form* of moral imperatives are distinguished (S. Ch. 5).

firm, but they are of particular importance here. They also relate very directly to what has been said before with regard to learning, categorization, and concept formation in the context of custom. This may be a good place to consider those issues.[1]

The first thing to keep in mind relates to the general way of thinking and forming notions. Thinking and perception take place in terms of categories and members of categories. In this sense, the term 'firm' stands for a category, like 'bird' or 'fruit'. These categories refer to entire classes of phenomena with vague demarcations; for example, there are many kinds of different birds— sparrows, eagles, emus, penguins—but none of them is in itself the equivalent of 'bird'. The term invokes the *schema* of a bird, i.e. a typical bird but with many features (e.g. colour) unspecified.[2] Such a schema refers not to an average case but rather to a particularly clear case. The schema of a 'triangle', for instance, relates to an equilateral triangle that is characterized by symmetry properties rather than by frequent occurrence. Other triangles are perceived as modifications of this clear case.

The category 'firm' has fuzzy boundaries. This is, again, similar to other categories. While it is clear that 'apple' is a fruit, such a categorization is less clear for 'pumpkin' or 'rhubarb'. Similarly, an independent and owner-directed factory, or a partnership of architects, is considered a firm, but demarcations become unclear with branch offices of franchise chains, conglomerates, or government agencies. This fuzziness of 'firm' has lead some authors to discard the term altogether, and go back to other notions. Yet this offers no escape, as it merely shifts the problem to these other notions. Fuzziness is common to *all* notions and categories that refer to real phenomena.

Only by employing concepts without any reference to real phenomena can fuzziness be avoided. The notion of 'contract', for example, has been widely used to substitute for the vague concept

---

[1] See Ch. 7. The position I am trying to develop is inspired by Asch (1952: Chs. 8 and 15). A recent philosophical attempt to deal with vagueness, going in a quite different direction, is T. Williamson (1994).

[2] See the discussion of schemata and categorization in Ch. 7. S. 7.9.

of a firm.[1] Firms are viewed as sets of contracting relationships; yet this substitutes for the vagueness of the term 'firm' the vagueness of the term 'contract'. 'Contract' refers, like 'firm', to a schema rather than to an empirical contract. The term is beset by the same fuzziness and vagueness that accompanies the notion of the firm. Empirical contracts range from explicit conditional promises to vague statements of intent. They may be implicit to the point of being indistinguishable from custom. In the end, exactitude in thinking may be lost rather than gained by such a substitution. In any case, there is no alternative to thinking in vague notions. Otherwise all abstract terms would have to be discarded. An antiseptic approach to social phenomena is not feasible. Theorists who insist on clear definitions do not appreciate this. John Maynard Keynes has pointed this out with regard to economics:

It is, I think, of the essential nature of economic exposition that it gives, not a complete statement, which, even if it were possible, would be prolix and complicated to the point of obscurity, but a sample statement, so to speak, out of all the things which could be said, intended to suggest to the reader the whole bundle of associated ideas, so that, if he catches the bundle, he will not in the least be confused or impeded by the technical incompleteness of the mere words which the author has written down, taken by themselves.[2]

Given the difficulty of the vagueness of categories, it may be tempting to seek that level of classification which permits defining the clearest notions, while discarding the more vague. This temptation should be resisted for two reasons. The first is that a set of vague notions, employed conjointly, may give a rather clear picture. The description 'white bird, swimming on a pond, with a long thin neck, and a flat orange bill' may come closer to describing a swan than any single one of the attributes and notions mentioned. The usual approach of denying the existence of a swan in view of the vagueness of the term, and of maintaining that it is just a bunch of feathers and proteins with a certain shape (long

---

[1] See S. 13.5.   [2] Keynes (1973: 470).

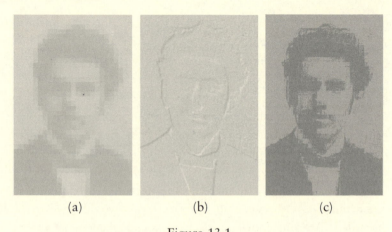

(a)   (b)   (c)

Figure 13.1
**Superimposing Two Vague Portraits (a) and (b) Yields an
Improved Portrait (c) of Max Wertheimer**

neck?), is also not very helpful. To restrict the description to the clearest terms involved in the characterization would amount to concentrating on the pond and the bill and discarding the rest. The terms 'bird', 'long', and 'thin' are very vague, yet these help considerably to clarify the picture. The context helps to sharpen their meaning.[1] The process going on here may be compared to the reconstruction of an extinct language from the clues contained in a set of related living languages. Such a reconstruction is unlikely ever to be perfect, but it is nevertheless possible to obtain some contours by combining many such clues. Even if each of them is vague, it contributes to the picture. It would therefore be foolish to neglect the information contained in it. Proto-Indo-European has been reconstructed in this way.[2] By superimposing two vague pictures, a somewhat improved (although still imperfect) picture may be obtained (Fig. 13.1). Vague notions thus may be fruitfully employed, notwithstanding their vagueness, and it would be wrong to discard them.

[1] Asch (1952: 429) summarizes a set of psychological findings related to the understanding of assertions as follows: 'The meaning of an assertion—its cognitive content—is determined by the role it has in its context.'
[2] Diamond (1991: 225–49).

Vagueness is not, however, a virtue. It is to be avoided as far as possible—but no further. Vague observations are of value only in so far as they contain *some* useful information; if they do not, however, they should be discarded. In this spirit, the notion of the firm, vague as it is, is maintained.

An explicit acknowledgement and defence of vagueness is needed because the modern stress on formal rigour has, as an unintended by-product, nearly suffocated the ability to think in vague terms in an exact manner. This implies a dissolution of important links linking theory to reality. Institutional analysis must rely—more than other branches of inquiry—on this supple way of thinking exactly.[1] Some people may be annoyed by this insight. Others may embrace the problems as intellectually more demanding than mechanical formalism. Whether welcomed or resented, the nexus has to be acknowledged as a datum, set by reality, and has to be spelled out accordingly.

13.4 *The Firm as a Social Entity*

A second reason for maintaining the notion of a firm is that the term is employed in the economic dealings of everyday life. In that, it is part of reality. People think in terms of firms, families, and churches. The theory of the firm ought to elucidate what is involved when talking about firms as they are commonly understood. It is of no great help simply to insist that 'firms' do not exist.

The negation of the existence of 'firms' as social entities may, for the purpose of economic theory, be seriously misleading. It may be said that firms exist because people think in these terms and base their action on this thinking. In so far as these notions influence behaviour, it would be absolutely wrong to deny the existence of the underlying notion. A theoretical position that

---

[1] The formal theorist tends not to grasp supple theorizing and concludes that it must be nonsense. This conclusion is wrong. Supple theorizing is actually quite demanding, and good supple theorizing is quite rare.

assumes firms away tacitly introduces the behavioural assumption that allegiance to a firm does not affect behaviour. From a psychological viewpoint, this seems to be highly improbable. All regularities of commitment, attribution, ownership, and rule preference point definitely and strongly to the opposite position. These effects cannot be ruled out in an axiomatic way, unless we 'wish to shut our eyes to realities and construct an edifice of pure crystal by imagination'—but then there are better fields for satisfying prodigious artistic ambitions.[1]

As a matter of terminology, the firm will be considered a social entity if a worker's self-perception of working for a firm, rather than working as an independent supplier, changes his behaviour, or if the owner's self-perception of owning the firm, rather than merely administering various contracts, influences his conduct. If neither is the case, 'the firm' is just a label. It will be argued below that firms are social entities in the sense that they *do* influence behaviour. Yet even if a different conclusion were reached, it would be unacceptable to assume away a possibly important aspect of institutional structure at the outset, merely on the grounds of an intellectual preference for schematization.

13.5 *The Nominalistic View of the Firm*

Consider first a view that negates explicitly any autonomy of the firm as a social institution. It takes the term 'firm' as being just a label, a shorthand expression for a collection of relations between individuals. This may be termed the *nominalistic* view of the firm.[2]

According to this view, a 'firm' emerges if some individuals form a team and contribute various inputs—their work, their capital, their skills—in ways and under conditions that are specified by a set of contracts. The 'firm' is conceived as a 'legal fiction

---

[1] Pirouette skating occurs to me in this context. The quotation paraphrases Marshall (1890: 644).

[2] For this view of the firm, see Alchian (1984). For individualism v. holism, see Asch (1952: ch. 9) and App. A (S. A.5–A.7). Alchian has changed his position, however; see Alchian (1991).

that serves as a nexus for contracting relationships'.[1] Such a 'firm' may take many forms, according to the conditions under which it operates. It may be run as a partnership among partners who enjoy equal control rights. If collectively exercised control proves too ineffective or too costly, however, it may be in the interest of the team members to organize control in a different manner.

Two cases are of particular interest. The first is where some team members obtain full control. This would occur if the exercise of control were more valuable to some team members than to others; they would thus acquire control from others who value it less.

There are several reasons why a centralization of control rights might be desired. An important one relates to 'specificity'.[2] An input is 'specific' for a certain use if the value of its productive contribution in that use exceeds the value it may generate in alternative uses. A machine that has been built for a particular use in a single firm is a specific input in this sense. Typically, the owners of inputs 'specific' to the firm will have a strong incentive to exercise control. Their inputs cannot readily be used elsewhere, and it will not be easy to withdraw them. This makes it possible for others to exploit them, *unless* the owners of firm-specific inputs themselves exercise control. Furthermore, investment in firm-specific inputs would not be made unless the investors were protected against future exploitation by holding the rights of control themselves. Therefore, in so far as firm-specific investment enhances the firm's performance, and no other means are available to protect the owners of firm-specific inputs against future exploitation, they will seek to gain control. Firms that are competitively

---

[1] Jensen and Meckling (1976: 310).

[2] See Alchian (1984) and O. E. Williamson (1985: 52–6) for recent statements. The specificity idea dates back at least to Marshall's (1890: 520) discussion of 'composite quasi-rents'. Modern reformulations include the distinction between specific and general training as introduced in the context of Becker's (1962) human capital theory; the discussion of 'idiosyncratic exchange' by O. E. Williamson *et al.* (1975); the discussion of the 'commitment problem' by Schlicht and von Weizsäcker (1977); the discussion of 'appropriable quasi-rents' by Klein, *et al.* (1978); and the discussion of transactional and psychological consequences of labour specificity in Schlicht (1979).

successful will end up with such a control structure. This will give rise to the picture of a firm that is commonly held.

From a nominalistic perspective, however, that picture is just fiction: 'As a result, the activities and operation of the team will be controlled and monitored by the firm-specific input owners, who gain or lose the most from the success and failure of the "firm". In fact, they are typically considered the "owners", or "employers", or "bosses" of the firm, though in reality the firm is a co-operating collection of resources owned by different people.'[1]

The second case is where the input owners may decide jointly to organize control. They may hire a director and hand some control rights over to him while retaining the right to control the director. This would require that the input owners all agreed permanently to restrict their own rights in order to enhance the performance of the 'firm'. This might involve long-term contracting and could introduce various rigidities. The 'firm' would still be no more than a set of individual contracts.

In reality, both ways of allocating control may be used in combination. Some input owners will exercise control rights jointly, while others will supply their inputs on a contractual basis. The 'owners' of the firm will bind themselves to the common project by long-term contracts in order to prevent individual input owners from breaking away or exploiting the investment of others.

Typically, the owners of fixed physical inputs—heavy specialized machinery, for instance—must be expected to exercise control. Fixed investments are specific to the production purpose, and it is costly to put them to different use. Yet firm-specific resources can also be human. Partnerships of lawyers, architects, or physicians are formed by members who make up a well-matched team. The team members are, as a result, less valuable elsewhere. This labour, specific to the firm, may use non-specific equipment, such as computers and buildings owned by others. The control rights must be expected to rest with the owners of the firm-specific

---

[1] Alchian (1987: 1032), misprint corrected. (The original reads '. . ."bosses" on . . .')

know-how, i.e. with labour, rather than with owners of equipment and buildings.[1]

The overall argument closely resembles the property rights argument described earlier.[2] Control rights, just like property rights, tend to be allocated in the most efficient manner, where 'efficiency' is defined by market success. This explains 'institutional' structure.

13.6 *Three Modes of Control*

The above account of the nature of the firm, given from a property rights perspective, rests critically on the way in which 'control rights' are allocated. In order to understand what is involved here, a close examination of the possibilities of controlling economic activity is appropriate.

Consider a worker who is required to perform a certain task. Regarding his motivation, several possibilities come to mind:

- *Exchange*: The worker is motivated by a reward attached to the performance of the task.
- *Command*: The worker has been ordered to perform the task, and he obeys the order.
- *Custom*: The worker performs because he thinks that it is his duty to do so; i.e. performing the task is part of his job.

'Control' may be exerted by each of these three modes of coordination: the performance may be brought about by offering a reward, by issuing a command, or by creating a set of customs and duties that induce the worker to perform the task spontaneously.

The three modes of control are not, of course, confined to firms. The distinction originated in economic anthropology, where it has

---

[1] Critics of the specificity view point to the possibility of safeguarding specific investments by means of long-term contracting (Demsetz 1988: ch. 9; Coase 1991: 69–74). I neglect this important and valid thought here for expositional reasons. A possible response is given in the next chapter. The overall conclusion given in the text is not, however, affected by this criticism.   [2] See S. 11.15.

been introduced for typifying modes of social organization.[1] Yet each of these control modes can be taken as a starting point for the theory of the firm. It is interesting to note that the same problems that are encountered on the level of the firm emerge also on the social level.

The three control modes give rise to three approaches to the theory of the firm. These will be discussed in the following sections. Subsequently it will be argued that each of the approaches stresses important features of firm organization, while the firm as a social institution emerges from a mutual adjustment and interaction of the control modes.

13.7 *Exchange: The Firm as a Specialized Market*

Some economists tend to deny the differences between the three control modes mentioned above. They see human motivation as being controlled exclusively by incentives. This view assimilates all action to exchange. Situational determinants of behaviour are neglected. The view is well illustrated by the following quotation:

It is common to see the firm characterized by the power to settle issues by fiat, by authority, or by disciplinary action superior to that available in the conventional market. This is delusion. The firm does not own all its inputs. It has no power of fiat, no authority, no disciplinary action any different in the slightest degree from ordinary market contracting between any two people. I can 'punish' you only by withholding future business or by seeking redress in the courts for any failure to honor our exchange agreement. That is exactly what any employer can do. He can fire or sue, just as I can fire my grocer by stopping purchases from him or sue him for delivering faulty products. What then is the content or the presumed power to manage and assign workers to various tasks? Exactly the same as one little consumer's power to manage and assign his grocer to various tasks. The single consumer can assign his grocer to the task of obtaining whatever the customer can induce the grocer to provide at a

---

[1] This draws on concepts developed in economic anthropology, adapted for our purposes. K. Polanyi *et al.*(1957: 250; see also K. Polanyi 1977: ch. 3) distinguishes between 'exchange', 'redistribution', and 'reciprocity'; and Heilbroner (1972: 21–8) uses 'market', 'command', and 'tradition'.

price acceptable to both parties. That is precisely all that an employer can do to an employee. To speak of managing, directing, or assigning workers to various tasks is a deceptive way of noting that the employer continually is involved in renegotiation of contracts on terms that must be acceptable to both parties. Telling an employee to type this letter rather than to file that document is like telling my grocer to sell me this brand of tuna rather than that brand of bread.[1]

The view expressed here fits nicely with the nominalist view of the firm. A firm is seen as a collection of individuals. These individuals are motivated by preferences, sanctions, and rewards. Their preferences remain unaffected by their joining a firm. In this sense, the label 'firm' has no real implications. Furthermore, authority and power are reduced to the possibility of offering rewards and administering sanctions. Commitment, loyalty, or obedience are disregarded as factors that may influence behaviour.

As a consequence, all actions are brought about by implicit or explicit bargains between the parties involved. If one party fulfils his contractual obligation by following an order or fulfilling his duty, he is doing so because he is avoiding the sanctions attached to disobedience. The moral element involved in disregarding a commitment is neglected. Those who exert control are essentially price-makers. They fix prices so as to reward certain desired activities and to punish undesired behaviour. By setting the right schedules, they coordinate economic activity. This requires them to supervise and monitor in order appropriately to administer the system of sanctions and rewards. In this sense, the firm may be viewed as a specialized market.[2]

From this point of view, the 'firm' is just a name tag for a set of specialized markets. The same type of coordination could be obtained among independent factory owners. Such a 'firm' may, for instance, be conceived as merely a controlling agency, with all the remaining input owners as independent suppliers. This would be a picture of the putting-out system rather than of a modern

---

[1] Alchian and Demsetz (1972: 119–20). Both authors have changed their views in the meanwhile, however; see Alchian (1991) and Demsetz (1988: ch. 9).

[2] The haggling envisaged by Alchian and Demsetz (1972: 119–20) would turn the market into a kind of bazaar.

enterprise.[1] A consistent defence of the thesis that the firm is a matrix of contracts can be expressed in a somewhat more positive way:

An implication of interpreting the firm as a nexus of contracts is that the 'firm' loses some analytical significance as attention is focused more on competition among individuals, their particular resources and on types of contractual relationships. Thinking of firms as the fundamental actors conceals *intra*-firm competition. . . . How much difference does it make when people compete within an existing firm rather than via new, small companies? . . . Entry of 'new firms' can be achieved by people moving from one firm to another, bringing resources and ideas either as an employee or as some other owner . . . Every entry or departure changes the firm. It is *not* silly to consider the entry of a new stockholder to be the creation of a new firm.[2]

Thus, it seems that this exchange view of the firm may contribute to an understanding of contractual relationships of various sorts, but that the firm itself thereby disappears as an entity. This is not surprising, since this was the assumption the argument started from.

13.8 *Command: The Firm as an Island of Authority*

Another view of the firm is obtained by allowing for command as a mode of control, as distinct from exchange. This is the position taken by Coase in his classic article on the nature of the firm.[3]

If a workman moves from department Y to department X, he does not go because of a change in relative prices, but because he is ordered to do so . . . Outside the firm, price movements direct production, which is coordinated through a series of exchange transactions on the market. Within a firm, these market transactions are eliminated and in place of the complicated market structure with exchange transactions is substituted the entrepreneur–coordinator, who directs production . . . we find

---

[1] Nutzinger (1978).　　[2] Alchian (1984: 46–7).
[3] Coase (1937). The view is also shared by other authors, e.g. Marx (1873: ch.13, s. 4), Simon (1951), and O. E. Williamson (1975).

'islands of conscious power in this ocean of unconscious cooperation like lumps of butter coagulating in a pail of butter-milk.'[1]

Although the price mechanism may sometimes be used to coordinate transactions, coordination within the firm is 'normally carried out without the intervention of the price mechanism'. The supersession of the price mechanism by command is, according to this view, the distinguishing mark of the firm.[2]

This view presupposes a difference between market and command. It is not unrealistic to do so. The Milgram experiments have established quite clearly the power of command as distinct from that of exchange.[3] The force of command relies on commitment. The worker has entered an employment contract and has committed himself to obey orders within limits, and under the conditions specified in the employment contract. The scope of command thus defines the boundaries of the firm.

The reason for the existence of firms, given this point of view, is the efficiency that can be achieved by using command rather than the market for purposes of coordination. One reason could be that theoretically people *prefer* coordination by command over coordination by exchange. Coase rules that out, 'for it would rather seem that the opposite tendency is operating if one judges from the stress normally laid on the advantage of "being one's own master".'[4] Thus, there must be efficiency advantages to be had from replacing the price system by a command system. Coase is here thinking mainly in terms of the costs involved in using the price mechanism relative to using command. Those transactions that can be cheaper when coordinated by command are organized within a firm; the other transactions are left to the market. The scope of command—and therefore firm size—may grow in response to changes that ease command; or it may shrink, if market transactions become easier to conduct. The role of the

---

[1] Coase (1937: 35). Coase takes the citation from Robertson (1928: 85) and remarks that the term 'entrepreneur' refers to 'the person or persons who, in a competitive system, take place of the price mechanism in the direction of resources', i.e. to management.
[2] Coase (1937: 36).   [3] See S. 8.3.   [4] Coase (1937: 38).

entrepreneur would be to coordinate activity in the most effective manner by issuing the right commands.

The workings of command may also be conceived in terms of entitlements and obligations. The employment contract establishes entitlements for the employer to have his orders obeyed within the specified limits; at the same time, it creates entitlements for the worker to obtain his remuneration. These entitlements go along with corresponding obligations of the other party. Seen in this manner, the employment contract establishes entitlements and obligations in various ways. One bundle of rights and obligations is exchanged for another. There is, however, no discernible equivalence of giving and taking in single acts, orders, or gratifications.

The exchange view of the firm would interpret command as just a special case of exchange. It is maintained that the firm 'has no power of fiat, no authority, no disciplinary action any different in the slightest degree from ordinary market contracting between any two people'.[1] This entails a behavioural assumption that appears arbitrary. The exchange explanation of the firm must assume that contracting is possible and that promises are kept with some probability. This is what the command view must presuppose.

13.9 Custom: The Firm as a Team

The command view of the firm has, however, some shortcomings. There are partnerships that cannot that easily be characterized in terms of command structures, yet they are firms. Furthermore, even in hierarchical firms the workers are not required primarily to obey commands. Rather, they are required to fulfil their duty and to do what their job requires. The term 'job' refers to the set of responsibilities and duties given to the worker who holds this job. The term would be quite meaningless without this background. The duties of the job might require the worker to react in a certain way to certain information. If the sales department provides the notifications that more production is needed, this is not a com-

---

[1] Alchian and Demsetz (1972: 119). See also the discussion in S. 13.7.

mand in the usual sense of the word: what it is is a piece of information that serves to coordinate various economic activities in accordance with a shared understanding of roles and responsibilities. If the foreman orders a worker to move from department Y to department X, this may appear as a command. The worker may react, however, by informing the foreman that additional help is needed: the foreman may respond positively, but the worker still will not have given a command to the foreman.

Under this view, the firm may be perceived as a system of interlocking social roles, embodied in job descriptions.[1] The role of the entrepreneur would be to influence these roles and responsibilities, introduce new roles, and shape role descriptions such that new exigencies can be met.

This view would thus see firms as systems of interconnected jobs. In this, a firm is very similar to a small tribe with its own particular culture. The recent discussion about 'corporate culture' has stressed this aspect.

13.10 *The Three Control Modes Considered Separately*

The various views of the firm expounded above have stressed different aspects of the way in which firms are organized. Exchange, command, and custom may be used to coordinate economic activity within a firm. Yet none of these views explains the existence of firms convincingly, as each of the mechanisms may be employed for solving coordination problems without necessitating an integration within a 'firm'.

Consider the exchange view, which relates the existence of the firm to asset specificity. The owners of specific resources will acquire control of the entire set of contracts in order to protect their specific investment. The standard argument against this view is that there are many other ways to protect specific investments, and that integration of ownership is only one of them. There is no reason to suppose that these problems cannot be dealt with by

---

[1] This view is due to Leibenstein (1960: 119–54).

suitable contracts.[1] In many cases, such contracts have actually been employed.

Regarding command, monitoring tasks and coordination problems do not necessitate integration. These problems can equally well be dealt with on a contractual base, quite independently of ownership. The team of architects or engineers in charge of supervising a construction site is usually not the 'owner' of the 'firm' that completes the construction. So comprehensive a firm is often not needed and does not exist. Command can be provided on a contractual base in the market without necessitating the establishment of a firm.

Regarding custom, long-term business relationships build very strongly on mutual responsibilities, mutually perceived entitlements, and obligations. These long-term contractual relationships tend to be largely routinized. They tend to be based on a shared history and a shared understanding that are functionally similar to job assignments at the firm level.

Each of the control modes can be used inside and outside a firm in various combinations. As a consequence, all productivity gains that can be obtained by employing these control modes can be realized without actually creating a firm. If a firm permits even better performance, the productivity gain cannot be attributed to the advantages offered by the control modes alone. To explain the existence of firms in a market economy, it must be assumed, in Alchian's words, that the establishment of a firm eases, in some 'mysterious' way, the task of coordination.[2]

13.11 *Jobs, Routines, and Custom*

In a firm, the control mechanisms discussed above are typically used conjointly. Market elements such as piece rates and incentive

---

[1] 'Asset specificity may be almost as easy to solve through contract as through vertical integration.' (Demsetz 1988: 152). 'I am very doubtful whether there is such a systematic relationship as that described . . . I came away with the clear impression that firms were able to resolve the problems inherent in long-term contracting, problems which seem to economists so intractable, without having to resort to vertical integration.' (Coase 1991: 68, 70).   [2] Alchian (1991: 233).

payments are encountered; so is authority resting with management and job assignments relying on custom and duty. The entire
system is sustained by habit and routine as well as by firm-specific
convictions and justifications.

Consider a 'job'.[1] It is defined in terms of a set of routines. A
routine involves how the worker is supposed to act and to respond
to various signals received from his environment. Each worker has
to 'know his job', but there is no need to know what other workers
are doing. Each worker has to understand, however, the particular
language and symbols used in the firm. The crane operator has to
understand the hand signal for 'a bit further down', and the
welder has to know how to interpret the scans provided by the
engineering department. These routines often work tacitly and
automatically, very similar to those involved in driving a car.

The prevailing set of routines embodies the firm's operational
knowledge. As the routines are largely automatic, the knowledge
embodied in them is mainly tacit and widely dispersed. Everyone
has to know how to do 'his job', but he will not, and need not,
know very much more. No one will be able to grasp fully the way
in which the firm operates as a whole.

The view of the firm as a team, coordinated by a set of job
descriptions and associated duties, and the view stressing routinization and habits are strongly intertwined. The first view emphasizes intentional motives, the second habit. Both work conjointly.
Intentional behaviour becomes habitualized, but may reappear in
consciousness. The relevant encoding and decoding processes have
been discussed before with regard to custom;[2] they appear here
again. The duties and routines that are attached to a job may be
envisaged in this light as a set of specialized customs. From this
point of view, all that has been said in the preceding chapters
about custom may be transferred directly to the theory of the firm.

The stress on customary aspects is characteristic of evolutionary
approaches to the theory of the firm. Many features that have been
discussed with regard to custom appear here. The problems of

---

[1] The following draws on Nelson and Winter (1982: ch. 5).   [2] See S. 1.6.

stabilization are similar, since the fuzziness problem appears here in an easily recognizable way:

Nominally, the workday in a particular organization may run from 9:00 to 5:00, but it may be the case (routinely) that very little activity that is productive from the organization's point of view gets done before 9:30 or after 4:45. . . . The priority system used by a particular member in allocating effort among tasks may make use, routinely, of the information contained in the overtones of panic or fury in the incoming messages. In short, routine operation is consistent with routinely occurring laxity, slippage, rule-breaking, defiance, and even sabotage. . . . Except for tasks involving very low levels of skill, performed under conditions favourable to close observation by a single supervisor, it is not practical to monitor and control behaviour so closely that only organizationally appropriate behaviours are permitted.[1]

This fuzziness poses the threat of erosion. Erosion can be checked in part by supervision. Certain workers may have the job of supervising others, and they will develop routines for doing so. Yet the problem of fuzziness is pronounced and cannot be coped with easily. Working 'strictly to rule' is a very severe threat to the firm's performance. It is occasionally used as an effective weapon in labour disputes. In a similar way, workers who insist on a tight reading of their 'job descriptions' while refusing to perform all other tasks will be detrimental to productivity. On the other hand, the supervisors may misuse their power. As much of what they are doing relates to their good judgement, there is no easy way of inducing them to perform in the firm's interest. Employment contracts will not specify clearly what each member is supposed to do. In so far as tacit knowledge is involved, this too will be impossible to spell out in detail.

The actual operation of the firm will in the end be stabilized by custom. Nelson and Winter describe this as a 'truce' between the members of the organization:

There is a truce between the supervisor and those supervised at every level of hierarchy. . . Like truce among nations, the truce among organization members tends to give rise to a particular symbolic culture

---

[1] Nelson and Winter (1982: 108–9).

shared by the parties. A renewal of overt hostilities would be costly and would also involve a sharp rise in uncertainty about the future positions of the parties. Accordingly, the state of truce is ordinarily considered valuable, and a breach of its terms is not undertaken lightly. But the terms of a truce can never be fully explicit . . . The terms become increasingly defined by a shared tradition, actions by individual members have connotations related to the truce. In particular, a contemplated action otherwise sensible both for the organization and for the member taking it may have to be rejected if it is likely to be interpreted as 'provocative'— that is, as signalling a lessened commitment to the preservation of the truce . . . On the defensive side, each member strives to protect his interests by standing prepared to deliver a firm rebuff not only to actions by others that clearly threaten his interests, but also to actions that might be quite innocuous were it not for their possible interpretation as probes of his alertness or determination to defend his rights under a truce.[1]

The analogy to territorial behaviour with animals is striking.[2] The 'truce' depends on perceived entitlements and obligations. Stabilization of the truce requires the prevailing rules prescribing these entitlements and obligations to be acknowledged. This follows the general pattern by which custom creates entitlements and obligations that render market transactions possible.[3]

13.12 *Chemical Interaction*

It is typical for firms internally to coordinate activity by combining elements of exchange, command, and custom. The result of this combination is, however, quite different from what could be expected by merely superimposing the effects that could be expected from using the elements alone. The close alignment of different control elements encountered in firms produces metamorphoses in each of them. In Mill's terminology, the control modes interact not 'additively', but 'chemically'.[4] The result obtained by combining them gives something different from a mere superposition of the single effects obtainable by using

---

[1] Nelson and Winter (1982: 110–11).   [2] See S. 11.13.
[3] See S. 2.6.   [4] See Mill (1925: 289), and S. A.2 below.

them separately. The web of interlocking reinforcements, characteristic of custom, works on the firm level, too.

The effect derives directly from the clarity principles governing human attitudes and motivation. Overall clarity creates overall interdependence. Consider the process of self-attribution. Individuals act from motives. They also infer their motives from their actions. The self-attribution of motives focuses on the clearest aspects and discounts other possible reasons. If there are several reasons for doing something, this creates 'overjustification'; one possible motive will be selected, and all others will be discounted.[1] Thus, human motivation creates a lumpiness with regard to control processes. Monetary incentives and duty cannot be combined smoothly. One motive ousts the other. As some psychologists say, motivation works in a 'hydraulic' rather than an 'additive' fashion.[2]

A piece rate may change such motivation by destroying the sense of duty. This may affect performance adversely. Insufficient performance may now easily be attributed to an insufficient piece rate rather than to any neglect of duty. This attribution would be impossible without a piece rate.[3] The conspicuous absence of piece rates in cases where observation of output is costless may serve the purpose of maintaining intrinsic motivation.

Similarly, the effectiveness of command rests on authority rather than side-payments. If the subjects in the Milgram experiments had been offered the choice of leaving the experiment in exchange for returning the few dollars they had received for participation, many presumably would have left.[4]

---

[1] See S. 9.3.   [2] Amabile (1983).

[3] The study of blood donations by Titmuss (1970) illustrates the mechanism in another field on a large scale. Many persons donate blood voluntarily, but cease to do so if a commercialized system is introduced whereby donors receive money for their donation. From the point of view developed here, the underlying reasoning is simple. Without a blood market, the individual donor will donate out of moral obligation ('If nobody donates, there would be no blood to help the injured'). With a market, this argument loses force, because the price mechanism now provides another means to secure blood supply ('If there is insufficient blood supply, the price must be raised'). Without a market, blood donations appear indispensable. The introduction of a blood market creates an improved possibility for obtaining blood and thereby destroys the moral obligation to make donations. Duty is substituted by money in a lumpy way.

[4] See S. 8.3.

Authority may also undermine custom and the sense of duty, very much in the same way as prices can do. If somebody is ordered to do something, the reason for doing it is to obey the order; the other reason—of performing the task out of duty—would provide overjustification and will be discounted.

These remarks illustrate that control mechanisms cannot be combined freely. If they are used conjointly—some authority, some monetary rewards, some work ethic—the joint effect will not be the sum of the three partial effects. The interaction is, in Mill's terminology, 'chemical' rather than additive.[1] The following sections elaborate this point.

13.13 *Piece Rates*

Consider piece rates. A system of optimally designed piece rates, as prescribed by economic theory, would not necessitate any kind of time measurement. The firm simply would have set prices that reflect the value of the additional piece to the firm. Standard economic theory suggests that this would make it worthwhile for the worker to exert himself up to the point where the additional costs are just covered by the additional value created. This would usually result in very high piece rates, but the firm could recover more than these expenses by reducing the base salary accordingly.

Such contracts are certainly very uncommon, if they exist at all.[2] Even the employees of car dealers and estate agents are clearly

---

[1] Mill(1925: 289); see also S. A.2 below.

[2] Two justifications are usually given to accommodate this observation. One relates to risk, the other to a balanced budget condition. Both are misleading in the sense that they do not apply for the bulk of work performed under piece-rate conditions. The risk argument, developed in Stiglitz (1975), posits that performance depends on effort and chance. If pay is tied to performance, the resulting income stream will be subject to random influences, and risk-averse workers will prefer a contract that entails some insurance. This implies a lower piece rate than the optimal one characterized in the text. However, workers receive not daily wages, but weekly or monthly wages. Such wages will average out most of the volatility arising from chance. In any case, smoothing may be achieved without spoiling incentives by distributing premia across several time periods. If risk aversion were strong, we should observe such reward spreading rather than an attenuation of incentives. The other argument goes in terms of balanced

and systematically rewarded much below the 'optimal' rate.[1] In reality, piece rates are determined in an elaborate manner, typically employing methods of time measurement to determine the amount of labour necessary for performing a certain operation. The practitioner's rationalization of these time measurements is that they serve to determine 'fair' piece rates. There is no reason to assume that this perception is wrong. The use of time measurement studies actually confirms the practitioner's interpretation, as firms feel no obligation to determine the labour content of other inputs they might purchase in the market. There is also no presumption to the effect that time studies measure productive contributions. Straightforward efficiency considerations would require speedier work if more expensive machinery is used. Additional incentives to achieve that end would also be suitable. Such considerations are entirely disregarded when determining 'work points'.

The use of time measurement rather than efficiency-related criteria for determining piece rates reconfirms the practitioners' view of piece rates as 'equitable rewards' for performing certain tasks. Textbooks on compensation policies stress the desideratum of 'internal consistency' in a firm's compensation policy. They mention the role of controlling the allocation of labour and of providing adequate incentives only as a goal of secondary importance.[2] This further confirms the interpretation of piece rates, rather than internal market prices, as just rewards. The conventions about time measurement and the corresponding practices and techniques contribute in turn to a matrix of firm-specific custom. One of their most important features is that they are

budgets. If several workers work together in a non-separable way and incentives are set in an optimal way, each of them will obtain the value of the entire team output minus a constant. This will usually conflict with the objective of a balanced budget. (Holmstrom 1982 has introduced this problem as a rationale for the existence of a firm.) Yet this poses not such a severe problem as is usually assumed. Each of several teams could be rewarded according to its own performance *minus* the average of the other team's performance. With similar teams, this would allow for an approximate balancing of the budget.

[1] Frank (1984) has established this empirically.
[2] See e.g. Milkovich and Newman (1984: 31).

clear. Lack of clarity will induce conflict. Piece rates operate like
social norms in society as a whole. They create entitlements and
obligations. Piece rates build on these standards. Rather than
rewarding individual tasks individually according to strain and
productive contribution, they reward general performance as measured according to custom.

Piece rates undoubtedly serve an important incentive function.
This, however, is achieved in an indirect way, through several
channels.[1] By attaching higher pay to 'work points', the worker's
attitude will change in favour of improved performance. This is
the direct first-round effect. Everybody will work a little harder.
This induces an indirect second-round effect. As the average performance standard increases, conformity induces each worker to
follow the change in average performance. In this way, the first-
round effect generates a second-round effect, and the process feeds
on itself. Any initial stimulus to increase performance will thus be
augmented by a 'social multiplier' that is generated by conformity.
The indirect effects may be much larger than the first-round
stimulus. This will hold particularly if conformity is strong.

Piece rates must be thus understood as working quite differently
from ordinary prices. They do not serve to coordinate action or to
clear some internal markets. Their *raison d'être* is to shape and
sustain routines. The integration of piece rates into firm-specific
custom transforms them from market prices to instruments maintaining morale. Integration changes their nature in a 'chemical'
manner.

13.14 *Hierarchy*

The same may be said with regard to hierarchy. Yet hierarchies
have very strong customary elements. This makes it more difficult
to spot 'chemical' interaction with custom. It is ubiquitous.

---

[1] The subsequent remarks draw on Schlicht (1981). They are not intended to be
exhaustive; their purpose is rather to illustrate some implications of the clarity view for
the theory of compensation and to indicate that 'additive' approaches, such as Vroom's
(1964) 'expectancy theory', seem misleading.

It is obvious that legitimate command must be rule-bound. Even if a supervisor or the owner of a firm is legally entitled to select freely from a set of options and to give orders accordingly, he has to do this in a consistent way; if he reacts, without any apparent reason, in a different manner to a similar problem, he will appear incompetent. This will undermine his authority. His authority presupposes that he is better informed than those who have to obey him. Evidence contradicting this presumption weakens morale. Commands that work in this manner are dysfunctional. Similarly, commands that contradict established routine without any apparent reason will undermine the customary base of inter-action within the firm. Each command that is issued in response to a new problem creates a precedent and generates entitlements that hinge upon the expectation that the precedent will be a guide to future action. In this sense, command serves to establish routines, entitlements, and obligations, rather than to control action directly.

The use of precedents has efficiency advantages in that it suffices to give an order only once. Such an order establishes the duty for the worker subsequently to deal with similar cases in the same manner, and to ask the supervisor for further instructions only if new circumstances arise. This obviously economizes on resources. It raises the problem that the supervisor may lose touch with what happens on the shop floor; the customs that he may have initiated by issuing an order may develop a life of their own without his knowledge.

Controlling a firm by command is thus quite different from controlling a computer by keying in some commands. The com-puter will not care about consistency, and will not check whether the style of the command conforms to the established routines. The machine will not, at the present stage of technology, tacitly revise its internal routines in order to conform to the style of the new command. It will not automatically erase routines that are no longer in use or that produce inconsistencies. A firm, on the other hand, *will* respond in this manner. It will do so because it will be driven by clarification processes in the minds of its employees. Just as custom works towards overall clarity in society, so the firm-specific customs may be viewed as integrating new elements in an all-encompassing schema. The psychological 'rubber-bands' of analogies, style, and coherence create a set of interlocking customs. In this way, the underlying clarification processes integrate the various elements that contribute to the functioning of the firm. They provide the source for 'chemical' interaction. This chemical integration is the basis of a firm's productivity advantages. It entails the uniqueness, or 'corporate identity', that is encountered in successful firms. 'All happy families', it has been said, 'are more or less dissimilar; all unhappy families are more or less alike.'[1] This applies to firms too, and for similar reasons.

13.15 Ownership: Instrumentalist Aspects

Current economic theories of ownership stress instrumental considerations centring around the question, 'Which ownership structure gives the best performance?' Such instrumentalism rules out any direct behavioural implications resulting from integration, and all constraints that arise from integration. They are, in this sense, nominalistic.[2]

Some arguments follow the spirit of the 'firm as a market' approach and relate closely to the specificity argument.[3] One of them stresses efficiency considerations with regard to investment decisions. An investment is profitable if the returns exceed the costs. If the returns from an investment go in part not to the investor, but to other firm members, this will dilute investment incentives. Some useful projects will not be undertaken because the private returns do not cover the investment outlays. If other contractual means are not sufficient to protect the returns,

---

[1] Nabokov (1969: 3).

[2] On the nominalistic conception of the firm, see S. 13.5. The juxtaposition of 'the firm as a commodity' and 'the firm as an association' proposed by Putterman (1988) touches important issues that are closely related to (and go in several ways beyond) the contrast of instrumental and psychological aspects of ownership discussed in this and the following section.   [3] See S. 13.7.

ownership—in the sense of a right to receive the full return—may solve the problem.[1] The specificity argument described earlier belongs to this group.

Another line of argument stresses the 'horizon problem'.[2] The reasoning may be explained by contrasting firm ownership by the owners of capital with firm ownership by the workers. If firm ownership is tied to capital, the capital owners will have an incentive to enhance the long-term prospects of the firm, even if they expect to sell their ownership rights in the near future. The price that they obtain will reflect the long-term prospects, and the capital market will align short-run and long-run aspects of performance. This argument would explain the prevalence of capitalist firms and the relative unimportance of labour-managed firms in market economies.

There is a similar solution to the horizon problem for labour-managed firms. It has been proposed as a theoretical possibility, and even as a practical solution.[3] The shortcomings of that solution illustrate nicely a fundamental problem in the marketing of labour. This difficulty contributes to an understanding of the firm's organization as emerging from the non-marketability of certain inputs. Theoretically, each worker in a labour-managed firm may be the 'owner' of his job. If he leaves his job, he may 'sell' it to another worker. This solves the horizon problem, since such an arrangement will make each worker interested in the long-term value of his job. Even if he intends to the leave the firm in the near future, he will be interested in getting a high price for his job. This will make him interested in long-term prospects even if he himself has a rather short horizon. The solution is analogous to the one obtained in the capital market where the individual inves-

---

[1] The mechanism invoked here is largely mysterious, because nothing observable or tangible is changed by shuffling nominal titles defining property. More involved applications of the same idea deal with joint investment, which results in joint ownership, again in a largely mysterious way. Hart and Moore (1990) assume for instance that the assignment of property rights influences bargaining. (The mystery is enshrined in Shapley-values lacking any rational or behavioural justification.)

[2] Pejovich (1973), Furubotn (1974; 1976).

[3] Schlicht and von Weizsäcker (1977), Fehr (1993a; 1993b).

tor is interested in the long-term profitability of the firm even if he plans to sell his share immediately.

The solution of tradable job rights is, however, excluded because it is not possible to standardize labour in a team context.[1] To make the point simple, consider the case where there are only three different types of worker: inferior, average, and good. An inferior worker has an outside option—another possibility to earn money—of 1, an average worker has an outside option of 2, and a good worker has an outside option of 3. Consider a team of four workers and assume that the team product is precisely the sum of the individual productivities given by the outside options. Initially, the team is composed of four average workers. Team output is 8, and output per head is 2. One team member considers selling his job. If he sells it to a poor worker, team output will drop to 7, and average output will drop to 1.75. If he sells the job to an average worker, team output will remain at 8, and per capita output will remain 2. If he sells his job to a good worker, team output will increase to 9, and per capita output will increase to 2.25. Thus, a good worker will not enter the firm, because his outside option of 3 exceeds the 2.25 that he can expect in the firm, but a poor worker would be happy to join since his outside option of 1 falls short of 1.75 obtainable in the firm. So the team member may obtain the best price from selling his job to a poor worker, and the worst price (actually a negative price of 0.75 in the example) to a good worker. The remaining team members would prefer that the job is sold to a good, rather than a poor, worker. So there is a conflict of interest that cannot be resolved easily, because the quality of the workers cannot be judged outside of the team context. If the team had a veto power by setting quality standards, this would destroy the transferability of job rights; if each worker were free to choose his replacement, the team would deteriorate in quality. Moreover, each worker may threaten to work poorly in order to force the team to agree to his selling his job to a sub-standard worker.[2]

[1] Schlicht and von Weizsäcker (1977).
[2] In other words, labour is a 'plastic' resource, and that generates market problems; see Alchian and Woodward (1987: 115–17).

Owing to a lack of standardization of labour in a team context, there cannot be a market for job rights. This would explain why labour-centred ownership structures are not prevalent in market economies. The result would be the same even if they were, in some sense, economically more efficient than capitalist ownership structures.[1]

The importance of the horizon problem is, of course, reduced if labour ceases to be mobile. In this case the members of the firm will be tied to the organization. They will be forced therefore to take an interest in the long-term consequences of their decisions.

The instrumentalist explanations for firm ownership relate ultimately to contracting problems. Certain contracts cannot be administered and enforced, and ownership emerges in such a way as to minimize contractual problems. In this way, according to the theory, the mechanism of competition selects among organizational forms. It may be remarked that competition will not necessarily select the most efficient organizational form: rather, it will select the variants that grow the fastest and outperform the others. A labour-managed firm may be the most efficient, for instance, but it may be surpassed by less efficient capitalist firms that expand and multiply more quickly.[2]

13.16 *Ownership: Psychological Aspects*

The instrumentalist explanations of firm ownership relate the allocation of control rights to competitive success. In this sense, they build on rights, and on the behavioural impact of alternative distributions of rights. This presupposition is introduced as an assumption that is not analysed further. All direct motivational effects that might emerge from alternative allocations of rights are

---

[1] This modifies Putterman's (1988: 244) claim that 'efficiency dictates that the entity that hires labour should itself be a commodity'. Theoretically speaking, the commodification of the firm may induce inefficiencies beyond frustrating democratic control.

[2] Schlicht (1984d). The above account is, however, extremely superficial. 'Modes of production' may induce fundamental non-convexities and lock-in effects; see Vogt (1986) for a penetrating analysis.

neglected. The theory of property developed earlier stressed the motivational aspect of property.[1] Without such a motivational side to property, it has been argued, 'property' would be an empty term lacking any connection to reality and behaviour. This insight is also of importance with regard to firm organization. The economic effect of the allocation of property rights cannot be reduced to incentives alone. The same incentives can be provided quite independently of the allocation of property rights by delegation and the implementation of appropriate incentive contracts.[2] The clarity view suggests that firm ownership matters beyond incentives, because self-attribution is geared to the individual's perception of his role within an organization, and motivation must be expected to be affected by that. A small example may indicate what is involved here.[3]

In Germany there are two major firms that sell frozen food to households directly. One of them, 'Eismann', is organized as a chain of franchises, in which all the drivers are the owners of their (standardized) vehicles and sell the Eismann products on their own account. The other, 'bo*frost', is a traditional firm whose drivers are its employees. As the products and services supplied by the two firms are almost identical, an exclusive stress on incentives would suggest that a region served by any one driver, and the money obtained from selling, say, one packet of spinach, should be almost identical for both firms. In fact, the firms differ considerably in this way.[4] These differences suggest that the property rights structure plays a role beyond merely providing incentives.

It has been argued earlier that a firm may be defined from a psychological point of view as an entity that is perceived as a firm by the employees, the customers, and the owners.[5] The importance of this perception for real behaviour and interaction is, in a way, obvious, since individuals are guided in their actions by their

[1] See Ch. 11 and especially S. 11.19.
[2] See the discussion of the relevance of property rights in S. 11.16.
[3] For the following, see Kunkel (1994: 70–2).
[4] The region served by a bo*frost driver is considerably smaller than that served by an Eismann driver, but sales per driver are roughly the same. It seems, further, that bo*frost is competitively more successful than Eismann.   [5] See S. 13.4.

perceptions. These and similar effects have come to the fore recently in discussions about 'corporate culture'.[1] Legal rulings in labour and antitrust law often reflect prevailing social perceptions about business demarcations.[2] These social perceptions follow the same principles of categorization as all other perceptions. They stress similarity, simplicity, and straightforwardness. The perception of 'ownership' is induced by long-lasting connections between the individual and the firm. The founder of a firm will be related to the firm in this way. Long-lasting attachment to the firm will generate perceptions of entitlements that are close to ownership. A salaried manager may by analogy be considered as belonging to the group of 'owners', whereas a small shareholder may appear merely as an investor. In other words, the principles of occupancy, prescription, accession, and succession as described by Hume will apply here, too.[3]

Psychological aspects of ownership entail direct efficiency consequences in so far as alternative ownership structures generate different perceptions of individual responsibility and autonomy.

13.17 *Hume's Counterpoint Again*

The dualism of instrumentalist and psychological aspects of firm ownership reiterates the dualism between functionalist and psychological aspects of property epitomized by Hume's counterpoint.[4] As has been argued before, the functionalist and psychological aspects often reinforce each other, but occasionally they may come into conflict. To illustrate the interesting possibilities that may emerge here, consider the following scenario.[5]

Start with a capitalist economy. All firms are controlled by the owners of capital, and labour is hired on a contractual basis in the

---

[1] See Casson (1991), who offers a penetrating discussion of the issue.

[2] 'Is the National Football League a firm or is it 24 separate firms? . . . a judge declared the league to be 24 different firms, and therefore they were colliding. If, however, the league were a joint venture, or a single firm with franchises, the applicable legal rules would have been very different' (Alchian and Woodward 1987: 134). See also Wagner (1994: 145–56) for a good discussion of similar issues in the German context.

[3] See S. 11.7–11.10.   [4] See S. 11.3.   [5] Schlicht (1979).

labour market. Technical progress leads to automatization. All easy jobs are automated. All remaining jobs require much firm-specific knowledge, i.e. skills that are useful only in one particular firm. These skills are highly productive but require expensive on-the-job training. In such a setting, high turnover would render the creation of firm-specific skills unprofitable, whereas arrangements that curb turnover would enable the firms and the workers to capture the efficiency gains obtainable through training. Labour contracts will therefore emerge which tie the workers to the firms for long periods of time because it is efficient to do so. In such a scenario, labour turnover must be expected to be low.

As a consequence, workers will be attached to firms, and prescription will take place.[1] The long and uninterrupted association of the workers with their firm tacitly creates perceptions of entitlements and obligations which conflict with the legal ownership structure. It will appear 'natural' to associate the firm with its workers, rather than with anonymous shareholders. Problems of legitimization may occur for capitalist firms, and labour-managed firms may gain a competitive advantage, owing to these changes in social perception. Yet this may be detrimental to the efficiency of the economy. This would be the case for labour-managed firms, which will have no incentive to care for the unemployed, and less incentive to expand than their capitalist counterparts. In other words, it is conceivable that the emerging property rights, as generated by the mechanisms of psychological entitlements, conflict severely with functional requirements. This is, of course, merely a theoretical possibility, rather than a realistic prospect. It is mentioned to highlight the significance of Hume's counterpoint in the context of the theory of the firm.[2]

---

[1] See S. 11.8.
[2] The argument provides a psychological underpinning for Schumpeter's (1943) thesis, that capitalism generates values undermining its own foundations; but this fact does not render the necessary assumptions more realistic.

13.18 *Clarity and the Nature of the Firm*

The firm is, first and foremost, a perceptional unity, like a swan. It is important that those who work in the firm and those who control the firm share this perception, because it gives rise to specific behavioural responses. The perception of rules that are characteristic of the firm generates a tendency to follow the rules. Similarly, the urge to clarify tends to integrate the system of rules and to enhance the overall impression of unity. The forces that shape firms are the same as those that shape custom. In order to understand routines, rule-guided behaviour must be understood. In order to understand command, the phenomena of obedience and commitment must be understood. In order to understand the workings of incentives, the impact on motivation must be grasped, and also the effect on routines and command. It has been argued that the clarity view may help in understanding these phenomena. The 'chemical' interaction of control modes discussed above has been interpreted as the result of overall clarification processes which integrate routines, commands, and incentives and create various interdependencies.[1] The productivity advantages obtainable from firm organization derive from the behavioural effect of integration.

The perceptual view comes close to Coase's position that the firm emerges from a bundle of long-term contractual relationships.[2] Long-term contracts must be expected to lead to an integration of routines and customs at various levels such that a perceptual unity results. Yet this is not always the case. Coase himself has mentioned several examples of long-term relationships that have not entailed integration. Long-term contracting is not equivalent to the formation of firms.

---

[1] See S. 13.11–13.14.

[2] Coase (1991:68) reluctantly accepts that a nexus of long-term contracts may be a firm. This appears to me not entirely convincing, as it would imply that publishing houses comprise the workshops of all the typesetters, printers, and bookbinders who enjoy long-term business relationships, for instance. The legal length of a contract should not be taken as the measuring rod here. The employment contract is subject to comparatively short notice, and is in the legal sense not long-term.

It is tempting to say that the firm may be understood as a system of highly integrated routines, reward systems, and command structures.[1] This parlance would capture the elements so far discussed. It may mislead, however, because it opens an unwarranted possibility of excluding psychological forces. Only if 'integration' is understood as comprising *perceived* integration may such a parlance be adequate.

The stress on perception is important here, because human action is guided by human perception. The firm as a substantive, rather than nominalistic, entity shapes behaviour, and this effect is mediated by processes of perception and concept formation. A similar observation holds true for social analysis in general. Modern attempts to 'objectify' social science by treating institutions as collections of independent individuals may be compared to a reading of Shakespeare's works by looking at the statistical characteristics of the letter sequences occurring in the text while denying the existence of any meaning emerging from the patterns formed by these letter sequences.

---

[1] Alchian (1991: 233) calls this 'teamwork' and writes that 'a "firm" yields an output greater than could otherwise be achieved . . . That added gain comes mysteriously from teamwork.' I do not accept this terminology, however. It may wrongly suggest that productivity gains arising from the development of a set of well-matched routines are of less importance than face-to-face contact. The point has also been made by Marx (1873: 316) 'Apart from the new power that arises from the fusion of many forces into one single force, mere social contact begets in most industries an emulation and stimulation of the animal spirits that heighten the efficiency of each workman.'

Chapter 14

THE DIVISION OF LABOUR

14.1 *Economic Organization and the Division of Labour*

The division of labour entails the problem of economic coordination. For reasons of preference and efficiency, among others, the various members of society specialize in performing distinct activities. These specialized activities must be coordinated in such a way that a useful overall result is obtained. The three modes of control discussed in the context of the firm—exchange, command, and custom—are used not only for purposes internal to the organization of the firm, but for the good of society as a whole.[1] Thus, the executive branch of government relies on command, and so does the military. Social interaction is governed by customary and legal rules that are the social counterparts of duty at the level of the firm. The system of markets, finally, coordinates production and consumption across firms and consumers through the mechanisms of exchange.

It is a Marxian misapprehension to think that the social division of labour is organized exclusively by the market and the division of labour within firms is organized exclusively by command.[2] Both the

---

[1] See S. 13.10.
[2] Marx (1873: ch. 12.4). This view is shared by many non-Marxists and is reflected, e.g., in the title *Markets and Hierarchies* chosen by O. E. Williamson (1975).

firm and the market rely on custom. All three control modes—custom, command, and exchange—work in various combinations, both at firm level and society level.

With regard to economic activity, the firm and the market are complementary institutions for organizing the division of labour. In order to understand the emergence of firms in a market system, it is necessary to analyse which *kinds* of activities are better organized within firms, and which by markets. Those kinds of coordination better performed by the market ought to be left to the market; those better performed without market interference, on the other hand, will give rise to the formation of firms. Accordingly, the fundamental coordination problem associated with the division of labour entails both the theory of the firm and the theory of the market.

This chapter is devoted to the problem of the division of labour, and the conditions under which that division of labour is better organized by the firm or by the market. Firms, as islands of custom, emerge in the market because coordination by custom is in many ways more efficient than coordination provided through the market. However, custom has a severe drawback, because the mutual reinforcement of a system of interlocking customs entails rigidity and inflexibility. The inherent inertia of coordination by means of custom renders the firm inferior to the market with regard to certain types of adaptation and change. The organizational alternative of coordinating a given task within a firm or through a market may be understood as engendering institutional competition between these two modes of organization. The institutional mix between firm and market which emerges in a society may be understood as arising from this competition. The firm thrives on the advantages of custom, and the market thrives on the flexibility attainable through standardization in an anonymous setting. In order to better understand the advantages and shortcomings of custom as a device for organizing the division of labour, the subsequent sections will be devoted to looking more closely into the coordination problems posed by the division of labour.

14.2 *The Division of Labour and the Extent of the Market*

The classic position with regard to the division of labour is encapsulated in 'Smith's theorem': the division of labour is limited by the extent of the market.[1] The usual reading of the theorem, suggested by Smith's own account, is, however, different. It may better be phrased as 'The division of labour is *determined* by the extent of the market.' The two versions should be distinguished.

Smith argues that specialization leads to an increase in productivity resulting from 'increasing returns to specialization'. These result from the increasing returns to scale that occur in performing any task or sub-task. As a consequence, all specialization increases the productivity of the economy as a whole. If there are two persons who divide their time equally between producing one unit of good A and one unit of good B, the joint output will be 2 units of A and 2 units of B. If both of them specialize, however, joint output increases: the first person produces more than 2 units of A and the second person will produce more than 2 units of B. They are able to do this because of increasing returns to scale. This amounts to increasing returns from specialization.

As to the reasons for increasing returns to specialization, Adam Smith mentions four of them. The first two are straightforward. One is that specialization leads to improved dexterity:

A common smith, who, though accustomed to handle the hammer, has never been used to make nails, will scarce be able to make above two or three hundred nails a day, and those too very bad ones. A smith who has been accustomed to make nails, can seldom make more than eight hundred or thousand nails a day. I have seen several boys under twenty years of age who had never exercised any other trade but that that of making nails and who could make, each of them, upwards of two thousand three hundred nails a day.[2]

---

[1] Smith (1776: 17) The name 'Smith's theorem' is due to Stigler (1951), who interprets it as indicated in the following text. For an interesting discussion of the division of labour, see Leibenstein (1960: ch. 7); for a good survey of views about the division of labour, see Groenewegen (1987).   [2] Adapted from Smith (1776: 7–8).

The second reason is that time can be saved that would be required 'in passing from one sort of work to another'.[1]

The third reason given by Smith is more intricate. It relates to the conditions of technical progress and the introduction of machinery:

I shall only observe, therefore, that the invention of all those machines by which labour is so much facilitated and abridged, seems to have been originally owing to the division of labour. Men are more likely to discover easier and readier methods of attaining any object, when the whole attention of their minds is directed towards that single object, than when it is dissipated among a great variety of things. But in consequence of the division of labour, the whole of every man's attention comes naturally to be directed towards some one very simple object.[2]

The fourth reason that Smith mentions relates to 'differences in natural talents in different men'. He is, however quite cautious here and adds that it is in reality 'much less than we are aware of; and the very different genius which appears to distinguish men of different professions, when grown up to maturity, is not upon many occasions so much the cause, as the effect of the division of labour'.[3]

Adam Smith's 'theorem' results from combining the idea of increasing returns to specialization with the causal variable of the size of the market. If a market is small, specialization in either good A or good B cannot occur. The joiner will produce both window casements and doors to meet the demand of his village. Although he could produce window casements more cheaply if they were demanded in larger quantities, the demand is not large enough to permit specialization. If the market expands because, say, transportation costs are reduced, conditions may change. It may then be worthwhile for joiner A to specialize in window casements and supply customers in the surrounding villages as

---

[1] Smith (1776: 8).

[2] Smith (1776: 9). Smith develops the idea further by introducing more specialists ('philosophers and machine-makers'), who exploit further advantages of specialization along the same lines.   [3] Smith (1776: 15).

well; the other joiners then may each specialize in supplying the enlarged market with other specific items.

14.3 Fixed Costs and Increasing Returns from Specialization

It is illuminating to rephrase some aspects of the reasons for increasing returns to specialization, as given by Smith, in terms of fixed costs. Fixed costs are costs that are independent of the level of production. They are setup costs incurred while establishing the possibility to produce. Many aspects of the arguments given by Smith relate to fixed costs in a straightforward way, but this view also sheds light on some other aspects of increasing returns from specialization.

Explicit training costs can be viewed as fixed costs. A modern statement stresses this aspect: 'A specialist such as a surgeon is an indivisible resource. He has a training of 10 years and then operates for 30 years. He cannot simply be replaced by two half surgeons who each are trained for 5 years and operate on half as many patients only every other day'.[1]

The fixed-cost parlance would also cover costs related to machinery. A joiner who builds window frames only occasionally will not find it worthwhile to buy specialized machinery; a carpenter specializing in windows, on the other hand, would be much more likely to make regular use of such equipment. Specialization renders it worthwhile to invest in specialist machinery. This leads to additional returns from specialization that go beyond the aforementioned increase in dexterity.

Important fixed costs relate to information and innovation. A lawyer specializing in certain cases may find it worthwhile to subscribe to a specialized data bank for finding the relevant precedents quickly, but a less specialized lawyer would not find such a subscription worthwhile. Similarly, the design of a machine requires research and development. This entails fixed costs, and

---

[1] von Weizsäcker (1991: 106).

it will be worthwhile contemplating such a project only if a sufficient number of machines is to be produced. It should also be noted that the greater specialization of joiners would be likely to increase the demand for specialized machinery and would therefore make it more worthwhile to supply it.

Other important fixed costs relate to the establishment of organization and routines. Investment in 'organization' is indeed of the utmost importance.[1] It is of the same nature as any other fixed-cost investment. Firms that specialize in certain products will also have an incentive to develop routines that are specifically tailored to their production. This will lead, again, to increasing returns from specialization.

The case of on-the-job skill acquisition, as discussed by Smith, also fits into the fixed-cost framework, although on-the-job training also raises more intricate issues. Nevertheless, the costs of acquiring a skill have to be considered as fixed costs.[2]

14.4 *The Division of Labour and the Nature of the Task*

Smith's argument presupposes that gains from specialization will accrue whenever the division of labour is deepened. This is not true. Many tasks cannot usefully be further subdivided. There is no sense in subdividing the writing of a poem such that everybody specializes in certain rhymes; or in subdividing the writing of computer software such that each programmer specializes in writing one single line of code. Several factors limit the division of labour, and the extent of the market is only one of them. Another relates to the nature of the task.

Some tasks simply cannot be subdivided. This applies to tasks that are of a sequential nature, where each step requires knowledge of previous steps. Distributing steps among different workers would require the transmission of information about the previous

---

[1] Marshall (1890: 138–9) stressed this rightly by describing 'organization' as one of the fundamental 'agents of production', along with land, labour, and capital.
[2] This is elaborated in Becker (1962).

steps. This may be more difficult and more time-consuming than
actually performing these steps. If a programmer has started to
write a routine, it will be much easier for him to complete it than
for somebody else to do so. The errors that can occur in the
communication process will be avoided. Such continuity has
been stressed in software engineering:

Men and months are interchangeable commodities only when a task can
be partitioned among many workers *with no communication among
them*. This is true for reaping wheat or picking cotton; it is not even
approximately true of systems programming.
  When a task cannot be partitioned because of sequential constraints,
the application of more effort has no effect on the schedule. . . . Many
software tasks have this characteristic because of the sequential nature of
debugging.[1]

But even if tasks can be subdivided, this does not necessarily
increase overall output, because a finer subdivision will necessitate
more coordination. This aspect has been neglected by Adam
Smith, but has been recognized in the literature:

When tasks require coordination of a delicate and complicated variety,
the individual worker may be more efficient if he performs a variety of
tasks because the loss from non-specialisation is offset by the gains from
coordination. We expect a better painting from a single good artist, than
if the world's best specialist in clouds does a portion of the picture, and
the world's best specialist in trees another portion.[2]

The importance of this observation is usually not appreciated
fully, in spite of the literature on transaction costs. It is not of
marginal concern, but rather constitutes one of the central problems posed by the division of labour. Software engineering illustrates this, once again, and in a drastic way:

In tasks that can be partitioned but which require communication among
subtasks, the effort of communication must be added to the amount of
work to be done. Therefore the best that can be done is somewhat poorer
than an even trade of men for months.
  The added burden of communication is made up of two parts, training

[1] Brooks (1975: 16–17).   [2] Stigler (1952: 140); see also Stigler (1966: 168).

and intercommunication. Each worker must be trained in the technology, the goals of the effort, the overall strategy, and the plan of work. This training cannot be partitioned, so this part of the added effort varies linearly with the number of workers.

Intercommunication is worse. If each part of the task must be separately coordinated with each other part, the effort increases $n(n-1)/2$. Three workers require three times as much pairwise intercommunication as two; four require six times as much as two. If, moreover, there need to be conferences among three, four, etc., workers to resolve things jointly, matters get worse yet . . .

Since software construction is inherently a system effort—an exercise in complex interrelationships—communication effort is great, and it quickly dominates the decrease in individual task time brought about by partitioning. Adding more men then lengthens, not shortens, the schedule.[1]

The costs involved here are sometimes immense, and the problems generated by the difficulty of coordination are equally tremendous.[2]

In contexts that require much interaction, the problem of the division of labour poses itself in a way that differs from what Smith has envisaged. In order to appreciate the relative advantages of custom and the market in coordinating tasks of this type, it is useful to look more closely into the issues of timing, separability, and conceptual integrity as determinants of the nature of the task.

14.5 *Timing*

The issue may be phrased in a slightly more general fashion by introducing a rough classification between tasks, according to their nature. To fix the ideas, let us suppose that each task may be conceived of as involving a number of actions $a, b, c, \ldots$ These actions are subdivisions of tasks. The task of screwing two pieces of wood together may be seen as a sequence focusing on the action

---

[1] Brooks (1975: 17–19).
[2] See Brooks (1975: 31). Brooks is known as the 'father of the OS/360'. He was project manager for the development of this software system and later project manager during the design phase.

of turning the screwdriver *once*. By repeating this action, the task is eventually completed. 'Action' refers in the following to an action *relative* to a task. The term is not meant to denote some 'action atom' that cannot be subdivided further. It does seem not useful to assume that such atoms exist. The turning of the screwdriver may be viewed as a task in its own right, comprising actions of several fingers, the arm, and the body, for instance, and this could be subdivided even further.

Given that a task comprises several actions, a distinction between different tasks may be drawn according to the *timing* that is required to perform the actions. *A sequential task* requires the actions *a, b, c,* to be performed in sequence.[1] An example would be the weaving of a fabric, where one thread has to follow the other and where it is not possible (or is prohibitively costly), for technological reasons, to leave some gaps and fill them in later. Another example would be the sequence of producing and testing an item: the test cannot be performed before the production task has been completed.

A simultaneous task requires that actions *a, b, c,* are performed simultaneously in close coordination. Workers who want to lift a beam together have to concert their action. The performance of a piece of music by an orchestra requires much more than each player playing his part flawlessly: the musicians have to play their parts synchronously.

There are also tasks in which the actions required can be performed quite independently. These are *temporarily independent tasks*; entering numbers into a data bank or writing entries for a dictionary are examples.

In reality, no task fits neatly into one or the other category. Distinctions may be drawn, however, along the time dimension. The categories introduced above are intended to highlight what is involved here.

---

[1] See also Leibenstein (1960: 111–15).

14.6 *Separability and Interdependence*

Another way of distinguishing tasks relates to intrinsic interdependence. This aspect is of great importance for the present purposes.

Consider first a sequential task. Actions a and b have been performed, and an intermediate product B is obtained. By applying action c, this intermediate product can be transformed into another intermediate product C, and so forth. Often it is unnecessary to know specifics about actions a and b in order to perform c. All information is contained in the intermediate product B. Such a task may be denoted as *separable*.

A nice illustration of separable tasks is given by Demsetz: 'The economical use of industrial chemicals by steel firms does not require transfer of knowledge of how these chemicals are produced; similarly, the use of steel by industrial chemical firms does not require transfer of knowledge of how steel is produced.'[1]

Sequential tasks may, however, be far from separable. Adding another line of computer code requires knowledge of the preceding code. All preceding actions a and b must be known in order to perform action c. If the actions of a sequential task depend on each other in this way, the task is termed an *interdependent task*.

The distinction between separable and interdependent sequential tasks is not a sharp one. In a sense, the computer program with completed parts a and b may contain all the information that is necessary to perform action c in an appropriate manner. The intermediate product B contains that information, and in a formal sense the task may appear additive. In order to cope with this difficulty, interdependence may be conceived as a matter of degree. The larger the information needed about previous production steps, the stronger is this interdependence.

But even if all information required for taking step c were to be contained in the intermediate product B, the worker in charge of

---

[1] Demsetz (1988: 159). Demsetz (1988: 160) has stressed this informational aspect in his view of the firm: 'Roughly speaking . . . the vertical boundaries of a firm are determined by the economies of conservation of expenditures on knowledge.'

taking step c would have to retrieve the relevant information about the previous actions from the intermediate product B. For instance, he would have to try to comprehend the code written by the previous programmers. In such a case, it might be cheaper to have the worker who had performed the previous steps also perform the next step c. This would save the costs that arise from retrieval, and would reduce the danger of errors. This may be considered as still another form of interdependence.

It may be the case, however, that the intermediate product *does not contain enough clues* to retrieve the information that is necessary to undertake step c. It may even be cheaper to perform steps a and b again rather than to try unravel the plan that gave rise to the intermediate product B. This too would be a case of interdependence.

Consider next simultaneous tasks. Again, these may be either separable or interdependent. A separable task is one where each action can be performed without any technical knowledge of the other actions; action c can be executed without knowing precisely how a and b are performed. Measurements performed simultaneously at different points of the globe are separable. In such cases coordination is simple, as only a timing device is needed. Each measurement can be made independently, and the way in which the measurements are made is inessential. It is only important that each observer has an accurate watch, and that he is instructed about the time of measurement.

Simultaneous tasks may, however, be strongly interdependent. A piece of chamber music requires each player to react instantaneously to the playing of his partners. Each nuance of articulation has to be perceived by each player, and each has to adjust his playing in order to achieve a perceptual unity and coherence. It takes many years of continuous practice for an ensemble to perfect such a degree of coordination.

Software engineering is no less demanding. Large projects have to be split up into modules that are developed simultaneously. If module a uses subroutines of module b and module b uses subroutines of module a, separability may be achieved by standardization. The standards must, however, be established in such a way that they can be implemented. Typically, they have to be changed to incorporate new developments. This cannot be done without intense interaction.

With regard to temporarily independent tasks, and in order to exhaust the classification, there may again be either separability or interdependence. If each individual action does not require knowledge about the other actions, the task is separable; if each task requires knowledge about the other tasks, the task is interdependent. In many cases interdependence will lead to simultaneity, but this will not always be the result. The task of filling three circles with three different colours is, in a way, both temporarily independent—because the sequence does not matter—and interdependent—because the filling of each circle requires knowledge about the colours of the circles already being filled. Yet each worker can do his job whenever he likes.

14.7 *Conceptual Integrity and Clarity*

Interdependence may also be generated beyond the temporal dimension through the requirement of *conceptual integrity*. This requirement has been stressed in particular in software engineering, but it is of general relevance:

Most European cathedrals show differences in plan or architectural style between parts built in different generations by different builders. The later builders were tempted to 'improve' upon the designs of earlier ones, . . . So the peaceful Norman transept abuts and contradicts the soaring Gothic nave . . .

Against these, the architectural unity of Reims stands in glorious contrast. The joy that stirs the beholder comes as much from the integrity of the design, as from any particular excellencies. As the guidebook tells us, this integrity was achieved by the self-abnegation of eight generations of builders, each of whom sacrificed some of his ideas so that the whole might be of pure design . . .

Even though they have not taken centuries to build, most programming systems reflect conceptual disunity far worse than that of cathedrals. Usually this arises not from a succession of master designers, but from the separation of design into many tasks done by many men.

I will contend that conceptual integrity is *the* most important consideration in system design. . . . *Simplicity* is not enough. Mooers's TRAC language and Algol 68 achieve simplicity as measured by the number of distinct elementary concepts. They are not, however, *straightforward*. The expression of the things one wants to do often requires involuted and unexpected combinations. . . . It is not enough to learn the elements and rules of combinations; one must also learn the idiomatic usage, a whole lore of how the elements are combined in practice. Simplicity and straightforwardness proceed from conceptual integrity. Each part must reflect the same philosophies and the same balancing of desiderata. Every part must even use the same techniques in syntax and analogous notions in semantics. Ease of use, then, dictates unity of design, conceptual integrity.[1]

Overall clarity is, thus, an important functional requirement for a piece of software. This requirement ties the different parts together and creates strong interdependence in programming.

It should not be surprising that clarity requirements enter here. The principles that govern human behaviour in playing a game like Eleusis and those that underlie the formation of custom are equally relevant for dealing with a computer language, or any other advanced item.[2] It is for this reason that clarity is an important aspect of functionality. With respect to everyday staple products such as cars, computers, or television sets, this may just appear as 'good handling' and straightforward operation to the consumer, but it is important for assembly and maintenance. Unclear design will translate into high costs of repair and unreliability after repair. It will make for a poor product.

14.8 *The Enigma of Markets*

Consider now the organization of the division of labour. The fundamental question is, which tasks are most economically coordinated through the market, and which are more logically coordinated within firms?

For tasks that involve substantive interdependence, the market is

---

[1] Brooks (1975: 42–4).   [2] The card game Eleusis has been described in S. 7.2.

a poor instrument for coordination. 'Jointness of effort and activities . . . involves more cooperation among individuals than that of simple market exchange.'[1] While the interdependence may be reduced by defining standards for interfaces between production steps, this will not always be feasible, and it may be costly. Yet even such standards will not necessarily lead to the formation of markets. Decentralization of interdependent tasks may also occur on a large scale through custom. The rules of traffic illustrate a decentralization of interconnected activities without a firm or a market.

But even separable tasks may be organized more easily within a firm than through a market. All the incentives that the market provides could also, theoretically speaking, be provided within the firm, while the overhead of additional marketing costs could be saved. Coordination could only be improved, because the firm as an organization offers a vastly richer menu of coordination devices than does the market.[2] It is easier to develop specific routines, or particular languages, within the firm than in the market, and informal ways of cooperation are more readily available.[3] Inserting a market between two steps introduces marketing costs into the production process and drastically reduces the possibilities of coordination by other means.

Thus, while the market has strong drawbacks with regard to interdependent tasks, it is also difficult to pinpoint the advantages of market organization for separable tasks. Instead of asking 'why firms?' the difficult question to answer is 'why markets?'[4]

---

[1] Alchian (1991: 233). Demsetz (1988: 157–62) has articulated this view in terms of information costs.

[2] 'Perhaps the most distinctive advantage of the firm, however, is the wider variety and greater sensitivity of control instruments that are available for enforcing intrafirm in comparison with interfirm activities'. (Williamson 1971: 113).

[3] This has been stressed in particular by Hirschman's (1970) insistence that 'voice' be granted an important role in the theory of the firm.

[4] This has been stressed by various authors, e.g. Coase (1937: 43: 'Why is not all production carried on by one big firm?'); O. E. Williamson (1985: 132–8: 'A Chronic Puzzle'), Von Weizsäcker (1991: 100: 'It is difficult to prove, rather than simply state, that there are functions performed better by the market rather than any possible alternative.'). The problem is sometimes referred to as 'Williamson's puzzle' or the 'centralization paradox'; see Stiglitz (1991: 18). O. E. Williamson (1985: ch. 6) and, more recently, Putterman (1995) provide excellent discussions of various facets of the problem. My concern here relates to more general aspects and the nature of custom.

In answering the question 'why firms?', Coase rejected the idea that people might *prefer* to work in firms rather than for the market: 'Such individuals would accept less in order to work under someone, and firms would arise naturally from this. But it would appear that this cannot be a very important reason, for it would rather seem that the opposite tendency is operating if one judges from the stress normally laid on the advantage of "being one's own master".'[1] This suggests that people may have a preference for market transactions. However, at least if real-world experience may be taken at face value, this does not seem to be true. The misleading conclusion arises because Coase stresses command rather than custom as the distinguishing mark of the firm. A job offers a range of competencies and responsibilities, and the worker *is*, within the confines of his job, his 'own master'. He may actually perceive more autonomy in performing his job than he would have in organizing his work as an entrepreneur. If the firm were his own, he would then also have to be alert to changes in circumstances and market conditions. The desire of housewives to obtain jobs seems to flow from the perception of personal autonomy in a job. Further, the firm provides an environment for social interaction which is sometimes valued highly; the arguments against 'telecommuting' (working with a computer at home) illustrate this. In the end, there seems to be a preference for working in firms. This renders the question 'why markets?' even harder to answer.

14.9 *Two Faces of Integration*

The firm, as a system of highly integrated routines, reward systems, and command structures, benefits from integration. The productivity gains obtainable are due not only to improved coordination by means of specialized and well-matched routines, languages, and tacit ways of cooperation, but also to the strong impact on motivation arising from the formation of a group. The

---

[1] Coase (1937: 38).

firm generates group forces that emanate from the same clarification processes that lead to interlocking customs. A set of interlocking customs provides many diffuse reasons for working and thinking in a certain way. Self-attribution will not be able to link behaviour to such a diffuse pattern of causes. Thus, self-attribution will focus on intrinsic motivation and will generate corresponding attitudes and motives.[1] In this way, 'corporate culture'—or, better, 'corporate custom'—shapes cognition and motivation. It is a productive asset and arises from the same forces that shape different cultures. Such group forces can be fairly strong. (They occasionally cause war.) Firms make use of them.[2]

But a system of highly integrated routines, rewards, and command structures has drawbacks *because* it is highly integrated. While integration shapes motivation and bundles information in a most parsimonious manner, it ties everything together and in that way creates rigidity. What has been said about interlocking customs applies here, too.[3] Coordination by routines may be efficient, but it requires the routines themselves to be inflexible.

Such inflexibility relates to the rules rather than to the actions that they generate. A firm may respond very quickly to changes in circumstances as long as this change can be handled by the prevailing routines and command structures. An army is organized in order to respond quickly, but it does not use the market mechanism to achieve that aim: rather, the organization is designed for that purpose. The routines and command structures are themselves fairly rigid.

14.10 The Costs of Custom

Integration binds together everything within an organization. Consider pay. All textbooks on compensation stress the

---

[1] See S. 9.7.

[2] On the foundation of groups, see Asch (1952: p. III and V). Such group phenomena are obviously important and have been emphasized in quite early writings, as can be seen from the quotation of Marx given in fn. 1, p. 241 above. Yet the theory of the firm has not taken account of this, and has not even tried to refute group effects on factual, rather than paradigmatic, grounds.   [3] See S. 10.8.

overwhelming importance of 'internal consistency', and practitioners agree. The following quotation from a textbook on compensation illustrates this:

Internal consistency refers to pay relationships among jobs or skill levels within a *single* organization. It is one of the basic compensation policies. It involves equal pay for jobs of equal worth and acceptable pay differentials for work of unequal worth. But internal consistency involves more than the pay structure. Often called internal equity, a policy that emphasizes internal consistency places importance on the inner workings, the relationships and pressures found within an organization. Consequently it includes concerns for the fairness of the procedures used to establish the pay structure, as well as the structure itself.[1]

The phenomenon itself hardly needs further elaboration. The various techniques used to determine compensation demonstrate the practical importance of these considerations. The equity standards are undeniably of great importance within organizations. They cannot be interpreted merely as surface appearances of underlying economic considerations. Clarity requirements are not reducible to scarcity arguments or to the logic of rationality. A 50–50 split of outcomes, as used in the Halsley method of employee compensation, can hardly be explained in terms of scarcity and incentives alone:[2] it relates to symmetry and clarity. Similar observations apply to a host of other compensation methods.

These remarks should not be taken to suggest that incentives and scarcity do not play a role: incentives and scarcity are obviously of the greatest importance. The point is rather that clarity requirements *constrain* the possibilities of obtaining the full and complete return from these instrumental considerations. The costs of custom emerge, just as do the benefits, from the need for coherence.

Many examples illustrate this feature. Wages for the same type of work vary systematically across industries and firms.[3] Trans-

[1] Adapted from Milkovich and Newman (1984: 31–2).
[2] Milkovich and Newman (1984: 343). See also the criticism of game-theoretical approaches to custom in S. 10.2.
[3] These 'firm effects' and 'industry effects' may, however, also have other explanations; see Oi(1990), Krueger and Summers (1988), Blackburn and Neumark (1992).

portation may be contracted out in order to avoid compensating the truck drivers according to the firm's own corporate culture;[1] cleaning, maintenance, and service may be contracted out for similar reasons. Some takeovers occur because the merger largely voids the compensation practices of the firm that is swallowed up. This may be a profitable and painless way of replacing one set of constraints for another.[2]

Other constraints resulting from integration relate to standards of quality. Work routines are geared to such standards. Typically, each firm predominantly serves a particular quality segment of the market even in cases where substantial economies could be expected from integrating high-quality production lines with low-quality products.[3]

These consistency constraints are well known, but less well understood. Why, it may be asked, are they so important? It has been shown, after all, that people get used to nearly everything. Psychological studies of adaptation

suggest that any stable state of affairs tends to become acceptable eventually, at least in the sense that alternatives to it no longer readily come to mind. Terms of exchange that are initially seen as unfair may in time acquire the status of a reference transaction. . . . The gap between what people consider fair and the behaviour they expect in the marketplace tends to be rather small.[4]

Custom is adaptive, after all. This argument is misleading. Even if workers can adapt to the most unintuitive regulations, this attempt is bound to create control problems. If the set of routines is augmented by a routine that embodies a different philosophy and style, each of the earlier established routines will lose some of its imperative character and a part of its impact on behaviour. Similar effects are well-known in software engineering. An entire program may suffer if features are added that do not 'fit'; then,

---

[1] Kubon-Gilke (1997: S. 5.3.6).
[2] O. E. Williamson (1985: 158) reports on an acquisition that went wrong because of internal equity constraints.
[3] Wagner (1994: 107–25).
[4] Kahneman *et al.* (1986*b*: 731–2); see also Major and Testa (1989).

whenever a further feature is added, it is uncertain whether it follows the old style or the new one. The delays and errors induced by this uncertainty may easily outweigh the benefits of the added features.[1] Similarly, the rule to do one job quickly and the other with the utmost scrutiny will induce workers to perceive the approach to work as somewhat arbitrary. The labour force will not easily develop a coherent style, an appropriate set of habits, and a functional structure of motivation. Furthermore, a mixing of principles of compensation will put the entire compensation policy of the firm at risk. Each worker will perceive the benefits that would accrue to him if he were treated like the others in some particular aspects. He will not consider that he may be benefiting in other dimensions. This creates internal stress and is detrimental to corporate custom.

14.11 *The Use of Knowledge in Society*

The market has been interpreted as a system that enables economic agents to make use of widely dispersed knowledge in a parsimonious manner. Prices serve as signals that encode all relevant information about scarcities and make this knowledge available throughout the social and economic system. It is, thus, not necessary to enquire further about specific scarcities, wants, or production conditions.[2]

The earlier discussion of the role of routines within firms has stressed efficiency aspects of coordination by custom in a parallel manner.[3] Routines are maintained by following them; what is not repeated is forgotten. This implies that only useful knowledge survives. The routines embody that knowledge, even if the individuals are not aware of the fact. By allocating responsibilities to job holders, the idiosyncratic expertise of these workers can be used to the benefit of the organization. In this sense, a firm-specific set of

---

[1] See S. 14.7.   [2] Hayek (1945).
[3] See S. 13.11. Demsetz (1988: ch. 9) has argued e.g. that firms can thrive in a market environment because they are more efficient in economizing on information flows; see also the discussion of separability and independence in S. 14.6 above.

customs may be conceived as a mechanism that enables the members of the firm to make coordinated use of widely dispersed knowledge.

This observation holds true in society as well. There are national economies that are coordinated mainly by custom. People follow the established behavioural patterns, and an overall coordination is achieved without any explicit awareness. Each individual needs only to know how to perform his allotted task and to follow the role prescription. His entitlements and obligations, his duties and routines transmit all the information that is necessary for him to coordinate social and economic activity. The market mechanism is not unique in this respect. Hayek, who (following Menger) developed the view of the price system as making use of dispersed information, was quite clear about this:

We make constant use of formulas, symbols and rules whose meaning we do not understand and through the use of which we avail ourselves of the assistance of knowledge which individually we do not possess. . . .The price system is just one of those formations which man has learned to use.[1]

Custom is another formation of this kind. If the market is a marvel, custom is a marvel, too.

Furthermore, command may also be understood as economizing on information. By centralizing the power of decision-making, it is possible to set up an efficient means of gathering information, and to distribute to the individual actors only those pieces of information that are necessary for them to take the appropriate action.

Thus, all three control modes—exchange, command, and custom—can be viewed as economizing on the use and distribution of knowledge. The market is not necessarily the most efficient way to deal with informational issues. Rather, it is conceivable that there are several *kinds* of information, and that the different control modes have specific advantages or drawbacks with respect to gathering, channelling, and distributing that intelligence.

[1] Hayek (1945: 528).

It is, however, misleading to put exclusive stress on the informational aspects of economic allocation mechanisms. Motivation is equally important in the economy.

14.12 *Change*

It has been argued that the problem of economic coordination arises only under conditions of change.[1] Under stationary conditions, all transactions are repeated over and over, and the task of coordination vanishes. Once a transaction pattern is established, no further need for coordination arises. Mere repetition will suffice to organize the division of labour.

The organization of the division of labour becomes crucial— and becomes intricate under conditions of change. Change necessitates adjustment. It therefore becomes important to understand how the economic organization of society generates and digests the change that is needed.

The division of labour within a given society will rely on certain organizational structures which are fixed in the short run. This holds true for markets, hierarchies, and custom. Each of these control modes is characterized by a certain rigidity in the underlying rule system. This renders it possible to cope with certain types of change but not with others.

Consider markets. They work best with standardized products, because standardization renders it unnecessary to evaluate and communicate quality parameters. More generally, it has been argued that 'for anything approaching perfect competition to exist, an intricate system of rules and regulations would normally be needed'.[2] Commodity and stock exchanges provide examples.

Any hierarchical system of command, moreover, depends on a certain institutional structure. Competencies must be defined, and chains of command determined. In a similar way, control by custom relies on fixities of behavioural patterns.

---

[1] Hayek (1945: 524), von Weizsäcker (1991: 102–3,109–10).
[2] Coase (1988: 9).

Thus, all three modes of control exhibit rigidity in some dimensions and flexibility in others. This suggests that each of the control modes may enjoy a differential advantage in coping with certain *types* of change. Markets, for example, can cope more easily with changing demands and supplies, whereas hierarchies and customary forms of organization may find it more difficult to digest such changes.[1] Changing traffic flows can be better coordinated by a system of traffic rules rather than by the auctioning of priority rights. Fires and other disasters can be better dealt with by a hierarchical organization relying on command than by prices and markets designed to allocate rescue forces.

The organization of interdependent tasks poses difficulties for the market. The set of instruments available for direct coordination within and between firms is much richer than that available in the market. On the other hand, the market, in spite of informational shortfalls, is better for organizing independent tasks because it unleashes the forces of competition. Through competition, it overcomes the rigidity of custom that impedes dynamic advance in closely knit organizations.[2]

Yet the perceived interdependency of tasks can attenuate over time. Once routinization takes place, it leads to a standardization of task interfaces. Standardization greatly reduces the need for personal communication. Each task module becomes more separable (and, possibly, internally more interdependent). In this way, the use of the market as a coordination device is rendered feasible.

The picture emerging from this discussion is as follows. New technological developments are organized first *within* firms or as joint ventures *between* firms, without strong reliance on the market. This is because it is difficult to use the market for coordination purposes for entirely non-standardized and volatile interdependent tasks. In the course of time, the project takes shape, routinization develops and takes hold, and standardization becomes possible. This reduces task interdependencies, which in

---

[1] However, the internal organization of firms may respond to different challenges. Burns (1963) has argued, for instance, that change requires an 'organismic' rather than a 'mechanistic' organization structure.   [2] See S. 14.8-14.10.

turn renders it increasingly advantageous to introduce the market as a coordination device for organizing the division of labour. There emerges a tendency to organize non-standardized change within firms, and standardized change through the market.[1] Firms are, so to speak, the nurseries for new projects. Once the projects have achieved an independent identity, they will spin off as separate firms. Those firms will then develop a special organizational culture and a special set of customs of their own.

14.13 *The Firm, the Market, and the Division of Labour*

The clarity view thus implies a view about the division of labour between the firm and the market. Both the firm and the market rely on exchange, command, and custom, but the firm permits tight integration and the development of specialized customs. This eases production and enhances motivation. Yet the tight integration within the firm comes at the cost of internal rigidity. The mutual adjustment of routines, command structures, and internal pricing schemes renders it difficult to implement change. Market interaction is less specialized and unleashes competitive forces to overcome organizational inertia.

The argument comes down to explaining the organization of the division of labour within firms and across the market in terms of the costs and benefits of integration. Where the benefits of integration outweigh the costs, integration will occur; where the costs outweigh the benefits, transactions will be carried out in the market.

The last statement is, by itself, as empty as the statement that transaction costs determine integration. Yet the view expounded here puts things differently. It stresses that the functioning of institutions is not reducible to their various components in an additive way. The stress on 'chemical' interaction is directed

---

[1] A related view has been outlined by von Weizsäcker (1991: 109–13). He argues that firms are better in handling slow change, and markets are better in handling fast change, and that the incentive to innovate falls as market concentration increases, giving rise to an 'equilibrium theory of innovation'.

against nominalistic views of the firm, the market, and other institutions. The tight alignment of routines, pricing procedures, and command structures, both across the market and within firms, emanates from the same tendencies of the human mind that fashion customs in all spheres of life. They relate to processes of overall clarification.

Part III

REVIEW

Chapter 15

THE TEXTURE OF CUSTOM

15.1 *Custom and Clarity*

The preceding chapters have interpreted custom as engendered by clarification processes that work on the multi-faceted interactions of everyday life. This has been illustrated by discussing aspects of property, the law, the firm, and the market from a clarity perspective.

Put very abstractly, the argument was as follows. First, the formation and perception of customary regularities is intimately tied up with clarity requirements. There are usually many ways to describe a certain set of events. Simple enumeration would be an obvious way, but such a description would not qualify as a regularity, because it does not involve any restriction confining instances to a certain structured pattern. Rules must involve restrictions of this nature. Without such restrictions, there is no way to perceive and learn regularities of any kind. The rules of custom are no exception. The features that distinguish rules from non-rules are governed by principles of clarification.[1] The argument may be summarized by saying that customary rules can be perceived and learned because of their clarity properties.

---

[1] This has been elaborated in Ch. 7.

Second, clarification shapes preferences. Whereas the preference for clear patterns renders rule perception and rule inference possible, this desire is not confined to perception. The desire is much broader and carries over to emotion and action. One manifestation of this broad tendency has been described as 'rule preference'. In its simplest form, rule preference expresses itself as habit formation, or as the reflex and habitual adoption of convictions. On a more conscious level, rule preference leads to feelings of entitlement and obligation which are generated by perceiving regularities. The individual feels entitled to do things that are customary and feels compelled to meet customary obligations. In this way, the perception and inference of the regularities of custom affect behaviour. Justifications of various entitlements often derive from rule preference in this manner.

Phenomena of property and ownership are based on rule preference. Rule preference induces 'ownership effects' that link behaviour to the allocation of property rights. Without such a behavioural effect of property assignments, property rights would be irrelevant to behaviour, and economic processes building on property would break down. Furthermore, contracting and market exchange are rendered possible because individuals share a desire to follow prevailing or newly established patterns. People make promises and exchange them. This is possible because promises create entitlements—obligations and commitments—which affect behaviour. Individuals have a desire to respect these entitlements. Market processes rely in this way on rule preference.

Furthermore, business firms make use of firm-specific customs and routines because these rules and routines shape behaviour much beyond what would be attributable to the effects of outright sanctions and rewards. This is made possible, again, by rule preference. Job descriptions involving duties and entitlements can work as they do because behaviour is influenced by perceived demands and duties. In such a way, firms can rely on organizational devices for coordinating the division of labour for complex interdependent tasks in cases where the market would fail, or would perform poorly. They do so by allocating duties and responsibilities and by developing a set of well matched routines that allow for smooth and automatic coordination. All this draws on rule preference and is based on clarity.

Third, and on a somewhat deeper level, individuals have a desire to act reasonably. They want to relate their actions to principles and justifications. The urge for coherence and clarity goes much beyond the analytic rationality postulates of conventional preference theory. Clarification demands similar treatment of similar cases, plays on analogies, and strives for unity of behaviour and style. The desire for overall clarity shapes preferences, actions, cognitions, and emotions by tying them together.

The tendency towards clarification reconfirms and stabilizes custom in a tacit way. It tends to adjust cognitions, actions, and emotions to one another. The result is a set of well matched and highly integrated customs that support each other in various diffuse ways. This usually goes unnoticed. The custom of right-hand driving, for instance, pervades many aspects of everyday life that are quite unrelated to custom, such as keeping to the right on the sidewalk, and designing supermarkets to accommodate the customers' habit of keeping to the right. These features physically ingrain the habit, reinforce it tacitly, and underpin the custom.

The individual's justifications for customary behaviour will usually ignore these various vague influences and will settle for explanations in terms of conventions and preferences. Every-day attribution processes and prevailing assumptions with respect to custom share this desire for over-simplification. The desire is directly related to clarity: individuals try to find clear, rather than diffuse, explanations even in cases where the diffuse explanation, is the correct one. This is of particular importance for a set of well matched customs where everything is minutely adjusted to everything else. Such a complex supports each of its elements in various ways. Individuals try to relate their behaviour to regularities, but the vast and diffuse set of interdependencies does not lend itself easily to rationalization in terms of one single rule. In spite of this, a routine is developed, and a simple regularity is stipulated, or a simple causal attribution is made. In this way, rationalizations in terms of reasons, convictions, and self-attributions are developed. For reasons of clarity and coherence, preferences follow suit. In this way, the diffuse reasons that underpin various customs tacitly shape preferences that reaffirm and stabilize those customs.

15.2 *The Strength of Custom*

Prevailing theorizing on custom centres around conventions, preferences, and smooth adaptation. This renders custom passive. It appears wrongly as an inertial force, lacking direction and structure. The strong motivational aspect of custom, as well as its autonomous unifying force remains concealed and elusive. In contrast, the clarity view tries to comprehend customary phenomena as partially autonomous, capable of shaping individual action, rather than merely reflecting social interaction and slowing down adaptation. At the same time, the clarity view conceptualizes custom as arising from tendencies in the human mind, and not from anonymous collective forces of mystical origin. It tries, in this way, to keep clear of the fallacies of both individualism and holism.

The clarity view suggests that the strength of custom does not reside in any of its diffuse elements, or in its many underlying rationalizations and adaptations, but rather in the way in which these elements are tied together. It is the texture, rather than the stuff, that matters most. The amalgam of well matched customs gains its force because everything depends on everything else. Habits, attitudes, preferences, and convictions are closely tied together. Each reconfirms the other. This makes for a firm and supple fabric, in spite of the extreme flimsiness of the individual threads.

The strength of custom—its partial autonomy, rigidity, and direction—derives ultimately from the tendency of the human mind towards overall clarity of organization. As the possible states of the world differ in clarity, the tendency towards clarity may be envisaged by imagining a landscape with valleys and basins of clarity towards which things are tending. The partial autonomy of custom, as well as its rigidity and direction, derive from these tendencies towards clarity.

The objective nature of clarity accounts for the objectivity and the apparent autonomy of custom. Judgements concerning simplicity, analogy, symmetry, and good continuity share this feature. The rules of custom—the rules that govern property, for example—inherit their objective appearance from the objective nature of clarity judgements. This distinguishes them from other social phenomena—from, say, the more volatile aspects of fashion—that incorporate many features deriving from idiosyncratic tastes.

Customs differ widely across societies, however. Each society may be thought of as having settled in one particular basin or valley of the clarity landscape. The force of gravity works over the entire landscape, pulling everything down. Clarification affects all societies in a similar way, just as the force of gravity affects all kinds of matter. However, the particular place where a society has settled, or the particular mountainside down which it slides, is contingent on history and circumstance. The phenomenon of custom is universal; its particular manifestations are not.

15.3 *Custom and Change*

Custom has been described as an integrating force. It binds various aspects of everyday life together by urging overall clarity. Customary rules subsume various events under a single regularity, similar cases are treated similarly, and new events are integrated by employing analogies. All this illustrates the integrative force of custom.

This integrative force of custom induces change of an autonomous kind that will require further clarification and integration. But there are many other sources of change that emerge for quite unrelated reasons and that are a threat to cohesiveness. Climatic and ecological change, migration, and population growth induce new problems; changes in technology provide an incessant source of perturbation. Custom has to cope with these changes by integrating them into the prevailing set of habits, convictions, and valuations. It must assimilate new routines, views, and valuations to accommodate the new developments. The integrating force of custom may succeed in aligning these changes with received views and traditional ways of behaviour, or it may fail to achieve this alignment and may disintegrate. But even during phases of fragmentation, the urge to clarify will induce unceasing attempts to form new customs and establish new routines. Thus, disintegration of custom during such phases does not indicate the absence of clarification: it only signifies that the processes of clarification are failing at that moment to generate viable integrative solutions.

Clarification creates a pervasive mutual interdependence of all kinds of social phenomena. An improvement in the technology of communication, for instance, will not be confined to replacing letters with electronic mail while leaving society unchanged in all other respects. It may transform market structure, induce changes in the perception of property rights, change the law, undermine local habits of interaction. It may deeply affect social structure. The direct effects of the introduction of information technology may be small, but they are very numerous and diffuse. A vast number of interactions will be affected, each in a minor way. Modes of payment, communication, and delivery may be imbalanced. The organization of work and the monitoring routines within firms will be forced to adapt. Face-to-face interaction will be replaced by more impersonal forms of coordination in many ways.

All of this engenders a cumulative sequence of indirect effects. The many small changes will bring about changes in routines and mores. Their diffuseness will induce attributions to changed norms and convictions, rather than to the underlying technological change. The lack of personal communication may call forth more standardized forms of behaviour and a different etiquette in order to establish trust in anonymous settings. The new manners and routines will spill over on to the prevailing customs and change them accordingly. The integrating force of clarification processes may engender a flow of indirect effects. In this way, custom channels change while being shaped by change, like a river meandering through time.

Appendix A
NOTES ON METHOD

A.1 *The Traditional View*

The traditional—and still largely dominant—view of how custom and economics relate to each other was stated 150 years ago by the great classical economist, John Stuart Mill. In the chapter in his *Principles* entitled 'Of Competition and Custom', he wrote:

Under the rule of individual property, the division of the produce is the result of two determining agencies: Competition and Custom. It is important to ascertain the amount of influence which belongs to each of these causes, and in what manner the operation of one is modified by the other.

Political economists generally, and English political economists above others, have been accustomed to . . . exaggerate the effect of competition, and to take into little account the other and conflicting principle [of custom]. . . . This is partly intelligible, if we consider that only through the principle of competition has political economy any pretension to the character of a science. So far as rents, profits, wages, prices, are determined by competition, laws may be assigned to them. Assume competition to be their exclusive regulator, and principles of broad generality and scientific precision may be laid down, according to which they will be regulated. The political economist justly deems this his proper business: and as an abstract or hypothetical science, political economy cannot be required to do, and indeed cannot do, anything more.[1]

The argument rests on the idea that the effects of competition fruitfully may be analysed by abstracting from all influences of custom. This involves very specific assumptions about the interaction of competition and custom, assumptions that are not necessarily valid.

A.2 *Additive and 'Chemical' Interaction*

Mill himself was aware of the problem. Generally, he said, influences may combine either 'mechanically' or 'chemically'. In the former case, the outcome can readily be understood as a superposition of the individual effects. The demand for umbrellas, for example, may be influenced by price and climate. The influence of price may be studied for a given climate, and the influence of climate may be studied for a given price. The joint effect of price and climate may be understood simply by

[1] Mill (1909: 242). The first edition of this book was published in 1848.

combining these considerations. Economic analysis largely proceeds in this way when discussing economic effects under the *ceteris paribus* assumption that 'everything else remains unchanged'. This isolating approach is appropriate if forces combine 'mechanically' or 'additively'.[1] If they do, each of the forces may be analysed separately, and the separate considerations may be combined later on to obtain a complete picture of the processes under study.

Mill noted, however, that causes may work together to produce an outcome that cannot readily be predicted from a knowledge of the individual effects alone. Two drugs may be each quite harmless, and even beneficial, but their joint effect could be lethal. This would be the result of a 'chemical' interaction.[2] Custom and competition may be said to interact chemically, if their joint effect flows from genuine interaction and cannot be understood in terms of a superposition of their separate and quasi-independent influences. If custom and competition interact in such a chemical way, the influence of competition cannot usefully be analysed while abstracting from the influence of custom. The isolating approach suggested by Mill would be quite inappropriate, even with regard to purely economic processes.

A.3 *The 'Chemical' View of Custom*

Mill's position clearly depends on the assumption that the forces of custom and competition combine additively rather than chemically. This is an assumption about the factual nature of social processes. It is not an innocuous methodological choice made for purposes of theoretical convenience alone. There are certainly many cases in which such an assumption is appropriate, and for these cases Mill's position can be defended. According to Marshall, however, 'Mill exaggerated the extent to which this can be done'.[3]

The general position adopted by Mill is extremely problematic, if not severely misleading. The problem is this. Customs are not independent givens: rather, they are produced by a 'chemical' combination of sundry forces. Under a long-term perspective, custom is the *result* of social interaction, rather than an independent driving force. It affects social and economic processes strongly. It may furnish explanations for purposes of short-term analysis, but in the long-term custom cannot be taken as given.

This 'chemical' view of custom underlies the arguments presented in

---

[1] The issue is extensively discussed in Schlicht (1985*a*).
[2] Mill (1925: 289). [3] Marshall (1890/1920: 771 n).

this book. It is very closely related to the 'reciprocity' view advocated by Jones.[1]

A.4 *Individualism v. Holism*

One of the age-old themes in the social sciences is the tension between methodological individualism and holism. The former insists that the only autonomous originators are the discrete individuals, and that all theory has to start from their actions. The latter maintains that social phenomena are not understandable in terms of the properties of the individuals alone. Individual action is conditioned by cultural forces, and must be understood in terms of these forces.

These two views—often related to economics and sociology—are based on two different views of man: the individualistic and the socio-logical view, respectively.[2]

A.5 *The Individualistic View*

The individualistic view holds that individuals are the only real actors in society. Social phenomena are *results* of an uncountable number of indi-vidual endeavours. They must, therefore, be theoretically interpreted as such.[3]

This thesis basically may take two forms, linked to the fields of psychology and economics. The first holds that individuals—through conditioning, learning, or in other ways—develop certain patterns of behaviour that ultimately give rise to social phenomena such as customs. Much of traditional psychology has stressed 'irrational' impulses such as drives, conditioned responses, or desires arising from subconscious pro-cesses. The economic view stresses the 'rational' aspects of behaviour while assuming that the relevant preferences are given. Behaviour is determined ultimately by the set of prevailing preferences, competitive processes and rational choice on the side of the individuals.[4]

---

[1] E. Jones (1995).

[2] The views have been aptly described as 'undersocialized' and 'oversocialized'; see Granovetter (1985) for an excellent account. The terminology is due to Wrong (1986).

[3] This paraphrases a formulation by the great Austrian economist, Carl Menger, concerning economics; see Menger (1883: 87). Max Weber's 'methodological individu-alism' as well as his 'ideal types' are closely related to the views held by his former teacher.

[4] The situation in economics is actually somewhat more complicated than portrayed here, since the rationality assumption is often used in an 'as if' sense. This does not, however, affect the conclusions drawn here. The problem is extensively elaborated in Schlicht (1990*a*).

Once it is conceded that preferences must be acquired, and that people are guided by their urges as well as by custom and reasoning, the psychological and economic views are compatible with one another. As 'rational' strategies may be routinized, habitualized, or encoded emotionally in various ways, it seems difficult, if not futile, to classify behaviour along the rationality-drive dimension.[1] It seems better to avoid that distinction and to treat the two views jointly.

The individualistic approach seems to be sound as far as it goes, but it is often stretched further. This is the case if it is postulated that there are two classes of phenomena, belonging to different layers of reality: individuals and social relations. The former are real, the latter are theoretical fictions. Terms like 'firm', 'family', or 'nation' refer to nothing with an identity of its own, but are shorthand terms that summarize in an abstract way the actions and interactions of many individuals. 'Customs' would arise because individuals have chosen to behave in a certain concerted fashion, or have learnt to do so, but the term refers to an abstraction.[2] Such a view seems untenable. Individuals and social relations coexist. The presence of one of these elements implies the presence of other, and there is no point in insisting that one of those elements is real while the other is an abstraction. Such a position would 'force us to say that the disturbance at a given point on a surface of water is a thing, although the wave-form generated by these disturbances is an abstraction'.[3]

Another frequent connotation of the individualistic thesis regards causality: the individuals are seen as the actors, and causality must start from them. This view is often presented as something axiomatic, but it actually involves factual assumptions about the nature of social interaction that are not necessarily true, and confounds proximate and ultimate causation. This issue will be discussed in the next section.

A.6 *The Sociological View*

The sociological view 'begins with the observation that when men live and act in groups, there arise forces and phenomena that follow laws of their own and which cannot be described in terms of the properties of the individuals composing them. Language, technology, kinship relations are not the product of individual minds and motives. These are processes

---

[1] See S. 1.6 above on emotional encoding.
[2] This is well illustrated in economics, where it is held that institutions like firms are 'legal fictions which serve as a nexus for a set of contracting relationships among individuals' (Jensen and Meckling 1976: 310).   [3] Asch (1952: 245).

over and above those that we find in individuals taken singly and which can no longer be traced back to them.'[1]

This idea is familiar in biology. While the genes may provide the proximate causes for the shape and colouring of a butterfly, the colouring may better be explained in terms of survival value. Some quite remote causes—the preferences of the birds and the colours of the plants—will explain the colouring along with the relevant properties of the genes. Some very rough premises about the reproductive processes—the principles of genetic transmission and variation—suffice to make such an argument. In explaining the shape of organisms by evolutionary principles, ultimate causes rather than proximate causes are evoked. These ultimate causes rest in the shape and behaviour of other organisms in the environment. The shape and behaviour of these organisms is explained similarly.

For social processes, the same may hold true. Social phenomena may take on a certain identity of their own. Once individual behaviour is influenced by social interaction, it may to a large extent be explicable in terms of social structure. Generally speaking, self-regulatory systems will stabilize certain features. The elements of such systems may adapt to these stable features, and in this sense individual behaviour may be understood as a consequence, rather than a cause, of social processes.[2] Individualistic positions tend to disregard this possibility.

A.7 *The Position Adopted Here*

So far as it goes, the sociological view is acceptable. There is no conflict with individualism once genuine social interaction is taken into account. Yet the sociological view is often held to imply that assumptions about individual behaviour are entirely irrelevant to the analysis, because the

---

[1] Asch (1952: 424). The account given in Asch's book of the 'group mind thesis' on the one hand and the 'individualistic thesis' on the other, written more than 40 years ago, provides a balanced view, still unsurpassed.

[2] It is sometimes maintained that 'an explanation . . . of system behavior in terms of actions and orientations of lower-level units is likely to be more stable and general than an explanation which remains at the system level' (Coleman 1990: 3). This belief is unfounded. Schlicht (1985a: 85–93) provides an example to the contrary. Within an economic model of growth and distribution, it turns out that the aggregate savings rate is stabilized independently of individual savings propensities, and income distribution adjusts in such a way that this aggregate outcome is obtained. In this example, the aggregate savings rate is determined by system properties and is independent of individual decisions, although it is just the sum of individual savings. The macro model exhibits, in this example, 'more' stability than the corresponding micro model. This phenomenon has been stressed by structuralist sociologists who insist that 'individuals come out of relations' (White 1992: 298).

individual himself is socially conditioned. Individual behaviour is assumed to be perfectly plastic. The true causes of individual action, therefore, must rest in system properties and cultural forces.

This seems an untenable position. There is no hope of explaining social phenomena while disregarding the properties of the individual. In order to explain the system properties themselves, the properties of individuals must be considered. Those system properties must result from general and universal traits of human nature, just as the laws of biological evolution are ultimately to be determined by general traits of the reproductive process.[1] If human behaviour were in fact infinitely plastic, no definite and stable social structure could emerge. But the human mind is *not* infinitely malleable. Its invariant properties account for social regularities like customs that occur everywhere but take vastly different forms in different societies. As these phenomena appear across cultures, an explanation for these features must be culture-invariant as well. Whereas the sociological perspective is often held to imply cultural relativism, the present view rejects it.

The approach pursued here thus combines elements of both the individualistic and the sociological points of view. It aims at understanding social processes while retaining the prime reality of individual and social phenomena, the two permanent poles of all social processes.[2]

A.8 *The Paradigmatic Approach*

There is, however, still another view on these matters that is widely shared among economists. This posits that economic analysis refers not so much to a specific field of study as to a particular paradigm— the paradigm of rational choice. It has been asserted that economics should try to explain as many phenomena as possible from optimizing behaviour, or should ask how the world would look if men were guided solely by economic motives—the striving for utility and profit.[3]

---

[1] In the example mentioned in the preceding footnote, the system properties are generated not only by the prevailing external conditions, but also by the type of behaviour of the individuals. The result holds, for example, only for a *range* of individual attitudes to saving: if individuals either save too much or do not save at all, the relevant system properties will break down.

[2] This paraphrases Asch (1952: 250). It is to be noted here that such a position is increasingly reflected in recent theoretical writings, e.g. Kuran (1995: 329–31).

[3] This paraphrases Menger (1883: 59), who was quite extreme on this. He did not deny the existence of other (non-economic) influences. They might even override the economic factors. Yet exact economics should not consider this. The other social sciences ought to deal with the other forces.

This view appears in the passage from Mill cited above where economics is described as an 'abstract or hypothetical science'.[1] A defence could run as follows. All theories are hypothetical, and realism can never be achieved. All that matters is consistency. Such consistency can be obtained only by conforming to a well-defined paradigm. The paradigm itself is seen as an organizational device that helps to pose empirically 'meaningful' questions and to offer consistent explanations— in fact, rationalizations—of empirical findings.

This view is not particularly helpful. Even if full realism can never be achieved, these theories may differ vastly in their degree of realism. Furthermore, a number of 'consistent' but otherwise arbitrary paradigms can be invented.[2]

The paradigmatic view comes down to one of the following two alternatives. First, economic theory may be taken as a language that is independent of the phenomena under study and tells next to nothing about the nature of social processes. Second, economic theory may be concerned with extracting the hypothetical implications of an arbitrarily chosen definition of economic motivation. The latter appears to be as shallow as the exercise that is suggested by the former alternative.

The other aspect of Mill's defence—'that only through the principle of competition has political economy any pretension to the character of a science'—suggests that a paradigmatic approach is necessary for any true 'science'.[3] This seems a highly irrelevant concern. No one, apart from economists, will be interested in whether or not economics is classified as a 'science'. If the only choice is either doing 'science' in cloud-cookoo-land or understanding economic reality, the economist's preference should be clear.

The position adopted here rejects the paradigmatic view. The field of study is not perceived as delineated by a theoretical paradigm. Rather, it is demanded that the phenomena under study ought not to work back to what has been presupposed. They must be separable in a real sense in order to lend themselves to isolated analysis. This separability require-ment defines the boundaries of fields. If economic and other influences combine in a chemical way, it is misleading to analyse these factors in

---

[1] See S. A.1 above.

[2] Coase (1988: 3–4) has suggested for instance that 'there is no reason to suppose that most human beings are engaged in maximising anything unless it be unhappiness, and even this with incomplete success'. The general identification problem is discussed in the context of the 'Eleusis' game in Ss. 7.2–7.5.   [3] Mill (1909: 242).

isolation. The view rests, thus, on (testable) assumptions about conceivable interactions.[1]

A.9 *Comments on the Use of Psychology*

It has been stressed repeatedly that custom is rooted in psychological regularities and cannot adequately be grasped without this background. The approach has been used to elucidate the phenomena of property, the law, the firm, and the market. The stress on psychological mechanisms runs against the grain of modern economic analysis. The purpose of the following remarks is to reflect on the aversion to using psychological arguments in the social sciences.

The widespread desire to sidestep psychological issues may be for two reasons. First, scientists may fear using arguments from other 'fields' because they do not feel sufficiently competent. Such a position favours hypotheses that are entirely paradigm-driven, and effectively excludes straightforward ideas that transgress the customary boundaries of any particular discipline.[2] In this way, a host of challenging ideas is excluded from scientific discourse. Köhler has commented on this as follows:

Of course nobody can be forced to participate in the solution of a fascinating problem. But is it not depressing that the task of having to travel through several fields of science is sometimes regarded not as an alluring prospect but as a disagreeable demand?[3]

The other reason for the aversion may lie in a fear of introducing subjectivity and arbitrariness by trespassing on the customary boundaries of the disciplines. In view of modern developments in psychology, this fear is understandable. Fortunately, it is substantively unfounded.

Modern developments in psychology have indeed taken a problematic turn. Asch summarizes this as follows:

Historical circumstances make for odd alignments, and this is what happened with the peculiar affiliation during the 1930s in America between the alien and mostly incompatible currents of behaviorism and psychoanalysis. Mainly they shared one affinity: both worked (although in distinctive ways) from the premise

---

[1] The view sketched above is closely akin to what Alfred Marshall (1920) advocated and practised. It is elaborated in Schlicht (1985*a*). New institutional economists such as Ronald Coase and Oliver Williamson pursues this 'realistic' tradition, but the abstract approach is still dominant; see the Williamson–Posner controversy (O. E. Williamson 1993*a*, 1993*b*; Posner 1993*a*, 1993*b*; Scott 1993; Coase 1993).

[2] See also the discussion in S. A.8 above.   [3] Köhler (1940: 113).

of human irrationality; both strove for a general psychology on that foundation
. . . And is not the current cognitive psychology, despite the striking change of
language it introduced, perhaps too often a guise for a newly attired behaviorism,
a species of the increasingly mentioned 'cognitive behaviorism'? . . . is this
discipline perhaps on the wrong track?[1]

Modern Gestalt psychology has taken a hopelessly subjectivist turn as
well. The following quotation by Fuller contrasts this modern view with
the 'classical' Gestalt position entertained by Wolfgang Köhler:

To come right to the point, the basic shortcoming of Köhler's approach—and
with it that of classical Gestalt psychology as a whole—is its objectivism. Köhler
holds psychology to the scientific ideal of an objective science of physical processes. . . . Psychological organization (law-governed dynamic self-distribution)
for Köhler is an objective causal process taking place in the cortex by reason of
spreading and interacting electric currents. The essentials of Gestalt formation
thus are viewed as occurring transphenomenally in the objective brain. . . . Existential phenomenology finds that meanings originate in an internal and external
signifying of one another in existential space, on meaning's own level, and not in
the causal forces presumed operative in objective space.[2]

While I am agnostic regarding Köhler's specific hypotheses about electric
fields in the brain, I do take Gestalt formation, which I termed 'clarification processes', as objective phenomena rooted in the objective structure
of the human nervous system. I side with the classical Gestalt psychology
and with Köhler—and Hume, who spoke about 'a faculty, which nature
has antecedently implanted in the mind, and render'd unavoidable'.[3]

This position avoids the problems of subjectivism by pointing out that
laws of perception are facts that can be studied and understood. Even
vague terms like 'style' and 'readability' can, in principle, be objectified.
There are wordprocessing programs that evaluate style and readability.
These programs are beset with problems, but it is remarkable that it is
possible to agree on *why* they are unsatisfactory. In other words, the
objective character of the problems encountered with 'operationalizing'
vague notions witnesses the non-subjective character of the phenomena in
question.

In Schumpeter's *History of Economic Analysis*, there is an interesting
paragraph dealing with Gestalt psychology:

Gestalt Psychology (Ehrenfels, Köhler, Koffka, Wertheimer, Riezler) develops
from a single basic fact: no individual element of any set of elements is perceived
or appraised or interpreted individually—a sound in a song, a color in a carpet, or
even a glass of wine that is part of a dinner is never 'experienced' in isolation and,

[1] Asch (1952: vii, x).   [2] Fuller (1990: 162–5).   [3] Hume (1740a: 183).

if it were, it would mean to us something quite different from what it does mean actually, that is, as part of the definite set in which it occurs. All we need to say about this evidently highly important discovery—for it was nothing less, though my formulations sound trivial enough—is . . . that among the many uses to which Gestalt psychology may be put in the social sciences, there is at least one of considerable importance. Gestalt psychology may be used in order to arrive at a sensible and non-metaphysical concept of psycho-sociological collectives—such as society itself.[1]

This is suggestive of the approach taken here. However, in spite of its obviousness, and in spite of Hume's elaborate arguments pointing in the Gestalt direction, the idea has not been pursued in the social sciences in a significant way. The book *Social Psychology* by Solomon Asch, published in 1952, is an outstanding exception. My attempt, in this book, has been to resuscitate this line of thought.

[1] Schumpeter (1954: 798).

Appendix B
THE PRINCIPLE OF RELATIVITY

B.1 Cultural Relativism

The position of cultural relativism has been stated and defended as follows. It is all very well to speak of the importance of the Platonic concept of 'ideal truth' and to make the metaphysical, or metacultural, postulate of objective reality as a constant that is independent of the observer. This intellectual position is known to exist. In terms of our knowledge of psychocultural processes relating to enculturation, however, the relativist once again can only pose his basic query: '*Whose* objective reality?'[1] In other words, relativism holds that reality, and in particular social reality, is a cultural construct. Truth in the social sciences is considered a matter of custom. The relativistic position would severely undermine the present attempt to approach the phenomenon of custom in universalistic terms. The purpose of this appendix is to criticize the position of cultural relativism and to suggest that Einstein's 'Principle of Relativity' ought to be maintained not only in the natural sciences, but in the social sciences as well.

The relativistic argument is simple. Cultural variation in norms, convictions, cognitions, and customs is endless, and no human being is in a position to detach himself from his own social background. This renders all theories about social phenomena thoroughly culture-dependent. It is argued that this position is a 'well established truth'.[2] The position is still dominant in large segments of the social sciences.[3]

B.2 A Critique of Cultural Relativism

The argument of relativism is not, however, entirely convincing, for several reasons.

First, the fact of cultural diversity may be interpreted in different ways. Different cultures may be brought about by universal laws, in the same manner in which subatomic particles combine in sundry combinations and form a host of chemical elements while obeying the universal and invariant laws of subatomic interaction. The social sciences may be construed analogously as aiming at understanding different social for-

---

[1] This paraphrases Herskovits (1958: 271).
[2] P. F. Schmidt (1955: 782). The relevant passage is quoted in Herskovits (1958: 266).
[3] A prominent, and rather extreme, position may be found in Geertz (1973).

mations in terms of universal principles.[1] Cultural relativism makes the unfounded predictive assumption that universalistic principles can never be established. In order to defend such an assumption, we must try to refute it. This requires adopting a universalist position as a working hypothesis.

Second, the idea of truth may be maintained even if we know that we are not able to grasp it.

Third, the thesis of relativism, if true, must be interpreted as being prompted by one specific culture. As all convictions are held to be social constructs, this must apply for the relativistic thesis itself. The relativistic thesis, if true and applied to itself, implies that it is arbitrary. In this sense it is self-contradictory. It cannot claim universal validity because it denies the possibility of truth independent of culture.

Fourth, the argument that human beings cannot detach themselves from their own culture (and that all analytic schemata must be culture-dependent for this reason) seems theoretically and practically misleading. Formally, the same argument could be made for any kind of story. Stories must be told in one language or another. They cannot, in that sense, be detached from language. Yet it is possible to translate a story from one language into another, and it is possible to recognize the different versions as the 'same' story. Even if a story must be told in one language, it makes sense, theoretically and practically, to think of the content of the story as being independent of language. In the same vein, we may think of social regularities as independent of culture, although it is impossible to formulate them in a culture-free way.

Fifth, those anthropologists who insist on cultural relativism are making their case by pointing to the variety of cultural practices, to the diverse meanings attached to them, and to the inner logic prevailing in alien cultures. Such cultural baggage differs radically from the understandings prevailing in our own culture. But American anthropologists, for instance, are apparently able to understand and explain Indonesian culture.[2] Foreigners learn to live in another culture and to grasp essential cultural particularities—perhaps not fully, but in a surprisingly comprehensive way. This suggests that it is possible for members of one culture to understand phenomena in other cultures. It points to universal regularities shared by all cultures.

---

[1] This analogy has been stressed by Lévi-Strauss (1955: 178). The position adopted here differs from that suggested by Lévi-Strauss; see p. 146 above, Asch (1952: ch. 13), and Duncker (1939).   [2] Geertz (1973).

B.3 *An Analogue to Einstein's Principle*

It is interesting and important to note how the problem of relativism has been dealt with in physics. Quite contrary to current misperceptions, and in contrast to the view embraced by cultural relativists, Einstein's theory of relativity is not concerned with asserting that 'everything is relative'. Instead, Einstein *postulates* that the laws of physics *must be conceived in such a way that they are independent of the point of reference chosen.* This is taken as axiomatic. Einstein's 'Principle of Relativity' presupposes that 'all bodies of reference . . . are equivalent for the description of natural phenomena (formulation of the general laws of nature)'.[1]

An analogous principle of relativity, pertaining to the social sciences, would thus read: 'The laws of social interaction are to be conceived as independent of the cultural position of the observer.' This principle summarizes the position adopted in this book. It underlies the stress on psychology, which is as ultimate to the social sciences as physics is to the natural sciences.[2]

It is to be emphasized, however, that the principle of relativity does not take any one culture as the natural reference point for social analysis, just as Einstein's position does not identify the heliocentric world-view as the natural one. Just as Einsteinian physics aims at formulating the laws of nature independently of the system of reference, so social analysis must aim at formulating its insights in ways that are invariant with respect to the cultural point of view taken.

Furthermore, the principle of relativity does not proclaim culture-specific theories to be worthless. Rather, they are to be considered as building blocks, or limiting cases, of universal regularities. A comparison may be found in physics, where Newton's system is a special case of Einstein's. Culture-specific studies are of universalistic significance precisely because they instance universal regularities of social interaction. For the purposes of social science, we may legitimately concentrate on specific cultures first, in order to find a foothold for developing theories of more general validity. The approach to custom proposed in this book is guided by this idea.

---

[1] Einstein (1961: 61).
[2] Asch (1952: xi). This concern has induced me to stress the independence of clarity and culture; see S. 6.7–6.12.

Appendix C
HUME'S LAW

C.1 *Surprises with Hume*

The account of Hume's theory of property may have surprised psychologists because of its stress on cognition.[1] It may have also surprised philosophers and social scientists. Some of them would be inclined to think that 'Hume's Law', so familiar to them, and typically associated with ethical relativism, is somewhat at odds with the universalist stance taken by Hume with regard to the foundation of property. They would also find it at variance with his simultaneous stress on property being intimately related to cognitive processes. They are right. 'Hume's Law', as usually interpreted, entails a view about an independence of cognition and valuation that runs counter to Hume's ideas. In this sense, the usual interpretation of Hume's Law is misleading.

The purpose of this appendix is to discuss the relationship between ethical relativism, Hume's Law, and the position taken by Hume on ethical issues, which is universalist.

C.2 *Ethical Relativism*

The position of ethical relativism asserts a fundamental arbitrariness of ethical valuations. Ethical relativism is usually confounded with cultural relativism by virtue of the argument that ethical valuations are determined by culture. Yet cultural relativism and ethical relativism are formally separate issues. The reason is that a social scientist who believes in the possibility of a positive universalist social science may still consider ethical valuations to be independent of factual judgements. He will thus see them as ultimately arbitrary and culturally contingent.[2]

The position of ethical relativism can be defended along two lines. The first defence is to treat ethical relativism as a special case of cultural relativism; the second is to assert the independence of ethical from factual judgements. The first line of argument has been discussed earlier and will not be dealt with here. The second line of argument is based on Hume's Law.

---

[1] See Ch. 11.
[2] This position is akin to that entertained by many economists. The logical independence of cultural and ethical relativism has been stressed by Herskovits (1958: 267). On cultural relativism, see App. B.

C.3 *Two Versions of Hume's Law*

There is no explicit statement of the law by Hume himself. The conventional view of the law is well captured by the following quotation, taken from the *Oxford Dictionary of Philosophy*:

Hume's law. A name for the contested view that it is impossible to derive an 'ought' from an 'is', or in other words, that there is no logical bridge over the gap between fact and value. Hume's own statement is in the *Treatise of Human Nature, iii.* 1.1, where he wrote that it seems 'altogether inconceivable that this new relation [ought] can be derived from others, which are entirely different from it'. The 'law' in fact appears as something of an afterthought to other discussion.[1]

Another dictionary of philosophy is more decisive:

Hume's law. The increasingly popular label for Hume's insistence that the 'naturalistic fallacy' is indeed a fallacy; and hence that conclusions about what ought to be cannot be deduced from premises stating only what was, what is, or what will be—and the other way round.[2]

A brief statement of the first version of Hume's Law is as follows:

The Loose Law: An *ought* cannot be derived from an *is*.

This 'law' can, however, be further elaborated. Granted that an *ought* cannot be derived from an *is*, it is still possible to derive an *ought* from an is in conjunction with another *ought*. The normative statement 'You ought to cure your cough' and the positive statement 'Your cough will disappear if you keep warm' imply the normative statement 'You ought to keep warm.' The last statement is a *derived* valuation.[3] Any value that is not derived is termed basic. This gives rise to the second formulation of Hume's Law:

The Tight Law: Any value is either basic or derived.

These laws look very similar. Both are consistent. They differ only in that the Tight Law introduces a distinction between basic and derived values that is not to be found in the Loose Law. This distinction is to be found in Hume, although he has not used the terms 'basic' and 'derived'.[4]

---

[1] S. Blackburn (1994: 180).

[2] Flew (1975: 146). It must be mentioned that the entry in the same dictionary on the 'naturalistic fallacy' is less simple-minded.

[3] This is in conformity with Hume (1740*a*: 459, 462); for the distinction between basic and derived values, see also Sen (1970: 59–64).

[4] Hume (1740*a*: 459, 462).

C.4 *The Loose Law, the Tight Law, and Ethical Relativism*

Consider how these versions of Hume's Law relate to the issue of ethical relativism.[1]

The Loose Law suggests the arbitrariness of values, because values cannot be derived from factual judgements. This is precisely the position of ethical relativism. A relativistic reading would take the law as vindicating all kinds of ethical relativism. There would be no factual basis for universal human rights. The very idea of rights, morality, good, and bad would appear arbitrary, a matter of taste or cultural contingency.

A similar conclusion seems to emerge from the Tight Law. As basic values, by definition, are not justifiable any further, they are arbitrary and non-rational. In so far as the law implies the existence of basic values, it would suggest the relativistic interpretation. Yet this is not the case.

The Tight Law says nothing about the existence of basic values. This may be clarified by a formally identical argument about numbers. We may define a natural number as *derived* if it can be obtained by taking the difference of two other numbers, and as *basic* if it is not derived. It is true that any number is either basic or derived, but all numbers are derived, and none is basic. Each number is based on another one. For that reason, there exists no basic number. Moral values may formally be related in the same way. All values may be based on others, without any basic value being required or implied.

The tight interpretation does not imply any kind of ethical relativism. This can be seen from an argument in analogy to the argument about basic and derived numbers. Assume that there are two sets of mutually exclusive values, say $\{A, B, C\}$ and $\{a, b, c\}$. The value A is assumed to be incompatible with a, in the sense of being 'just the opposite'. This is denoted by $(A) \perp a$, which reads 'A is incompatible with a'. Under a similar assumption for the other valuations, it is assumed that

$$(A) \perp a, (B) \perp b, (C) \perp c$$

holds true.

Assume now that there is a set of factual knowledge, known to be true. Together with this knowledge, each value judgement can be derived from

---

[1] The following argument is very simple and straightforward but is not well known. It is related to Albert's (1968: ch. 12) discussion of 'Brückenprinzipien'. Recent contributions on the topic, e.g. Sen (1970: 59–64) and Sugden (1986: 153–4; 175) seem to misrepresent the case. The issue is of some importance for the problem of cultural relativism; therefore I state it here again. (An earlier statement is in Schlicht 1974.) For a good discussion of cultural relativism, see Asch (1952).

others. As a matter of notation, $(A, B) \to C$ denotes that 'factual knowledge allows the derivation of value C from values A and B.'

Assume the following inferences to be possible in this way:

$$(B, c) \to A, \; (a) \to B, \; (A, b) \to C,$$

$$(C, b) \to a, \; (c) \to b, \; (a, B) \to c.$$

All values A, B, C, a, b, c are derived values. They can be derived from other values by means of factual knowledge. Yet the set of valuations is uniquely determined as (A,B,C). This can be seen as follows. Note first that this set of norms violates none of the above implications. So it is a possible system of values, given the factual knowledge. But what about other norm systems like (A, b, c) that could be obtained by combining other alternatives? They can all be ruled out. Consider each of the alternative valuations. If a were right, B would be right. This in turn would imply c to be right. B and c imply A—a contradiction, since a and A are incompatible. So a is wrong and A is right. Assume now that b is right. As A is right, this would imply C to be right, and this would imply a to be right. This cannot be the case, because A has been shown to be right. So B is right, and b is wrong. Assume now that c is right. This implies b to be right, but this cannot be the case, because B has been shown to be right. This proves that the set of values (A, B, C) is uniquely determined by the factual knowledge available.

Thus, the Tight Law does not imply ethical relativism. To be precise, it does not imply *anything* concerning the issue of ethical relativism. It does not rule out a multiplicity of possible value systems, it does not rule out uniqueness, and it does not rule out the non-existence that may come about if no value system can be found that is consistent with the postulated inferences.

The above example has shown that the Tight Law is compatible with uniqueness. In this sense the Loose Law, although compatible with the Tight Law, is misleading. The following, after all, is implied by *both* versions:

First implication: It may be the case that an *ought* can be uniquely determined from an *is* under the assumption that an *ought* exists. This does not presuppose the existence of basic values.

This seems to be a better version than the Loose Law because it does not suggest, incorrectly, that valuations *must* be arbitrary. There is no reason to make such a contention about values. However, another implication can be obtained from this discussion. That implication is indeed very universalist in spirit:

Second implication: Additional knowledge may reduce the set of possible values, but will never increase it.

This implication stresses the dependence of values on knowledge, rather than stating that valuations are arbitrary. Thus, even if it is assumed that Hume's Law is correct, the law certainly cannot be used as a defence of any kind of ethical relativism.

C.5 *The Existence of an* Ought

Hume's concern, however, went in a quite different direction. The first section of book III, part I of the *Treatise* is entitled 'Moral distinctions not deriv'd from reason'. It is followed by a second section, 'Moral distinctions deriv'd from a moral sense'. The usual discussion of Hume's Law relates to the first section and neglects the second. The omission leads to misunderstanding. It neglects the way in which the moral sense relates to reason. The 'law' is actually a consequence of the way in which Hume distinguishes 'reason' and 'moral sense'. The law is an *implication of a theoretical distinction drawn between reason and moral sense*— nothing more, nothing less.

Hume would accept both implications. He has actually dealt with the possibility of uniqueness mentioned in the first implication:

In order, therefore, to prove that the measures of right or wrong are eternal laws, *obligatory* on every rational mind, 'tis not sufficient to shew the relations upon which they are founded: We must also point out the connexion with the will; and must prove that this connexion is so necessary, that in every well-disposed mind, it must take place and have its influence.[1]

This highlights what Hume's discussion is aiming at. Right and wrong are not external to human beings and derivable *more geometrico*: they relate to the will and are active forces. Reason is passive:

The merit and demerit of actions frequently contradict, and sometimes controul our natural propensities. But reason has no such influence . . . [It] is the discovery of truth and falshood. . . . Moral distinctions, therefore, are not the offspring of reason. Reason is wholly inactive, and can never be the source of so active a principle as conscience, or a sense of morals.[2]

Therefore, reason cannot establish the *existence* of an *ought*. The problem is not that of a relativism of values, but that of existence. The *existence* of an *ought* cannot be derived from judgements about truth and

---

[1] Hume (1740*a*: 465).   [2] Hume (1740*a*: 458).

falsehood. Yet reason can contribute to establishing what possible *oughts* there might be.

This question about the *existence* of an *ought* is quite different from the problem about the *contents* of the *ought*. Usual discussions, however, refer typically to the latter. A correct version of Hume's Law would read:

> The existence of an *ought* cannot be inferred from a judgement about the true and the false. This is not necessarily the case with the contents of the *ought*.

In this sense, the usual interpretation given to Hume's Law is wrong, or at least severely misleading. It is especially misleading in its relativistic interpretation, since the problem of the existence of an *ought* is phrased in a universalistic way. The very question presupposes the *ought* to be not arbitrary.

C.6 *The Moral Sense*

The interpretation of Hume's Law given above follows modern deductive reasoning, but runs against Hume's view of the way in which moral judgements are formed. He makes the argument that the existence of an *ought* cannot be derived from reason in order to establish the existence of a 'moral sense'. In this, he aims to relate moral judgement to psychology. It is interesting that this idea has not been taken up by either philosophy or psychology.[1] It would not be appropriate to give a comprehensive account here.[2] A sketch of Hume's ethical theory must suffice.

Reason cannot give rise to an *ought*. Hume concludes from this that moral judgements are brought about by 'impressions' arising from the individual's 'moral sense' in a direct way:

> Thus the course of the argument leads us to conclude, that since vice and virtue are not discoverable merely by reason, or the comparison of ideas, it must be by means of some impression or sentiment they occasion, that we are able to mark the difference betwixt them. . . . The next question is, Of what nature are these impressions, and after what manner do they operate upon us? Here we cannot remain long in suspense, but must pronounce the impression arising from virtue, to be agreeable, and that proceeding from vice to be uneasy.[3]

Yet these impressions are not just impressions of pleasure or uneasiness; they are of a 'peculiar kind':

---

[1] The Gestalt psychologists Wertheimer (1935) and Köhler (1938) are exceptions.

[2] For an excellent introduction to Hume, see MacNabb (1967). This article contains an annotated list of critical works on different aspects of Hume's philosophy, including his moral philosophy. The point I am going to make—assimilating Wertheimer (1935) and Hume (1777a)—is somewhat different from the issues discussed in that literature.

[3] Hume (1740a: 470).

An action, or sentiment, or character is virtuous or vicious; why? because its view causes a pleasure or uneasiness of a particular kind. In giving a reason, therefore, for the pleasure or uneasiness, we sufficiently explain the vice or virtue. To have a sense of virtue is nothing but to *feel* a satisfaction of a particular kind from the contemplation of a character. The very *feeling* constitutes our praise or admiration. We go no farther; we do not enquire into the cause of the satisfaction. We do not infer a character to be virtuous, because it pleases: But in feeling that it pleases after such a particular manner, we in effect feel that it is virtuous. The case is the same as in our judgements concerning all kinds of beauty, and tastes, and sensations. Our approbation is imply'd in the immediate pleasure they convey to us.[1]

Pleasure (or, in today's terminology, utility) is, however, a term that comprises many different impressions:

A good composition of music and a bottle of wine equally produce pleasure; and what is more, their goodness is determin'd merely by pleasure. But shall we say upon that account, that the wine is harmonious, or the music of a good flavor? . . . the satisfaction is different . . . Nor is every sentiment of pleasure and pain of that *peculiar* kind, which makes us praise and condemn.[2]

The particular kind of sentiment relates to a detached view of events, later formulated by Adam Smith as the point of view taken by an 'impartial spectator'. Hume phrased this as follows:

The good qualities of an enemy are hurtful to us; but may still command our esteem and respect. 'Tis only when a character is considered in general, without reference to our particular interest, that it causes such feelings or sentiment, as denominates it morally good or evil.[3]

This way of forming moral judgements is deeply rooted in human nature.

These sentiments are so rooted in our constitution and temper, that without entirely confounding the human mind by disease or madness, 'tis impossible to extirpate and destroy them.[4]

Moral sentiment relates, further, not to *single* features of an action, but to *overall* evaluations of an entire pattern, just like perceptions of beauty. 'The same principles produce, in many instances, our sentiments of morals, as well as those of beauty.'[5] In that, it relates directly to the tendency towards overall clarification discussed above:[6]

---

[1] Hume (1740*a*: 471).   [2] Hume (1740*a*: 472).
[3] Hume (1740*a*: 472). For Smith's theory involving an impartial spectator, see Smith (1759).   [4] Hume (1740*a*: 474).
[5] Hume (1740*a*: 577).   [6] See S. 8.1.

Attend to Palladio and Perrault, while they explain all the parts and proportions of a pillar. They talk of the cornice, and frieze, and base, and entabulature, and shaft, and architrave; and give the impression and position of these members. But should you ask the description and position of its beauty, they would readily reply, that the beauty is not in any of the parts or members of a pillar, but results from the whole, when that complicated figure is presented to an intelligent mind, susceptible to those finer sensations.[1]

The perception of morality arises from the human constitution, like the perception of 'sounds, colours, heat, or cold'.[2] The impressions are 'involuntary and necessary.'[3] They are universal:

Tho' the rules of justice be *artificial*, they are not *arbitrary*. Nor is the expression improper to call them the *Laws of Nature*; if by natural we understand what is common to any species, or even if we confine it to mean what is inseparable from the species.[4]

It is, thus, perfectly clear that Hume cannot be considered a defender of any kind of ethical relativism.

C.7 *An Afterthought*

Another criticism of Hume's Law can be formulated as follows.

Suppose I have developed a positive theory of ethical judgements which describes and predicts how ethical judgements flow from impressions, tastes, and deliberations. Such a theory must be, by necessity, *both* positive and normative, in the sense that my own ethical judgements must follow the rules established in my positive ethical theory; otherwise, my positive theory would be false. Thus, a purely positive theory, if true,

---

[1] Hume (1777a: 292). This later view, not to be found in the *Treatise*, may be seen as a development of the relation between beauty and virtue, as elaborated in the *Treatise*. It is reminiscent of Wertheimer's (1935) view of morality. Wertheimer (1934) would insist, however, on treating logic *and* morality as being generated by the same principles of 'Prägnanz', 'requiredness'—or, as I say, 'clarity'. I agree with Wertheimer (see S. 8.1). This does not necessarily imply any substantive disagreement with Hume. I simply think that the theoretical distinction he has drawn for his own philosophical purposes may lead to severe misunderstandings and should be followed with care.
[2] Hume (1740a: 469). These are 'not qualities of objects, but perceptions of the mind'. The extreme subjectivism expressed here thus pertains not only to morality, but to reason as well: 'Reason is nothing but a wonderful and unintelligible instinct in our souls, which carries us along a certain train of ideas, and endows them with particular qualities, according to their particular situations and relations' (Hume 1740a: 179). This does not justify cultural relativism either. Those who read Hume in a relativistic manner should be careful enough to declare that the entire world—including their own existence and their own theoretical statements—is as arbitrary as they declare morality to be. I would not object.
[3] Hume (1740a: 608).   [4] Hume (1740a: 484).

rules out ethical judgements that do not conform to the theory. A positive theory, therefore, carries normative implications.

In conclusion, there are strong reasons for challenging the validity of what became erroneously known as 'Hume's Law' and what seems incompatible with Hume's universalism and his writings.

REFERENCES

Abbott, R. (1975), *Kartenspiel als Kunst*. German trans. by W. Hochkeppel, (Ebenhausen bei München: Langwiesche-Brandt). First published as *Abbott's New Card Games*, (New York: Stein and Day, 1963).

Adams, J. S. (1963), 'Toward an Understanding of Inequity', *Journal of Abnormal and Social Psychology*, 67: 422–36.

Akerlof, G. A. (1976), 'The Economics of Caste and of the Rat Race and Other Woeful Tales', *Quarterly Journal of Economics*, 90: 599–617; cited from the reprint in G. A. Akerlof, *An Economic Theorist's Book of Tales* (Cambridge: Cambridge University Press, 1984: 23–44).

—— and Dickens, W. T. (1982), 'The Economic Consequences of Cognitive Dissonance', *American Economic Review*, 72: 307–19.

Albers, W. and Albers, G. (1983), 'On The Prominence Structure of the Decimal System', in R. W. Scholz (ed.), *Decision Making under Uncertainty* (Amsterdam: Elsevier, 271–87).

Albert, H. (1968), *Traktat über Kritische Vernunft*, 5th edn. (Tübungen: J. C. B. Mohr, 1991).

Alchian, A. A. (1984), 'Specificity, Specialization, and Coalitions', *Journal of Institutional and Theoretical Economics*, 140: 34–9.

—— (1987), 'Property Rights', in J. Eatwell, M. Milgate, and P. Newman (eds.), *The New Palgrave: A Dictionary of Economics*, (New York: Stockton, iii. 1031–4).

—— (1991), 'Development of Economic Theory and Antitrust: A View from the Theory of the Firm', *Journal of Institutional and Theoretical Economics*, 147: 232–4.

—— and Demsetz, H. (1972), 'Production, Information Costs, and Economic Organization', *American Economic Review*, 62: 777–95; cited from the reprint in Demsetz (1988: 119–43).

—— and Woodward, S. (1987), 'Reflections on the Theory of the Firm', *Journal of Institutional and Theoretical Economics*, 143: 110–36.

Amabile, T. (1983), *The Social Psychology of Creativity* (New York: Springer).

Anderson, J. R. (1980), *Cognitive Psychology and its Implications*, (San Francisco: Freeman).

Armstrong, M. (1993), *Melbourne City Guide* (Hawthorn: Lonely Planet).

Armstrong, S. (1991), 'Female Circumcision: Fighting a Cruel Tradition', *New Scientist*, 2: 22–7.

Arrow, K. J. (1974), *The Limits of Organization* (New York: Norton).

—— (1990), Interview, in Richard Swedberg, *Economics and Sociology* (Princeton: Princeton University Press, 133–51).

Asch S. (1952), *Social Psychology* (Oxford: Oxford University Press 1987).

Austin, W. and Hatfield, E. (1980), 'Equity Theory, Power, and Social Justice', in G. Mikula (ed.), *Justice and Social Interaction* (New York: Springer, 25–61).

Axelrod, R. (1984), *The Evolution of Cooperation* (New York: Basic Books).

Ayer, A. J. (1954), *Philosophical Essays* (London: Macmillan).

Barley, N. (1986), *A Plague of Caterpillars: A Return to the African Bush* (London: Penguin).

Barnard C. (1938), *The Functions of the Executive*, (Cambridge, Mass.: Harvard University Press).

Bartlett, F. C. (1932), *Remembering* (Cambridge: Cambridge University Press).

Basu K. (1984), *The Less Developed Economy* (Oxford: Basil Blackwell).

—— (1994), 'Group Rationality, Utilitarianism, and Escher's Waterfall', *Games and Economic Behavior*, 7: 1–9.

—— Jones, E., and Schlicht, E. (1987), 'The Growth and Decay of Custom: The Role of the New Institutional Economics in Economic History', *Explorations in Economic History*, 24: 1–21.

Beaglehole, E. (1931), *Property* (London: George Allen and Unwin).

Becker, G. S. (1962), 'Investment in Human Capital: A Theoretical Analysis', *Journal of Political Economy*, Supplement: 9–49.

Bell-Krannhals, I. (1990), *Haben um zu geben: Eigentum und Besitz auf den Trobriand-Inseln, Papua New Guinea*, Basler Beiträge zur Ethnologie, 31 (Basel: Wepf).

Bernheim, B. D. (1994), 'A Theory of Conformity', *Journal of Political Economy*, 102, 841–77.

Binmore, K. and Samuelson, L. (1994), 'An Economist's Perspective on the Evolution of Norms', *Journal of Institutional and Theoretical Economics*, 150: 45–63.

Blackburn, M., and Neumark, D. (1992), 'Unobserved Ability, Efficiency Wages, and Interindustry Wage Differentials', *Quarterly Journal of Economics*, 107: 1421–36.

Blackburn, S. (ed.) (1994), *The Oxford Dictionary of Philosophy* (Oxford: Oxford University Press).

Blau, P. M. (1955), *The Dynamics of Bureaucracy: A Study of Interper-*

sonal Relations in Two Government Agencies (Chicago: Chicago University Press).

Braeuer, W. (1981), *Urahnen der Ökonomie: Von der Volkswirtschaftslehre des Altertums und des Mittelalters* (München: Ölschläger).

Brandes, W. and Weise, P. (1995), 'Motivation, Moral, und Arbeitsleistung', in K. Gerlach and R. Schettkat (eds.), *Determinanten der Lohnbildung* (Berlin: Sigma, 233–54).

Brehm, J. W. (1966), *Responses to Loss of Freedom: A Theory of Psychological Reactance* (New York: Academic Press).

Brooks, F. P. (1975), *The Mythical Man-Month: Essays in Software Engineering* (reprint with corrections: Reading: Addison-Wesley, 1982).

Buchanan, J. (1994), 'Choosing What to Choose', *Journal of Institutional and Theoretical Economics*, 150: 123–35.

—— and Brennan, G. (1985), *The Reason of Rules* (New York: Cambridge University Press).

Bull, C. (1983), 'Implicit Contracts in the Absence of Enforcement and Risk Aversion', *American Economic Review*, 73, 658–71.

Bunzel, R. (1938), 'The Economic Organization of Primitive Peoples', in F. Boas (ed.), *General Anthropology* (Washington: Heath, 1938: 327–408).

Burns, T. (1963), 'Industry in a New Age', *New Society*, 31 January 17–20.

Calabresi, G. and Melamed, A. D. (1972), 'Property Rules, Liability Rules, and Inalienability: One View of the Cathedral', *Harvard Law Review*, 85: 1089–1128.

Carmichael, L. (1985), Can Unemployment Be Involuntary? Comment', *American Economic Review*, 75, 1213–14.

Casson, M. (1991), *Economics of Business Culture: Game Theory, Transaction Costs and Economic Performance* (Oxford: Clarendon Press).

Chang, J. (1991), *Wild Swans: Three Daughters of China* (London: Harper-Collins).

Cheung, S. N. S. (1969), *The Theory of Share Tenancy* (Chicago: Chicago University Press).

Chimelli, R. (1992), 'Frankreichs Regierung will hart bleiben', *Süddeutsche Zeitung* 153, (6 July): 6.

Cialdini, R. B. (1984), *Influence: How and Why People Agree to Things* (New York: Morrow).

—— (1988), *Influence: Science and Practice* (Glenview; Ill.: Scott, Foresman.

Coase, R. H. (1937), 'The Nature of the Firm', *Economica*, n. s. 4: 386–405; cited from the reprint in Coase (1988: 33–55).

—— (1960), 'The Problem of Social Cost', *Journal of Law and Economics*, 3: 1–60; cited from the reprint in Coase, (1988: 95–156).

—— (1977), 'Economics and Contiguous Disciplines', in M. Perlman (ed.), *The Organization and Retrieval of Economic Knowledge* (London: Macmillan; cited from the reprint in R. H. Coase, *Essays on Economics and Economists* (Chicago: University of Chicago Press, 1994: 34–46).

—— (1988), *The Firm, the Market, and the Law* (Chicago: University of Chicago Press).

—— (1991), 'The Nature of the Firm: Influence', in O. E. Williamson and S. Winter (eds.), *The Nature of the Firm: Origins, Evolution, and Development* (Oxford: Oxford University Press, 61–74).

—— (1993), 'Coase on Posner on Coase', *Journal of Institutional and Theoretical Economics*, 149: 96–8.

Cohen, F. S. (1933), *Ethical Systems and Legal Ideals* (New York: Falcon Press); quoted from the reprint (Westport: Greenwood Press, 1976).

Coleman, J. S. (1990), *Foundations of Social Theory* (Cambridge, Mass.: Harvard University Press).

Colman, A. M. (1988), *What is Psychology? The Inside Story*, 2nd edn. (London: Routledge).

Dahlgren, K. (1985), 'The Cognitive Structure of Social Categories', *Cognitive Science*, 9: 379–98.

Dahlman, C. J. (1980), *The Open Field System and Beyond: A Property Rights Analysis of an Economic Institution* (Cambridge: Cambridge University Press).

David, P. A. (1985), 'Clio and the Economics of QWERTY', *American Economic Review*, 75: 332–7.

Davies, N. B. (1978), 'Territorial Defence in the Speckled Wood Butterfly (*Pararge aegeria*): The Resident Always Wins', *Animal Behavior*, 26: 138–47.

Deci, E. L. (1971), 'The Effects of Externally Mediated Rewards on Intrinsic Motivation', *Journal of Personality and Social Psychology*, 18: 105–15.

Dembo, T. (1931), 'Der Ärger als Dynamisches Problem', *Psychologische Forschung*, 15: 1–144.

Demsetz, H. (1967), 'Toward a Theory of Property Rights', *American Economic Review*, Papers and Proceedings, 57: 347–59; cited from the reprint in Demsetz (1988: 104–16).

—— (1988), *Ownership, Control, and the Firm: The Organization of Economic Activity*, (Oxford: Blackwell).

Derham, D. P., Mahler, F. K. H., and Walker, P. L. (1971), *An Introduction to Law*, 2nd ed. (Melbourne: Law Book Company).

Diamond, J. (1991), *The Rise and Fall of the Third Chimpanzee*, Vintage ed. (London: Random House).

Duncker, K. (1939), 'Ethical Relativity? An Inquiry Into the Psychology of Ethics', *Mind*, 48: 39–57.

Ehrenfels, C. von, (1890), 'Ueber Gestaltqualitäten', *Vierteljahresschrift für Wissenschaft und Philosophie*, 14: 249–92.

Ehrlich, I. (1973), 'Participation in Illegal Activities: A Theoretical and Empirical Analysis', *Journal of Political Economy*, 81: 521–65.

Eibl-Eibesfeld, I. (1975), *Ethology: The Biology of Behavior*, 2nd ed., trans. from German by E. Klinghammer (New York: Holt, Rinehart and Winston).

Einstein, A. (1961), *Relativity: The Special and the General Theory*, trans. from German by R. E. Lawson (New York: Crown Publishers).

Eisenberg, M. A. (1988), *The Nature of the Common Law* (Cambridge, Mass.: Harvard University Press).

Ellickson, R. (1991), *Order without Law: How Neighbors Settle Disputes* (Cambridge, Mass.: Harvard University Press).

Ellis, L. (1985), 'On the Rudiments of Possessions and Property', *Social Science Information*, 24: 113–43.

Englund, G. and Otto, C. (1991), 'Effects of Ownership Status, Weight Asymmetry, and Case Fit on the Outcome of Case Contests in Two Populations of *Agrynia Pagetana* (*Trichoptera: Phryganeidae*) Larvae', *Behavioral Ecology and Sociobiology*, 29: 113–20.

Eysenck, H. J. (1976), 'The Biology of Morality', In T. Luckona (ed.), *Moral Development and Behavior*, (New York: Holt, Rinehart and Whinston, 108–23).

Eysenck, M. W., and Keane, M. T. (1990), *Cognitive Psychology: A Student's Handbook* (Hillsdale, NJ: Lawrence Erlbaum).

Fehr, E. (1993*a*), 'The Labor–Capital Partnership: Reconciling Insider Power with Full Employment', in A. B. Atkinson (ed.), *The Economics of Partnership* (New York: St Martin's Press, 50–77).

—— (1993*b*), 'The Simple Analysis of a Membership Market in a Labor-Managed Economy', in S. Bowles, H. Gintis, and B. Gustafsson, *Markets and Democracy: Participation, Accountability, and Efficiency* (Cambridge: Cambridge University Press, 1993: 260–76).

—— Gächter, S., and Kirchsteiger, G. (1996), 'Reciprocity as a Contract Enforcement Device: Experimental Evidence'. Manuscript, Institute for Empirical Research in Economics, University of Zürich.

Festinger, L. (1957), *A Theory of Cognitive Dissonance* (Evanston, Ill.: Row, Peterson).

—— and Carlsmith, J. M. (1959), 'Cognitive Consequences of Forced Compliance', *Journal of Abnormal and Social Psychology*, 58: 203–11.

Field (1984), 'Microeconomics, Norms, and Rationality', *Economic Development and Cultural Change*, 32: 683–711.

Flew, A. (ed.) (1975), *A Dictionary of Philosophy* (New York: St Martin's Press).

—— (1986), *David Hume: Philosopher of Moral Science* (Oxford: Blackwell).

Frank, R. H. (1984), 'Are Workers Paid their Marginal Products?' *American Economic Review*, 74: 549–71.

—— (1988), *Passions within Reason: The Strategic Role of Emotions* (New York: Norton).

—— (1989), 'Beyond Self-Interest', *Challenge*, 32(2): 4–13.

Franke Stevens, E. (1988), 'Contests between Bands of Federal Horses for Access for Fresh Water: The Resident Wins', *Animal Behavior*, 39: 1–9

Franz, W. (ed.) (1990), *Hysteresis Effects in Economic Models* (Heidelberg: Physica).

Frey, B. S. (1995), 'How Intrinsic Motivation is Crowded Out and In', *Rationality and Society*, 6: 334–52.

—— and Stroebe, W. (1980), 'Ist das Modell des Homo Oeconomicus "unpsychologisch?"', *Journal of Institutional and Theoretical Economics*, 136: 82–97.

Fuller, A. R. (1990). *Insight Into Value: An Exploration of the Premises of a Phenomenological Psychology*, (Albany, NY: State University of New York Press).

Fuller, L. L. (1967), *Legal Fictions* (Stanford: Stanford University Press).

—— (1968), *Anatomy of Law* (New York: Praeger).

—— (1981), *The Principles of Social Order*, ed. K. I. Winston (Durham, NC: Duke University Press).

Furubotn, E. (1974), 'Bank Credit and the Labor Managed Firm: The Yogoslav Case', *Canadian-American Slavic Studies*, 8: 89–106.

—— (1976), 'The Long-Run Analysis of the Labor-Managed Firm: An Alternative Interpretation', *American Economic Review*, 66: 104–24.

—— and Richter, R. (1997), *Institutions and Economic Theory* (Ann Arbor: Michigan University Press).

Geertz, C. (1973), *The Interpretation of Cultures* (New York: Basic Books).

Glason, J. B. (1973), 'Code Switching in Children's Language', In T. E. Moore (ed.), *Cognitive Development and Acquisition of Language* (New York: Academic Press, 159–68).

Gottschaldt, K. (1926), 'Über den Einfluß der Erfahrung auf die Wahrnehmung von Figuren', *Psychologische Forschung*, 8: 261–317;

English excerpt in W. D. Ellis (ed.), *A Source Book of Gestalt Psychology* (London: Routledge and Kegan Paul, 1938: 109–35).

Gouldner, A. W. (1960), 'The Norm of Reciprocity: A Preliminary Statement', *American Sociological Review*, 25: 161–78.

Granovetter M. (1985), 'Economic Action and Social Structure: The Problem of Embeddedness', *American Journal of Sociology*, 91: 481–510.

—— (1991), 'The Social Construction of Economic Institutions', in A. Etzioni and P. R. Lawrence (eds.), *Socio-Economics* (Armonk; NY: Sharpe, 75–81).

Greenwald, A. G. and Banaji, M. R. (1995), 'Implicit Social Cognitions: Attitudes, Self-Esteem, and Stereotypes', *Psychological Review*, 102: 4–27.

Groeben, N. (1975), 'Gestalttheorie als Irrationalismus?' in S. Ertel, L. Kemmler, and M. Stadler (eds.), *Gestalttheorie in der modernen Psychologie* (Darmstadt: Steinkopff, 134–45).

Groenewegen, P. (1987), 'Division of Labour', in J. Eatwell, M. Milgate, and P. Newman (eds.), *The New Palgrave: A Dictionary of Economics* (New York: Stockton, i. 901–7).

Grotius, H. (1625), *The Rights of War and Peace*, trans. from Latin by A. C. Campbell (Washington: Dunne, 1901; reprint Westport, Conn.: Hyperion Press, 1979).

Güth, W. and Tietz, R. (1990), 'Ultimatum Bargaining Behavior: A Survey and Comparison of Experimental Results', *Journal of Economic Psychology*, 11: 417–49.

—— Schmittberger, R., and Schwarze, B. (1982), 'An Experimental Analysis of Ultimatum Bargaining', *Journal of Economic Behavior and Organization* 3: 362–88.

Hallpike, C. R. (1986), *The Principles of Social Evolution* (Oxford: Clarendon Press).

Hardin, R. (1988), *Morality within the Limits of Reason* (Chicago and London: University of Chigago Press).

Harrod, R. (1956), *Foundations of Inductive Logic* (London: Macmillan).

Hart, O. and Moore, J. (1990), 'Property Rights and the Nature of the Firm', *Journal of Political Economy*, 98: 1119–58.

Hartung, F. E. (1954), 'Cultural Relativity and Moral Judgements', *Philosophy of Science*, 21, 118–26.

Hayek, F. A. (1945), 'The Use of Knowledge in Society', *American Economic Review*, 35: 519–30.

—— (1952), *The Sensory Order* (London: Routledge & Kegan Paul; quoted from the 1976 reprint).

—— (1955), *The Political Idea of the Rule of Law* (Cairo: National Bank of Egypt).

—— (1964), 'The Theory of Complex Phenomena', in M. Bunge (ed.), *The Critical Approach to Science and Philosophy* (London: Free Press of Glencoe).

—— (1973), *Law, Legislation and Liberty, i, Rules and Order* (London: Routledge and Kegan Paul).

—— (1975), *The Rule of Law* (Menlo Park, Calif.: Institute for Humane Studies).

—— (1976), *Law, Legislation and Liberty, ii, The Mirage of Social Justice* (London: Routledge and Kegan Paul).

Hecker, D. (1990), *Eigentum als Sachherrschaft: Zur Genese und Kritik eines besonderen Herrschaftsanspruchs* (Paderborn: Schöningh).

Heider (Rosch), E. (1972), 'Universals in Color Naming and Memory', *Journal of Experimental Psychology*, 93: 10–20.

Heider, F. (1958), *The Psychology of Interpersonal Relations* (New York: Wiley).

Heilbroner, R. L. (1972), *The Making of Economic Society*, 4th ed. Englewood Cliffs, NJ: Prentice-Hall). First published in 1962.

Herskovits, M. (1958), 'Some Further Remarks on Cultural Relativism', *American Anthropologist*, 60: 266–73.

Hilgard, E. R. and Bower, G. H. (1966), *Theories of Learning*, 3rd edn. (New York: Appleton-Century-Crofts).

—— Atkinson, R. C., and Atkinson, R. L. (1971), *Introduction to Psychology*, 5th edn. (New York: Harcourt).

Hirschman, A. O. (1970), *Exit, Voice, and Loyalty* (Cambridge, Mass.: Harvard University Press).

—— (1985), 'Against Parsimony', *Economics and Philosophy*, 1, 7–21.

Hobbes, T. (1651), *Leviathan*, ed. by C. B. Macpherson. (Harmondsworth: Penguin, 1968).

Hodgson, G. (1993), *Economics and Evolution: Bringing Life Back into Economics* (Cambridge: Polity Press).

Hoffmann, R. C. (1975), 'Medieval Origins of the Common Fields', in W. N. Parker and E. L. Jones (eds.), *European Peasants and their Markets* (Princeton: Princeton University Press, 23–71).

Hofstadter, D. E. (1979), *Gödel, Escher, Bach* (New York: Basic Books).

Holmstrom, B. (1982), 'Moral Hazard in Teams', *Bell Journal of Economics*, 13: 324–40.

Homans, G. C. (1961), *Social Behavior: Its Elementary Forms* (New York: Harcourt Brace Jovanovich).

Hume D. (1740*a*), *A Treatise on Human Nature*, ed. L. A. Selby-Bigge (Oxford: Clarendon Press, 1888).

—— (1740*b*), *An Abstract of A Treatise of Human Nature* (Cambridge: Cambridge University Press, 1938).

—— (1777*a*), *Enquiries Concerning the Human Understanding and Concerning the Principles of Morals*, ed. L. A. Selby-Bigge, 2nd edn. (Oxford: Clarendon Press, 1902).

—— (1777*b*), *The Natural History of Religion*, in G. C. A. Gaskin (ed.), *David Hume: Principal Writings on Religion including Dialogues Concerning Religion and The Natural History of Religion* (Oxford: Oxford University Press, 1993).

Iannaccone, L. R. (1992), 'Sacrifice and Stigma: Reducing Free-riding in Cults, Communes, and Other Collectives', *Journal of Political Economy*, 100: 271–91.

Jeffreys, H. (1961), *Theory of Probability*, 3rd edn. (Oxford: Clarendon Press).

Jensen, M. C. and Meckling, W. (1976), 'Theory of the Firm: Managerial Behavior, Agency Costs, and Ownership Structure', *Journal of Financial Economics*, 3: 305–60.

Jevons, W. S. (1878), *The Theory of Political Economy*, 2nd edn. (London: Macmillan). First published 1871.

Jones, E. I. (1981), *The European Miracle* (Cambridge: Cambridge University Press).

—— 1995, 'Culture and its Relationship to Economic Change', *Journal of Institutional and Theoretical Economics*, 151: 269–85.

Jones, S. R. G. (1984), *The Economics of Conformism* (Oxford: Blackwell).

Kahneman, D. (1994), 'New Challenges to the Rationality Assumption', *Journal of Institutional and Theoretical Economics*, 150: 18–36.

——, Knetsch, J. L., and Thaler, R. H. (1986*a*), 'Fairness and the Assumptions of Economics', in R. M. Hogarth and M. W. Reder (eds.), *Rational Choice: The Contrast between Economics and Psychology* (Chicago: University of Chicago Press).

—— —— —— (1986*b*), 'Fairness as a Constraint on Profit Seeking: Entitlements in the Market', *American Economic Review*, 76, 728–41.

—— —— —— (1990), 'Experimental Tests of the Endowment Effect and the Coase Theorem', *Journal of Political Economy*, 98, 1325–48.

Katz, D. and Braly, K. (1933), 'Racial Stereotypes in One Hundred College Students', *Journal of Abnormal and Social Psychology*, 28: 280–90.

Kelley, H. H. (1967), 'Attribution Theory in Social Psychology', in D. Levine (ed.), *Nebraska Symposium on Motivation*, 51 (Lincoln: University of Nebraska Press).

—— (1973), 'The Process of Causal Attribution', *American Psychologist*, 28: 107–28.

Keynes, J. M. (1973), *The Collected Writings of John Maynard Keynes, xiii, The General Theory and After. Part I: Preparation*, ed. D. Moggridge (London: Macmillan).

Killias, M. (1985), 'Die Bedeutung von Rechtsgefühl und Sanktionen für die Konformität des Verhaltens gegenber neuen Normen', *Jahrbuch für Rechtssoziologie und Rechtstheorie*, 10, 257–72.

Klein B. (1985), 'Self-Enforcing Contracts', *Journal of Institutional and Theoretical Economics*, 141: 594–600.

—— Crawford, R. G. and Alchian, A. A. (1978), 'Vertical Integration, Appropriable Rents, and the Competitive Contracting Process', *Journal of Law and Economics*, 21: 297–326.

Koffka, K. (1935), *Principles of Gestalt Psychology* (London: Routledge & Kegan Paul).

Kohlberg, L. (1983), *The Psychology of Moral Development*, 3 vols. (New York: Harper and Row).

Köhler, W. (1938), *The Place of Values in a World of Facts* (New York: Liveright).

—— (1940), *Dynamics in Psychology* (New York: Liveright).

—— (1971), 'The Naturalistic Interpretation of Man (The Trojan Horse)', in M. Henle (ed.), *The Selected Papers of Wolfgang Köhler* (New York: Liveright, 337–55).

Krueger, A. B., and Summers, L. (1988), 'Efficiency Wages and the Inter-Industry Wage Structure', *Econometrica*, 56: 259–93.

Kubon-Gilke, G. (1990), *Motivation und Beschäftigung* (Frankfurt: Campus).

—— (1995), 'Evolutionstheoretische Begründungen der Reziprozität', *Gestalt Theory*, 17, 217–25.

—— (1997), *Verhaltensbindung und die Evolution ökonomischer Institutien* (Marburg: Metropolis).

—— and Schlicht, E. (1993), 'Gefordertheit und institutionelle Analyse am Beispiel des Eigentums', *Gestalt Theory*, 15: 256–73.

Kuhn, T. (1970), *The Structure of Scientific Revolutions*, 2nd edn. (Chicago: University of Chicago Press).

Kummer, H. and Cords, M (1991), 'Cues of Ownership in Long-Tailed Macaques', *Animal Behaviour*, 42: 529–49.

Kunkel, M. (1994), *Franchising und asymmetrische Information* (Wiesbaden: Deutscher Universitäts-Verlag).

Kuran, T. (1987), 'Preference Falsification, Policy Continuity and Collective Conservatism', *Economic Journal*, 97: 642–65.

—— (1991), 'Cognitive Limitations and Preference Evolution', *Journal of Institutional and Theoretical Economics*, 147, 241–73.

Kuran, T. (1995), *Private Truths, Public Lies* (Cambridge, Mass.: Harvard University Press).

Leacock, E. (1954), 'The Montagnes "Hunting Territory" and Fur Trade', *American Anthropological Association*, 36, Memoir no. 78.

Leibenstein, H. (1960), *Economic Theory and Organizational Analysis* (New York: Harper).

Lepper, M. R., and Greene, D. (1978), 'Overjustification Research and Beyond', in M. R. Lepper and D. Greene (eds.), *The Hidden Costs of Rewards: New Perspectives on the Psychology of Motivation*, (Hillsdale, NJ: Lawrence Erlbaum, 109–48.

Lévi-Strauss, C. (1949), *Structural Anthropology*, trans. from French by C. Jacobson and B. G. Schoepf (Harmondsworth: Penguin, 1972).

—— (1955), *Tristes Tropiques*, trans. from French by J. Weighman and D. Weighman (London: Jonathan Cape, 1973).

Lewis, D. K. (1969), *Convention: A Philosophical Study* (Cambridge, Mass.: Harvard University Press).

Liebowitz, S. J. and Margolis, S. E. (1990), 'The Fable of the Keys', Journal of Law and Economics, 33: 1–25.

Lips, J. E. (1938), 'Government', in F. Boas (ed.), *General Anthropology* (Washington: Heath, 487–534).

Llewellyn, K. N. (1931), 'What Price Contract? An Essay in Perspective', *Yale Law Journal*, 40: 704–51.

—— (1962), *Jurisprudence: Realism in Theory and Practice* (Chicago: University of Chicago Press).

Loewenstein, G. and Adler, D. (1993), 'A Bias in the Prediction of Taste', Working Paper, Carnegie-Mellon University, Pittsburgh.

Lorenz, K. (1973), *Behind the Mirror*, Trans. from German by R. Taylor (New York: Harcourt Brace Jovanowich, 1977).

Macaulay, S. (1963), 'Non-Contractual Relations in Business', *American Sociological Review*, 28: 55–70.

McCloskey, D. N. (1975), 'The Persistence of English Common Fields', in W. N. Parker and E. L. Jones (eds.), *European Peasants and their Markets* (Princeton: Princeton University Press, 1975: 73–160).

McCloskey, M. E., and Glucksberg, S. (1978), 'Natural Categories: Well-Defined or Fuzzy Sets?' *Memory and Cognition*, 6: 462–72.

McGuire, W. J. (1966), 'The Current Status of Cognitive Consistency Theories', in S. Feldman (ed.), *Cognitive Consistency* (New York: Academic Press, 1–46).

MacIntosh, J. H. (1973), 'Factors Affecting the Recognition of Territory Boundaries by Mice (*Mus musculus*)', *Animal Behavior*, 21: 464–70.

Mackie, J. L. (1977), *Ethics: Inventing Right and Wrong* (Harmondsworth: Penguin).

—— (1980), *Hume's Moral Theory* (London: Routledge).

MacNabb, D. G. C. (1967), 'Hume', in *Encyclopedia of Philosophy*, ed. P. Edwards, (New York: Free Press, iv. 74–90).

MacNeill, I. R. (1974), 'The Many Futures of Contracts', *Southern California Law Review*, 47: 691–816.

Major, B. and Testa, M. (1989), 'Social Comparison Processes and Judgements of Entitlement and Satisfaction', *Journal of Experimental Social Psychology*, 25: 101–20.

Manis, M. (1971), *An Introduction to Cognitive Psychology* (Belmont, Calif.: Brooks/Cole).

Margolis, H. (1987), *Patterns, Thinking, and Cognition* (Chicago: University of Chicago Press).

Marshall, A. (1885), 'The Present Position of Economics', in A. C. Pigou (ed.), *The Memorials of Alfred Marshall* (London: Macmillan 1925: 152–74).

—— (1890), *Principles of Economics*, 8th edn. (London: Macmillan, 1920).

—— (1961), *Principles of Economics*, ii, 9th (variorum) edn, ed. and annotated by C. W. Guillebaud (London: Macmillan).

Marx, K. (1873), *Capital: A Critical Analysis of Capitalist Production*, i, trans. from the 3rd German edn. by S. Moore and E. Aveling and ed. by F. Engels, with a supplement ed. and trans. by D. Torr (London: George Allen and Unwin, 1946).

Mauss, M. (1924), *The Gift: Forms and Functions of Exchange in Archaic Societies*, trans. from French by I. Cunnison (Washington: Smithsonian Institute).

Menger, C. (1883), *Untersuchungen über die Methode der Sozialwissenschaften und der politischen Ökonomie insbesondere* (Leipzig).

Milgram, S. (1974), *Obedience to Authority: An Experimental View* (London: Tavistock).

Milkovich, G. T., and Newman, J. M. (1984), *Compensation*, 3rd edn. (Homewood, Ill.: Irwin, 1990).

Mill J. S. (1909), *Principles of Political Economy*, ed. W. Ashley (London: Longmans). First published in 1848.

—— (1925), *System of Logic*, new impression (London: Longmans). First published in 1843.

Moriarty, T. (1975), 'Crime, Commitment and the Responsive Bystander: Two Field Experiments', *Journal of Personality and Social Psychology*, 31: 370–6.

Mossner, E. C. (1980), *The Life of David Hume*, 2nd edn. (Oxford: Clarendon Press).

Murphy, G. L., and Medin, D. L. (1985), 'The Role of Theories in Conceptual Coherence', *Psychological Review*, 92: 289–316.

Nabokov, V. (1969), *Ada or Ardor: A Family Chronicle* (London: Weidenfeld and Nicolson).

Nelson R. R. and Winter, S. G. (1982), *An Evolutionary Theory of Economic Change* (Cambridge, Mass.: Harvard University Press).

Nippold, W. (1954), *Die Anfänge des Eigentums bei den Naturvölkern und die Entstehung des Privateigentums* (S'Gravenhage: Mouton).

North, D. C. (1990), *Institutions, Institutional Change and Economic Performance* (Cambridge: Cambridge University Press).

—— (1993), 'Institutions and Credible Commitments', *Journal of Institutional and Theoretical Economics*, 149: 11–13.

—— and Denzau, A. T. (1994), 'Shared Mental Models: Ideologies and Institutions,' *Kyklos*, 47, 3–31.

Nutzinger, H. G. (1978), 'The Firm as a Social Institution: The Failure of the Contractarian Viewpoint', *Economic Analysis and Worker's Management*, 10:217–37; reprinted in G. M. Hodgson (ed.). *The Economics of Institutions* (Aldershot: Edward Elgar 1993), 369–88.

Oi, W. Y. (1990), 'Employment Relations in Dual Labor Markets ('It's Nice Work If You Can Get It')', *Journal of Labor Economics*, 8(1, pt 2): S124–S149.

Opp, K.-D. (1982), 'The Evolutionary Emergence of Norms', *British Journal of Social Psychology*, 21: 139–49.

Paton, G. W., and Derham, D. P. (1972), *A Textbook of Jurisprudence*, 4th edn. (Oxford: Clarendon Press).

Pejovich, S. (1973), 'The Banking System and the Investment Behavior of the Yugoslav Firm', in M. Bronstein (ed.), *Plan and Market: Economic Reform in Eastern Europe* (New Haven: Yale University Press).

Peter, K. and Withaker, I. (1981), 'The Acquisition of Personal Property among the Hutterites and its Social Dimensions', *Anthropologica*, 23: 145–55.

Piaget, J. (1967), *Biologie et Connaissance* (Paris: Gallimard).

Platteau, J.-P. and Abraham, A. (1987), 'An Inquiry into Quasi-Credit Contracts: The Role of Reciprocal Credit and Interlinked Deals in Small-Scale Fishing Communities', *Journal of Development Studies*, 23: 641–90.

Polanyi, K. (1977), *The Livelihood of Man*, ed. H. W. Pearson (New York: Academic Press).

—— Arensberg, C., and Pearson, H. (1957), *Trade and Market in the Early Empires* (New York: Free Press).

Polanyi, M. (1962), *Personal Knowledge* (New York: Harper and Row). First published in 1958.

Posner, R. A. (1993*a*), 'The New Institutional Economics Meets Law and Economics', *Journal of Institutional and Theoretical Economics*, 149: 73–87.

—— (1993*b*), 'Reply', *Journal of Institutional and Theoretical Economics*, 149: 119–21.

Putterman, L. (1988), 'The Firm as an Association versus the Firm as a Commodity', *Economics and Philosophy*, 4: 243–66.

—— (1995), 'Markets, Hierarchies, and Information: On a Paradox in the Economics of Organization', *Journal of Economic Behavior and Organization*, 26: 373–90.

Rabin, M. (1993), 'Incorporating Fairness into Game Theory and Economics', *American Economic Review*, 83: 1281–1302.

Reese, H. W. (1989), 'Rules and Rule-Governance: Cognitive and Behavioristic Views', in S. C. Hayes (ed.), *Rule-Governed Behavior: Cognition, Contingencies, and Instructional Control* (New York: Plenum, 3–84).

Reichard, G. A. (1938), 'Social Life', in F. Boas (ed.) *General Anthropology* (Washington: Heath, 409–86).

Riechert, S. (1978), 'Games Spiders Play: Behavioral Variability in Territorial Disputes', *Behavioral Ecology and Sociobiology*, 3: 135–62.

Reisman, D. (1987), *Alfred Marshall: Progress and Politics* (New York: St Martin's Press).

Robertson, D. H. (1928), *Control of Industry*, 2nd edn. (Cambridge: Cambridge University Press).

Rogers, E. (1971), *Diffusion of Innovations*, 3rd edn. (New York: Free Press). First published in 1962.

Roget, P. M. (1992), *Roget's International Thesaurus*, 1992, 5th edn. ed. R. L. Chapman (New York: Harper).

Romer, D. (1984), 'The Theory of Social Custom: A Modification and Some Extensions', *Quarterly Journal of Economics*, 99: 717–27.

Rosch, E. (1972), *see* E. Heider (Rosch) (1972).

—— (1973), 'On the Internal Structure of Perceptual and Semantic Categories', in T. E. Moore (ed.), *Cognitive Development and Acquisition of Language* (New York: Academic Press, 111–44).

—— (1975), 'Cognitive Reference Points', *Cognitive Psychology*, 7: 532–47.

—— (1978), 'Principles of Categorization', in E. Rosch and B. B. Lloyd (eds.), *Cognition and Categorization* (Hillsdale, NJ: Lawrence Erlbaum, 27–48).

Ross, L. (1977), 'The Intuitive Psychologist and his Shortcomings', in L. Berkowitz (ed.), *Advances in Experimental Social Psychology*, x, (New York: Academic Press, 173–220).

Ross, L. (1990), 'Recognizing the Role of Construal Processes', in I. Rock (ed.), *The Legacy of Solomon Asch* (Hillsdale, NJ: Lawrence Erlbaum, 77–96).

Rotwein, E. (1987), 'Hume, David', in J. Eatwell, M. Milgate, and P. Newman (eds.), *The New Palgrave: A Dictionary of Economics* (New York: Stockton, ii. 692–5).

Rousseau, J. J. (1754), *The Social Contract and Discourses*, trans. from French by G. D. H. Cole, revised and augmented by J. H. Brumfitt and J. C. Hall (London: Dent, 1973).

Ryan, A. (1984), *Property* (Oxford: Blackwell).

—— (1987), 'Property', in J. Eatwell, M. Milgate, and P. Newman (eds.), *The New Palgrave: A Dictionary of Economics* (New York: Stockton, iii. 1030–1).

Savage, L. (1954), *The Foundations of Statistics* (New York: Wiley).

Schelling, T. C. (1978), *Micromotives and Macrobehavior* (New York: Norton).

—— (1980), *The Strategy of Conflict*, 2nd edn. (Cambridge, Mass.: Harvard University Press). First published in 1960.

Schiffman, H. R. (1982), *Sensation and Perception: An Integrated Approach*, 2nd edn. (New York: Wiley).

Schlicht, E. (1974), 'Die Theorie der kollektiven Entscheidung und der individualistische Ansatz', *Leviathan*, 2: 265–80.

—— (1977), *Grundlagen der ökonomischen Analyse* (Reinbek: Rowohlt).

—— (1979), 'The Transition to Labour Management as a Gestalt Switch', *Gestalt Theory*, 1: 54–67.

—— (1981), 'Reference Group Behaviour and Economic Incentives: A Remark', *Journal of Institutional and Theoretical Economics*, 137: 125–7 and 733–6.

—— (1984a), 'Cognitive Dissonance in Economics', In H. Todt (ed.), *Normengeleitetes Verhalten in den Sozialwissenschaften* (Berlin: Duncker und Humblot, 61–81).

—— (1984b), 'The Shadow Economy and Morals: A Note', in W. Gaertner and A. Wenig (eds.), *The Economics of the Shadow Economy* Springer-Verlag, 265–71).

—— (1984c), 'Die emotive und die kognitive Gerechtigkeitsauffassung', *Ökonomie und Gesellschaft*, 2: 141–54.

—— (1984d), 'Plant Closings, Worker Reallocation Costs and Efficiency Gains to Labor Representation on the Board of Directors: Comment on Furubotn/Wiggins', *Journal of Institutional and Theoretical Economics*, 140: 193–4.

—— (1985a), *Isolation and Aggregation in Economics* (Berlin: Springer-Verlag).

—— (1985*b*), 'Dismissal versus Fines as a Discipline Device: Comment on Shapiro and Stiglitz', mimeo, Institute for Advanced Study, Princeton, NJ.

—— (1990*a*), 'Rationality, Bounded or Not, and Institutional Analysis', *Journal of Institutional and Theoretical Economics*, 146: 703–19.

—— (1990*b*), 'A Critique of a Custom in Economics', in H. König (ed.), *Economics of Wage Determination* (Berlin: Springer-Verlag, 155–67).

—— (1993), 'On Custom', *Journal of Institutional and Theoretical Economics*, 149: 178–203.

—— (1994), 'Choosing What to Choose: Comment', *Journal of Institutional and Theoretical Economics*, 150: 142–4.

—— (1995*a*), 'Economic Analysis and Organized Religion', in E. L. Jones and V. Reynolds (eds.), *Survival and Religion: Biological Evolution and Cultural Change* (Chichester: Wiley, 111–60).

—— (1995*b*), 'Autonomous Wage Inflation', in K. Gerlach and R. Schettkat (eds.), *Determinanten der Lohnbildung* (Berlin: Sigma, 187–201).

—— (1996), 'Exploiting the Coase Mechanism: The Extortion Problem', *Kyklos*, 49, 319–30.

—— and von Weizsäcker, C. C. (1977), 'Risk Financing in Labour Managed Economics: The Commitment Problem', *Journal of Institutional and Theoretical Economics*, Special Issue (Profit Sharing): 53–66.

Schmidt, P. F. (1955), 'Some Criticisms of Cultural Relativism,' *Journal of Philosophy*, 52, 780–91.

Schmidt, W. (1939), 'Ursprung und Entwicklung des Eigentums', *Scentia*, 33: 47–58.

Schmitt D. R. and Marvell, G. (1972), 'Withdrawal and Reward Allocation as Responses to Inequity', *Journal of Experimental Social Psychology*, 225: 207–21.

Schmoller, G. (1923), *Grundriß der Allgemeinen Volkswirtschaftslehre*, i, 5th edn. (Berlin: Duncker und Humblot).

Schotter, A. (1981), *The Economic Theory of Social Institutions* (Cambridge: Cambridge University Press).

Schumpeter, J. A. (1943), *Capitalism, Socialism, and Democracy* (London: George Allen and Unwin).

—— (1954), *History of Economic Analysis* (Oxford: Oxford University Press).

Scott, K. (1993), 'The New Institutional Economics Meets Law and Economics: Comment', *Journal of Institutional and Theoretical Economics*, 149: 92–5.

Searle, J. R. (1964), 'How to Derive "ought" from "is"', *Philosophical Review*, 73: 43–58.

Segall, M. H., Campbell, D. T., and Herskovits, M. J. (1966), *The Influence of Culture on Visual Perception* (Indianapolis: Bobbs-Merrill).

Selten, R. (1994), 'New Challenges to the Rationality Assumption: Comment', *Journal of Institutional and Theoretical Economics*, 150: 42–4.

—— and Berg, C. C. (1970), 'Three Experimental Series of Oligopoly Games with Continuous Time', in H. Sauermann (ed.), *Beiträge zur experimentellen Wirtschaftsforschung*, ii (Tübingen: J. C. B. Mohr): 228–39.

Sen, A. K. (1970), *Collective Choice and Social Welfare* (Edinburgh: Oliver and Boyd).

—— (1973), 'On Ignorance and Equal Distribution', *American Economic Review*, 63: 1022–4.

Senar, J. C., Camerino, M., and Metcalfe, N. B. (1989), 'Agonistic Interactions in Siskin Flocks: Why Are Dominants Sometimes Subordinate?' *Behavioral Ecology and Sociobiology*, 25: 141–5.

Shapiro, C., and Stiglitz, J. (1984), 'Equilibrium Unemployment as a Worker Discipline Device', *American Economic Review*, 74, 433–44.

—— —— (1985), 'Can Unemployment Be Involuntary? Reply', *American Economic Review*, 75, 1215–17.

Sigg, H. and Falett, J. (1985), 'Experiments on the Respect of Possession and Property in Hamadrygas Baboons (*Papio Hamadrygas*)', *Animal Behavior*, 33: 978–84.

Silveira, J. (1971), '*Incubation: The Effect of Interrupting Timing and Length on Problem Solution and Quality of Problem Processing,*' Unpublished doctoral dissertation, University of Oregon.

Simon, H. A. (1951), 'A Formal Theory of the Employment Relation', *Econometrica*, 19: 293–305; reprinted in *Models of Man* (New York: Wiley, 1957).

—— (1978), 'Rationality as Process and Product of Thought', *American Economic Review*, 68: 1–16.

Smart, J. J. C. (1973), *Utilitarianism: For and Against* (Cambridge: Cambridge University Press).

Smith, A. (1759), *The Theory of Moral Sentiments* (Oxford: Clarendon Press, 1976).

—— (1776), *An Inquiry into the Nature and Causes of the Wealth of Nations*, ed. E. Cannan (New York: Random House, 1937).

Smith, N. K. (1941), *The Philosophy of David Hume: A Critical Study of its Origins and Central Doctrines* (London: Macmillan).

Stamps, J. A., and Krishnan, V. V. (1995), 'Territory Acquisition in Lizards: III. Competing For Space', *Animal Behavior*, 49: 679–93.

Stigler, G. J. (1951), 'The Division of Labor is Limited by the Extent of the Market', *Journal of Political Economy*, 59: 192–3; cited from the reprint in G. J. Stigler, *The Organization of Industry* (New York: Wiley, 1968: 129–41).

—— (1952), *The Theory of Price* (New York: Macmillan).

—— (1966), *The Theory of Price*, 3rd edn. (New York: Macmillan).

Stiglitz, J. E. (1975), 'Incentives, Risk, and Information: Notes towards a Theory of Hierarchy', *Bell Journal of Economics*, 6: 552–79.

—— (1987), 'The Causes and Consequences of the Dependence of Quality on Price', *Journal of Economic Literature*, 25: 1–48.

—— (1991), 'Symposium on Organizations and Economics', *Journal of Economic Perspectives*, 5(2): 15–24.

Sugden, R. (1986), *The Economics of Rights, Co-operation and Welfare* (Oxford: Blackwell).

—— (1989), 'Spontaneous Order', *Journal of Economic Perspectives*, 3(4), 85–97.

Summers, C. (1969), 'Collective Agreements and the Law of Contracts', *Yale Law Journal*, 78: 537–75.

Swedberg, R. (1993), 'Economics and Custom', *Journal of Institutional and Theoretical Economics*, 149: 204–9.

Swift, J. (1713), *Journal to Stella*, ed. H. Williams (New York: Barnes and Noble, 1975).

Telser, L. (1981), 'A Theory of Self-Enforcing Agreements', *Journal of Business*, 53: 27–44.

Thorndyke, P. W (1977), 'Cognitive Structures in Comprehension and Memory of Narrative Discourse', *Cognitive Psychology*, 9: 77–110.

Titmuss, R. M. (1970), *The Gift Relationship: From Human Blood to Social Policy* (London: Allen and Unwin).

Tochtermann, E. (1992), 'Handfester Streit um Taxi-Rechnung', *Süddeutsche Zeitung*, 178(4): 14.

Trivers R. L. (1971), 'The Evolution of Reciprocal Altruism', *Quarterly Review of Biology*, 35: 49.

Turner, J. C. (1987), *Rediscovering the Social Group* (Oxford: Blackwell).

Tversky A., and Kahneman, D. (1986), 'Rational Choice and the Framing of Decisions', *Journal of Business*, 59: 251–78.

Vanberg, V. (1988), 'Rules and Choice in Economics and Sociology', *Jahrbuch für Neue Politische ökonomie*, 7: 1–22 (Tübingen: Mohr).

—— (1994), 'Hayek's Legacy and the Future of Liberal Thought: Rational Liberalism Versus Evolutionary Agnosticism', *Cato Journal*, 4, 179–98.

Vogt, W. (1986), *Theorie der kapitalistischen und einer laboristischen Ökonomie* (Frankfurt-Campus).

von Weizsäcker, C. C. (1991), 'Antitrust and the Division of Labor', *Journal of Institutional and Theoretical Economics*, 147: 99–113.

Vroom, V. H. (1964), *Work and Motivation* (New York: Wiley).

Wagner, R. (1994), *Die Grenzen der Unternehmung* (Heidelberg: Physica).

Walker, E. L. (1980), *Psychological Complexity and Preference* (Monterey; Calif.: Brooks/Cole).

Waltzer, M. (1983). *Spheres of Justice: A Defense of Pluralism amd Equality* (New York: Basic Books).

Wang, G. and Greenfield, M. D. (1991), 'Effects of Territory Ownership on Dominance in the Desert Clicker (*Orthoptera: Acrididae*)', *Animal Behavior*, 42: 579–87.

Weber, M. (1922), *Economy and Society: An Outline of Interpretative Sociology* (Berkeley: University of California Press, 1978).

Weber, M. (1949), *The Methodology of the Social Sciences* (New York: Free Press).

Weise, P. (1992), 'Evolution in a Field of Socioeconomic Forces', in U. Witt (ed.), *Explaining Process and Change* (Ann Arbor: University of Michigan Press, 35–48).

Wells, G. L., and Petty, R. E. (1980), 'The Effect of Overt Head Movements on Persuasion: Compatibility and Incompatibility of Responses', *Basic and Applied Social Psychology*, 1: 219 – 30.

Wertheimer, M. (1922), 'Untersuchungen zur Lehre von der Gestalt, II'. *Psychologische Forschung*, 4: 301–50; (English exerpt in W. D. Ellis (ed.), *A Source Book in Gestalt Psychology* (New York: Harcourt, Brace, 1938).

—— (1934), 'On Truth', *Social Research*, 1: 135–46.

—— (1935), 'Some Problems in the Theory of Ethics', *Social Research*, 2: 353–67.

—— (1959), *Productive Thinking*, enlarged edn., ed. M. Wertheimer (New York: Harper).

White, H. (1992), *Identity and Control* (Princeton: Princeton University Press).

Williamson, O. E. (1971), 'The Vertical Integration of Production: Market Failure Considerations', *American Economic Review*, 61: 112–23.

—— (1975), *Markets and Hierarchies: Analysis and Antitrust Implications* (New York: Free Press).

—— (1985), *The Economic Institutions of Capitalism* (New York: Free Press).

—— (1993a), 'The Evolving Science of Organization', *Journal of Institutional and Theoretical Economics*, 149: 36–63.

—— (1993*b*), 'Transaction Cost Economics Meets Posnerian Law and Economics', *Journal of Institutional and Theoretical Economics*, 149: 99–118.

—— Harris, E. J., and Wachter, M. L. (1975), 'Understanding the Employment Relation: The Analysis of Idiosyncratic Exchange', *Bell Journal of Economics*, 6: 250–80; reprinted in Williamson (1975: 57–81).

Williamson, T. (1994), *Vagueness* (London: Routledge).

Witt, U. (1986), 'Evolution and Stability of Cooperation without Enforceable Contracts', *Kyklos*, 39, 245–66.

—— (1989), 'The Evolution of Economic Institutions as a Propagation Process', *Public Choice*, 62: 155–72.

Wrong D. (1981), 'The Oversocialized Conception of Man in Modern Sociology', *American Sociological Review*, 86: 183–93.

Wulf, F. (1922), 'Über die Veranderung von Vorstellungen (Gedächtnis und Gestalt)', *Psychologische Forschung*, 1: 222–373; English exerpt in W. D. Ellis (ed.), *A Source Book of Gestalt Psychology* (London: Routledge and Kegan Paul, 1938: 136–48).

Zeigarnik, B. (1927), 'Über das Behalten von erledigten und unerledigten Handlungen', *Psychologische Forschung*, 9: 1–85; English exerpt in W. D. Ellis (ed.), *A Source Book of Gestalt Psychology* (London: Routledge and Kegan Paul, 1938: 300–14).

Zimbardo, P. (1969), *The Cognitive Control of Motivation: The Consequences of Choice and Dissonance* (Glenview; Ill.: Scott, Foresman).

—— Weisenberg, M., and Firestone, I. (1969), 'Changing Appetites for Eating Fried Grasshoppers with Cognitive Dissonance', in P. Zimbardo, *The Cognitive Control of Motivation: The Consequences of Choice and Dissonance* (Glenview, Ill.: Scott, Foresman).

—— and Leippe, M. R. (1991), *The Psychology of Attitude Change and Social Influence* (Philadelphia: Temple University Press).

—— Ebbesen, E. B., and Maslach, C. (1977), *Influencing Attitudes and Changing Behavior*, 2nd edn. (Menlo Park, Calif.: Addison-Wesley).

Zukin S. and DiMaggio, P. (1990), 'Introduction', in S. Zukin and P. DiMaggio (eds.), *Structures of Capital* (Cambridge: Cambridge University Press, 1–36).

INDEX

Entries in bold denote main entries.